June Fourth

MW01073979

The Tiananmen protests and Beijing massacre of 1989 were a major turning point in recent Chinese history. In this new analysis of 1989, Jeremy Brown tells the vivid stories of participants and victims, exploring the nationwide scope of the democracy movement and the brutal crackdown that crushed it. At each critical juncture in the spring of 1989, demonstrators and decision makers agonized over difficult choices and saw how events could have unfolded differently. The alternative paths that participants imagined confirm that bloodshed was neither inevitable nor necessary. Using a wide range of previously untapped sources and examining how ordinary citizens throughout China experienced the crackdown after the massacre, this ambitious social history sheds fresh light on events that continue to reverberate in China to this day.

Jeremy Brown is Associate Professor of Modern Chinese History at Simon Fraser University.

New Approaches to Asian History

This dynamic new series publishes books on the milestones in Asian history, those that have come to define particular periods or to mark turning points in the political, cultural and social evolution of the region. The books in this series are intended as introductions for students to be used in the classroom. They are written by scholars whose credentials are well established in their particular fields and who have, in many cases, taught the subject across a number of years.

A list of books in the series can be found at the end of the volume.

June Fourth

*The Tiananmen Protests and Beijing
Massacre of 1989*

Jeremy Brown

Simon Fraser University, British Columbia

CAMBRIDGE
UNIVERSITY PRESS

University Printing House, Cambridge CB2 8BS, United Kingdom

One Liberty Plaza, 20th Floor, New York, NY 10006, USA

477 Williamstown Road, Port Melbourne, VIC 3207, Australia

314–321, 3rd Floor, Plot 3, Splendor Forum, Jasola District Centre, New Delhi – 110025, India

79 Anson Road, #06-04/06, Singapore 079906

Cambridge University Press is part of the University of Cambridge.

It furthers the University's mission by disseminating knowledge in the pursuit of education, learning, and research at the highest international levels of excellence.

www.cambridge.org
Information on this title: www.cambridge.org/9781107042070
DOI: 10.1017/9781107323728

First published 2021

A catalogue record for this publication is available from the British Library.

Library of Congress Cataloging-in-Publication Data
Names: Brown, Jeremy, 1976– author.
Title: June fourth : the Tiananmen protests and Beijing Massacre of 1989 / Jeremy Brown, Simon Fraser University, British Columbia.
Other titles: Tiananmen protests and Beijing Massacre of 1989
Description: Cambridge, United Kingdom ; New York : Cambridge University Press, 2021. | Series: New approaches to Asian history | Includes bibliographical references and index.
Identifiers: LCCN 2020055138 (print) | LCCN 2020055139 (ebook) | ISBN 9781107042070 (hardback) | ISBN 9781107657809 (paperback) | ISBN 9781107323728 (epub)
Subjects: LCSH: China–History–Tiananmen Square Incident, 1989. | China–History–Tiananmen Square Incident, 1989–Influence.
Classification: LCC DS779.32 .B77 2021 (print) | LCC DS779.32 (ebook) | DDC 951.05/8–dc23
LC record available at https://lccn.loc.gov/2020055138
LC ebook record available at https://lccn.loc.gov/2020055139

ISBN 978-1-107-04207-0 Hardback
ISBN 978-1-107-65780-9 Paperback

Contents

Figures

Preface

I was twelve years old in 1989. Growing up in Iowa City, Iowa, I watched plenty of television, including many Chicago Cubs baseball games. Each evening my mother watched Peter Jennings on *ABC World News Tonight*. As tens of thousands of protesters marched to Tiananmen Square on April 21, 1989, to commemorate the death of former Communist Party General Secretary Hu Yaobang, the Cubs were playing a night game against the Mets in New York. The baseball broadcast clashed directly with my mom's nightly news fix. Peter Jennings did mention the protests on April 21,[1] but I did not care. I cared about the Cubs' 8–4 win against the Mets. When, on April 27, 1989, hundreds of thousands of Beijing citizens marched to protest the previous day's *People's Daily* editorial about taking a "clear-cut stand against turmoil," the Cubs beat the Dodgers 1–0 in an afternoon game at home that finished well before Jennings spoke about the protests in Beijing at the top of the news. I might have started paying attention to China that day, although I had no inkling that I would ever learn Chinese, live in Beijing, and devote my career to Chinese history.

The date that most people remember about China in 1989 is June 4 (although the massacre of Beijing civilians by People's Liberation Army soldiers actually began on the night of June 3 and continued into the early hours of June 4). It was the weekend: June 3 was Saturday and June 4 was Sunday – a detail that Premier Li Peng would eventually reveal was central to the decision to forcibly clear Tiananmen Square by dawn on Sunday morning, to prevent massive crowds from hitting the streets on their day off.[2] Weekend afternoons were prime baseball-watching time for me. I could commandeer the television to watch the Cubs' important battles in St. Louis against the Cardinals (the Cubs lost on Saturday and won on Sunday), and a few hours later my mother could watch the news

---

[1] Vanderbilt Television News Archive, tvnews.vanderbilt.edu/broadcasts/121680.

[2] Zhang Ganghua, 李鹏六四日记真相 (The truth about Li Peng's June Fourth diary) (hereafter abbreviated as *LP*) (Hong Kong: Aoya chuban youxian gongsi, 2010), 292.

unimpeded, preserving family harmony. I was sad that the Cubs had lost in extra innings on June 3, but I definitely paid attention to the news that evening, when American television began reporting on the shooting and killing in Beijing.

My point is that unlike most authors of books about the Tiananmen Square protests and Beijing massacre, I had no personal stake in the events at the time. I was not in China and had no special interest or expertise in China. My life and worldview were not radically changed by what happened in June 1989. I was a child halfway across the globe who cared more about baseball than about China. But like many American kids whose parents watched television every night, I was aware that something was happening. Something that, by June 3, 1989, was unequivocally very bad and sad. While I am approaching this topic from the useful position of a detached outsider – a professional historian describing distant events – I am not a blank slate. My assumptions and framework for understanding June Fourth began to be shaped in 1989. North Americans who watched television coverage of the protests saw scenes of hope and joy in May when students, workers, officials, and retirees marched in support of democracy. Then they witnessed an authoritarian dictatorship killing young people who wanted to be like "us." Even though I paid no more than passing, preteen attention, my own view of China in 1989 was shaped by this melodramatic late Cold War framework provided by the American media. Only when I first went to Harbin, China, as a nineteen-year-old exchange student in 1997, did I begin to encounter different frameworks and to question my own.

I am writing this book because my students, many of whom were born in China, are fascinated by and obsessed with a months-long event that has come to be known as June Fourth. June Fourth can be divided into three parts: a nationwide democracy movement between April and June 1989, the Beijing massacre of June 3 and June 4, and a prolonged crackdown that persisted into 1990 and that in many ways has continued ever since. My students' interest is infectious. Everyone who learns about June Fourth intuitively grasps that it was a major turning point in Chinese history, one that threw many lives off course and eventually contributed to the arrival of millions of Chinese students in North American, European, and Australian universities. But what kind of turning point was it? What small turning points can we identify in April, May, and June 1989 that contributed to the larger watershed? How might things have gone differently? The more the Chinese government censors discussion and restricts research about 1989, the more curious students and I get and the more we want to dig into the facts. Studying an event that has been covered up and obscured means that it is necessary to start with the most basic questions of historical inquiry. What happened? What did it mean?

Viewing the Tiananmen protests and Beijing massacre as history is a new approach. It differs from the hundreds of previously published journalistic, memoir, and social science books about 1989. A historical approach allows for more comprehensive coverage of the protests, massacre, and aftermath in terms of focus, geographical space, and time. Many previous accounts have overemphasized the stories and influence of prominent student protesters, have focused on Beijing campuses and Tiananmen Square itself while downplaying what was going on in the rest of the city and the rest of China, and have stopped their story after the People's Liberation Army took control of the square as the sun rose on June 4, 1989. This has contributed to a skewed view that, pushed to its logical conclusion, blames students' arguments and missteps for provoking the authorities to order a military assault on Beijing.

Before I started doing research for this book, I shared this skewed view. When I received a promotional copy of Canadian author Denise Chong's book *Egg on Mao* in 2010, I had never heard of Lu Decheng. I was skeptical that a book needed to be written about Lu and two other working-class rabble-rousers from Hunan who threw eggs at Mao Zedong's portrait overlooking Tiananmen Square in May 1989. I was wrong. I had unwittingly internalized the Beijing-centric, student-focused narrative that saw the actions of nonelites as jeopardizing a protest movement led by students from China's elite universities. I overcame my reluctance and cracked open Chong's masterful book. It changed my mind and confirmed the value of looking beyond Beijing students. Chong's contribution greatly enriches the pages that follow.

A few years later, Chai Ling's publisher sent me a free copy of Chai's memoir. Like many people whose understanding of the history of 1989 comes from a Beijing student-centric view, I had an exceedingly negative impression of Chai, who was one of the most prominent student leaders in Beijing in 1989. My opinion was shaped primarily by the documentary *Gate of Heavenly Peace*, which depicts Chai as a selfish villain who recklessly tried to provoke the Communist Party to shed blood. Chai's book is as self-serving and defensive as most memoirs tend to be, but it is extremely revealing about what it was like to be a woman university student in the 1980s and how that experience could predispose someone to get involved in a risky protest movement. More crucially, it shows that no student leader deserves to be cast as a villain or blamed for a massacre.

My account recognizes the importance of Beijing students. But I see them as a diverse group living among an even more diverse mix of people whose actions and choices were far more significant than those of students from a few elite universities: ordinary residents of Beijing, worker activists pushing to establish independent unions, people outside China's capital, including Muslims and Tibetans, and the top Communist Party leaders who authorized deadly force against peaceful civilian protesters.

My inclination as a social historian is to focus on ordinary people instead of elite politicians. Plenty of regular people appear in this book. Their hopes and grievances created genuine possibilities for positive change during the spring of 1989. And most of the hundreds or thousands of people who died on June 3 and June 4 were ordinary residents of Beijing. Correcting the skewed student-centric view of 1989 and avoiding victim blaming, however, means paying significant attention to the people who could have prevented a massacre but instead caused one.

The top leader of China in 1989, the eighty-four-year-old Deng Xiaoping, decided to send in the army to forcibly clear Tiananmen Square by an arbitrary deadline. Contrary to accounts that portray Deng as unwilling, uninvolved, reluctant, or "manipulated" into imposing martial law by "hard-liners" who won a factional battle against "reformers," it is clear that Deng himself decided that the student movement was turmoil that had to be crushed by force.[3] Because of his revolutionary seniority, Deng was the ultimate decider in China to whom all others had to bow down. Deng was the one who manipulated reluctant colleagues, not the other way around. Many of the high-level politicians and military leaders around him did not initially support imposing martial law in Beijing and using force to clear Tiananmen Square. But once Deng's views became clear, almost everyone else fell into line, pledging their loyalty and parroting the elderly leader's language.

In treating the Beijing massacre as history, I have adopted a victim-centered approach, naming the names of people who were killed, naming the perpetrators of the massacre, and drawing on the efforts of the Tiananmen Mothers to chart who the dead were and what they were doing when they died. Many of those who were shot and killed were on the streets of Beijing not to resist the army but to witness an atrocity or to help save others. Some civilians who died were trying to get to work, going out for breakfast, or hiding in their own homes. Their deaths were

---

[3] Michael Dillon's biography of Deng promotes the thesis that Deng was manipulated; Ezra Vogel's biography more accurately depicts Deng as the "ultimate decision-maker" in 1989. Michael Dillon, *Deng Xiaoping: The Man Who Made Modern China* (London: Tauris, 2015); Ezra F. Vogel, *Deng Xiaoping and the Transformation of China* (Cambridge, MA: Harvard University Press, 2011), 595.

senseless and totally unnecessary. Their loved ones, instead of receiving apologies and compensation, have been treated as criminals and dissidents.

Because of the Communist Party's censorship and falsehoods about what happened in June 1989, we do not know precisely how many people died in Beijing in early June. The number of dead could have been as low as 478, as high as 3,000, or somewhere in between, such as 727 (a number released by an insider in 2012). Any of these numbers is horrible and unacceptable. What is surprising is that they are not higher, knowing as we do now that more than two hundred thousand soldiers invaded and occupied Beijing. While two military units in particular, the 38th Group Army and the 15th Airborne, shot directly at civilians and strafed apartment buildings wildly as they approached Tiananmen Square from the west and south, many other soldiers – hesitant, scared, or unwilling to target civilians – did not shoot. The massacre was a terrible atrocity. It would have been far worse if dozens of other units had been as eager to shoot as the 38th Group Army and 15th Airborne were.

No history of 1989 would be comprehensive without looking beyond Beijing and chronicling the months-long nationwide crackdown that followed the Beijing massacre. Deng Xiaoping and Premier Li Peng had imposed martial law in Lhasa in March 1989 and considered it a success, making military action Deng's preferred option in Beijing a few months later. In April and May, protesters in every province and autonomous region of China emulated protesters in Beijing while also directly influencing events in the capital, either by capturing Communist Party leaders' attention or by traveling to Beijing themselves. After June 4, angry resistance and state violence ebbed for months.

Outbursts of resistance to violence were paralleled by a movement during the second half of 1989 to punish and purge people who had participated in the protests. People reacted as if they had been forced to live with a dangerously abusive partner: silently going through the motions, lying, protecting others who depended on them, and occasionally standing up to bullying. This dynamic continues through the present day. The abuser's enablers remain in charge of China thanks to Deng's decision to use military force against civilians. They mostly conceal the abuse, but if necessary, they defend it, saying that they had no choice. Sadly, the enablers have worked hard to teach young people who did not live through 1989 that what happened is best forgotten, that the victims deserved it, that it had been necessary to get rough to preserve China's stability.

The massacre was not necessary or justifiable. Each part of this book concludes with a special chapter examining alternative paths and momentous turning points that Chinese people in China discussed during or after 1989. Because people had genuinely high hopes that China could become less corrupt and less repressive in April and May 1989, and because their aspirations were shattered so tragically by bullets and tanks, many survivors have obsessed over what could have been done to alter the course of history. Asking how things could have gone differently is a direct attack against the cynical argument that murdering civilians was an inevitable outcome or a necessary result.[4] It emphasizes agency and contingency. Agency means that individuals and groups were not passive pawns – they had the power to change history. Even though a diseased political system characterized by "old-man politics" facilitated Deng Xiaoping's domination of his colleagues,[5] millions of people stood up and resisted Deng's dictatorship. Their many successes should not be wiped away by the appearance of tanks and guns on June 3.

Contingency means that every action, choice, or event was dependent on countless other uncertain occurrences. For example, General Secretary Zhao Ziyang's ill-timed departure to North Korea on April 23, 1989, and Soviet leader Mikhail Gorbachev's arrival in Beijing for a summit on May 15, 1989, initially had nothing to do with a democracy movement in China, but they became key turning points. Many other small decisions by relatively unknown people added up to contribute to outcomes that, at the time, were shocking, surprising, and never foreordained.

While my historical approach is an attempt to be comprehensive, it is not exhaustive. This is partly because of source limitations and partly because by emphasizing people, places, and events that have previously been neglected, I am making conscious choices to downplay things that I believe have been overemphasized. For example, Beijing students play a prominent role in the story but I refrain from giving a blow-by-blow account of their debates or of elite urban intellectuals' theorizing. Nor do I dwell on symbols or symbolism. I will not be mentioning "tank man" or devoting more than a sentence to a statue called the goddess of democracy – these two symbols say more about North American and European observers' imagination than they do about what happened in

---

[4] Political scientist David Skidmore cites Henry Kissinger's statement that "no government in the world would have tolerated having the main square of its capital occupied for eight weeks by tens of thousands of demonstrators" as an example of the inevitability thesis as it applies to China in 1989. David Skidmore, "The 1989 Tiananmen Crackdown Was Not Inevitable," *The Diplomat*, April 10, 2020, thediplomat.com/2020/04/the-1989-tiananmen-crackdown-was-not-inevitable.

[5] Chung Yen-lin, "The Ousting of General Secretary Hu Yaobang: The Roles Played by Peng Zhen and Other Party Elders," *China Review* 19, no. 1 (2019): 89–122.

China in 1989.[6] Focusing on an unknown man who bravely provided a dramatic photo opportunity by standing in front of a row of tanks on June 5, 1989, is an insult to the suffering of thousands of people who were actually injured by or literally fought back against the PLA's guns and tanks, but whose courage was not documented by cameras.

The hierarchies of Chinese society in 1989 were patriarchal, sexist, antirural, and Han supremacist (meaning that the dominant Han ethnicity had set up a system that treated non-Han people, including Tibetans and Uyghurs, as inferior). Existing histories of June Fourth reproduce these harmful hierarchies. They overemphasize Han men. They overlook rural people's experiences and treat non-Han struggles for autonomy as peripheral. They downplay women's participation and viewpoints or even misogynistically belittle Chai Ling's effectiveness as a movement leader and blame her for inciting a crackdown.

North American authors writing about June Fourth do so in a society that is patriarchal, sexist, and white supremacist, a reality that has also shaped scholarly decisions about what is worth writing about. It has been a prolonged and ongoing learning process for me to first recognize and then push back against hierarchies of exclusion and discrimination that I am personally enmeshed in as a privileged white guy. But it is crucial to do so. I have amplified previously marginalized voices and have consciously built on the paradigm-shifting contributions of such authors as Chai Ling, Denise Chong, Chung Yen-lin, Louisa Lim, Rowena Xiaoqing He, and Wu Renhua. Citations of their work can be found throughout the footnotes of the pages that follow and also in the suggestions for further reading provided at the end of the book.

Ten years ago, my original plan was to teach seminars about June Fourth as a way to prepare myself for the day – sometime soon, I hoped – when it would be possible to openly conduct interviews and read archives about 1989 in China. Instead, research about relatively innocuous topics has become increasingly difficult and dangerous after Xi Jinping became China's top leader in 2012. Sources about 1989 remain woefully limited. The Chinese Communist Party's repression of victims, its enforced amnesia about the inclusivity and scope of the democracy movement, and its dishonest characterization of the massacre itself make it more important than ever to forge ahead in telling the history of June Fourth in spite of source limitations. The student

---

[6] Michael Dutton writes that "the scene of the man and the tank" is the only "streetscene in China worth remembering in Western eyes … The representation is so powerful that it demolishes other understandings." Michael Dutton, *Streetlife China* (Cambridge: Cambridge University Press, 1998), 17.

movement in Beijing was well documented at the time and source collections are plentiful outside China. Put together with the revealing (but also defensive and self-serving) memoirs of Premier Li Peng, General Secretary Zhao Ziyang, and journalists Lu Chaoqi and Zhang Wanshu and others, they provide a fuller picture of the interplay between top leaders, student activists, and ordinary citizens.

Many secrets about the massacre and its aftermath remain locked in inaccessible archives inside China, but leaked collections of internally circulated military and Communist Party documents, the dogged work of the Tiananmen Mothers and independent scholar Wu Renhua, interviews by dissident writer Liao Yiwu, and my own conversations with survivors make it possible to provide the most comprehensive account to date of the events of 1989.

One source I have not used is *The Tiananmen Papers*, which for a time was considered an authoritative collection but has not stood the test of time and cannot be considered reliable. Most of the primary sources excerpted in *The Tiananmen Papers* come from other collections, in which case I have consulted earlier versions. The few original sources in *The Tiananmen Papers* are impossibly detailed, unverifiable transcripts of dubious provenance purporting to reveal conversations among top leaders.[7] Omitting *The Tiananmen Papers* as a source, while critically analyzing memoirs and other materials, is a necessary step in pursuing a more credible and inclusive history of 1989 that goes beyond the machinations of high officials and student leaders.

Some of the sources I cite are only available on the internet, meaning that they could disappear at any time because of censorship, technical obsolescence, or something as mundane as failing to renew a domain registration. To guarantee perpetual access to online sources, I have archived all web pages cited in the footnotes at the Internet Archive's Wayback Machine. If a page has already disappeared at the time of publication, I provide a link to the archived page. If an original link in

---

[7] Alfred Chan's critiques of *The Tiananmen Papers* remain convincing, especially when paired with Joseph Torigian's assessment of a more recent, more reliable collection of leaked documents – *The Last Secret* – versus the contents of *The Tiananmen Papers*. See Alfred L. Chan, "The Tiananmen Papers Revisited," *China Quarterly* 177 (March 2004): 190–205; Alfred L. Chan, "Fabricated Secrets and Phantom Documents: the 'Tiananmen Papers' and 'China's Leadership Files,' A Re-rejoinder," June 19, 2005, publish.uwo.ca/~achan/Fabricated Secrets 2.pdf. See also Tsoi Wing-Mui, ed., *The Last Secret: The Final Documents from the June Fourth Crackdown* (Hong Kong: New Century, 2019), alongside Torigian's comments in Graeme Smith, Louisa Lim, Bao Pu, and Joseph Torigian, "Tiananmen's Final Secret," *Little Red Podcast*, June 2, 2019, omny.fm/shows/the-little-red-podcast/tiananmens-final-secret.

the notes becomes unusable in the future, readers can find the archived version at web.archive.org.

I am indebted to many people for their assistance and encouragement. My biggest thanks go to the Simon Fraser University students with whom I have studied June Fourth. My students' energy and curiosity, which they channeled into more than seventy original Wikipedia contributions, convinced me that writing the history of 1989 is too urgent to wait for ideal research conditions. I am also grateful to Denise Chong, who made a captivating and inspiring visit to the seminar; to Chai Ling, who answered students' questions in a Skype meeting; and to Louisa Lim, who talked with students about her amazing book via Skype.

Wu Renhua is the world's leading expert in June Fourth studies and has been extremely generous in sharing his knowledge with me. Timothy Cheek and Perry Link encouraged me from the very beginning. At the finish line they read the entire manuscript and gave detailed feedback, for which I am forever grateful. Conversations with Rowena Xiaoqing He, Chung Yen-lin, Geremie Barmé, and many people in China whose lives were changed by what happened in 1989 but who cannot be named here greatly enriched this book, as did online exchanges with Michael Sullivan, Joseph Torigian, and Wu Guoguang.

I thank Paul G. Pickowicz, Karl Gerth, and graduate students from San Diego and Irvine for inviting me to tag along on a trip to Stanford University's East Asia Library, where librarian Zhaohui Xue was extremely helpful. At a conference in La Jolla that grew out of the research trip, I received valuable feedback from Richard Madsen, Sara Schneewind, Jeffrey Wasserstrom, and the students in Pickowicz's seminar. I am also grateful to Arunabh Ghosh and to Robert Eisinger for giving me the chance to speak about the post-massacre purge to public audiences at Harvard University and Roger Williams University.

I appreciate Jasmine Chen and the artists and staff at the Arts Club Theatre Company in Vancouver for asking me to take part in a panel following a showing of Lauren Yee's wonderful play *The Great Leap*. Remarks by Mabel Tung and Anna Wang at the panel pushed me to think about June Fourth in new ways.

Librarians helped me to find and use many of the sources I draw from in the book. Aside from the interlibrary loan staff at Simon Fraser University, who did lots of searching, finding, and heavy lifting, I want to thank librarians at the Burnaby Public Library, the Fung Library Fairbank Collection at Harvard University, the National Central Library in Beijing, the National Central Library in Taipei, the National Chengchi University Library, the Universities Service Centre for Chinese

Studies at the Chinese University of Hong Kong, and the East Asian Library at the University of California, Los Angeles.

Chris Buckley of the *New York Times* was generous in sharing sources; I thank him and Andrew Jacobs for sharing notes from their dynamite reporting about the military dimension of June Fourth. Timothy Brook shared his VHS collection of propaganda documentaries twisting the truth of what happened in June 1989. As painful and infuriating as they were to watch, I needed to see them. Thanks, Tim, for making viewing possible.

Three research assistants helped me with newspapers, memoirs, diaries, and videos. I do not want to get you in trouble by naming you here, but you know who you are. Thank you.

I have been fortunate to work with three History Department chairs during my time at Simon Fraser University: Mark Leier, Hilmar Pabel, and Jennifer Spear. They fostered a humane work environment that allowed me to complete the book. I cherish the freedom to say, teach, and write what I want at SFU. Writing about June Fourth has been a constant reminder to never take this for granted. I appreciate my colleagues in the History Department, the Faculty of Arts and Social Sciences, the faculty association, and the university administration, who work together to protect and promote freedom, tolerance, equity, diversity, and inclusion. One inadequate but significant step in this process is respectfully acknowledging that I wrote this book while living and working on the unceded territory of the Squamish, Tsleil-Watuth, Musqueam, and Kwikwetlem peoples.

I am thankful to Marigold Acland at Cambridge University Press for originally pitching this project to me, and I owe deep thanks to Lucy Rhymer for helping me from start to finish. Six other key people greatly improved the book in concrete ways: Carolyn Brown read every word and polished and fixed the writing; Danny Frazier designed and drew compelling illustrations, allowing readers to visualize what happened in 1989; John Gaunt's careful copy-editing corrected too many errors to count; Cheryl Lenser completed a top-notch index; and Emily Sharp and Natasha Whelan ensured that production went smoothly. I am grateful for funding from Simon Fraser University's University Publications Fund, which supported indexing and illustration costs.

This book was stalled and going nowhere until a group of remarkable people entered my family's life and changed us for the better. Dr. Hamad Abdoul Raman got us on the right track and has kept us there – thank you so much. Equally huge thanks go to Cristina Abasolo, Nancy Barton, Mark Curry, Sarah Gatiss-Brown, Dave Gatiss, Kareem John, Noushaba Nousheen, Michelle Seigel, Catherine Williams, Pam Woronko, and other teachers and caregivers. The compassion and positivity that they have given (and continue to give) to me, Laura, Henry, and Leo cannot be overstated. During my final months of writing, a hip and back injury made life (and typing) difficult and painful. Nadine Nembhard of Restore Physiotherapy fixed the problem and gave me ways to get stronger. The caring and skilled people named in this paragraph may not have realized that they helped me finish this book, but they deserve credit for making it possible.

Chronology

November 5, 1986	More than ten thousand students march in Changsha.
December 1986– January 1987	Hu Yaobang purged as general secretary after student protests in Hefei, Shanghai, Beijing, and other cities.
December 1988	Thousands of Chinese students protest in Nanjing after a fight involving African students and a security guard at Hehai University.
March 1989	Security forces violently suppress Tibetan protesters in Lhasa, killing more than four hundred people. Li Peng declares martial law in Lhasa.
April 7, 1989	Protesting against restrictions on freedom of speech in Taiwan, publisher Cheng Nan-jung (also known as Nylon Cheng) commits suicide by setting himself on fire in his office in Taipei. April 7 is now commemorated as "Freedom of Expression Day" in Taiwan.
April 8, 1989	Hu Yaobang suffers heart attack during a Politburo meeting.
April 15, 1989	Hu Yaobang dies in hospital.
April 17, 1989	Örkesh Dölet (Wuerkaixi) speaks to a large crowd of students at Beijing Normal University.
April 18, 1989	Chai Ling is chased by police near Xinhua Gate, the entrance to the Communist Party's leadership compound.
April 22, 1989	Hu Yaobang's memorial service. Protesters in Changsha and Xi'an storm government compounds and are forcibly dispersed by police.
April 23, 1989	Zhao Ziyang departs for North Korea.

April 25–26, 1989	Official characterization of the protest movement as "turmoil" is broadcast on television and radio and published in newspapers nationwide.
April 27, 1989	Approximately one hundred thousand students march to Tiananmen Square.
April 29, 1989	Sham dialogue between students and officials in Beijing.
April 30, 1989	Zhao Ziyang returns to Beijing from North Korea.
May 4, 1989	Zhao Ziyang tells Asian Development Bank delegates that problems should be solved "democratically and legally" and that "major turmoil will not occur in China."
May 6, 1989	More than ten thousand Muslims march in Lanzhou protesting the book *Sexual Customs*. Censors in Beijing halt sales of the book and order the destruction of all existing copies.
May 11, 1989	Deng Xiaoping emerges from seclusion to meet with Iranian President Ali Khamenei.
May 12, 1989	Muslims protest against *Sexual Customs* in Beijing, Hohhot, Lanzhou, and Xining.
May 13, 1989	Students begin hunger strike in Tiananmen Square.
May 14, 1989	Dialogue meeting between student activists and officials ends in disarray in Beijing.
May 15, 1989	Soviet leader Mikhail Gorbachev arrives in Beijing. Rumors of imminent self-immolations circulate in and around Tiananmen Square. Approximately twenty thousand Muslims demonstrate in an officially approved march in Xi'an.
May 17, 1989	In a meeting at Deng Xiaoping's home, Deng tells Zhao Ziyang and other members of the Politburo Standing Committee that he has decided to implement martial law. Zhao says that he is unwilling to carry out martial law.
May 17–18, 1989	More than one million Beijing residents march in support of the hunger strikers.

May 18, 1989   Li Peng meets with hunger strikers in the Great Hall of the People. Thousands of Muslims protest in Yinchuan and Urumqi.

May 19, 1989   Deng Xiaoping tells elders, military officials, and Li Peng that he has selected Shanghai Party secretary Jiang Zemin to replace Zhao Ziyang as general secretary. Approximately 304,000 university students from the provinces arrive in Beijing on fifty-one separate trains. In Taipei, Chan I-hua commits suicide by self-immolation at Cheng Nan-jung's funeral.

May 20, 1989   Martial law goes into effect in urban Beijing at 10 a.m., but citizens block the troops' advance into the city. General Xu Qinxian, leader of the 38th Group Army, refuses to carry out the martial law order.

May 22, 1989   Lu Decheng, Yu Dongyue, and Yu Zhijian throw paint-filled eggs at Mao Zedong's portrait overlooking Tiananmen Square.

May 23, 1989   The Joint Liaison Group of All Circles in the Capital to Protect and Uphold the Constitution, or Capital Joint Liaison Group (CJLG), forms as an umbrella organization of protest groups.

May 24, 1989   People's Liberation Army (PLA) troops withdraw from Beijing and regroup.

May 28, 1989   Zhao Ziyang's political secretary Bao Tong is detained in Qincheng Prison; Bao's secretary Wu Wei is locked up in a security compound outside Beijing.

May 29, 1989   Li Peng chairs a Politburo Standing Committee meeting to discuss how the PLA should clear Tiananmen Square.

May 31, 1989   Deng Xiaoping and Yang Shangkun sign off on plans for the PLA to advance on and clear Tiananmen Square.

June 1, 1989   Eight hundred students from Nanjing head north on foot toward Beijing in a "long march" protest.

June 1–2, 1989   By 3 a.m. on June 2, twenty-five thousand soldiers and officers gather in the Great Hall of

	the People and other areas near Tiananmen Square.
June 3, 1989	PLA troops advancing toward Tiananmen Square open fire on civilian protesters after 10 p.m., killing hundreds, including teenagers Jiang Jielian and Wang Nan and others along Beijing's main east–west avenue. Xiao Bo, Wang Weiping, Xiong Zhiming, and others are shot and killed while trying to help others. Soldiers shoot and kill Liu Jinhua and Liu Zhenying while the two are out on separate trips trying to buy medicine for their children.
June 4, 1989	The Beijing massacre continues overnight and into the day. At least five students are reportedly shot and killed inside Tiananmen Square: Cheng Renxing, Dai Jinping, Huang Xinhua, Li Haocheng, and Zhou Deping. PLA soldiers kill the following people as they try to commute to or from work: Chen Ziqi, Dai Wei, Li Chun, Liu Junhe, Wang Hongqi, Wang Junjing, and Wang Qingzeng. A rampaging tank kills eleven students at Liubukou, including Dong Xiaojun, Gong Jifang, Lin Renfu, Tian Daomin, and Wang Peiwen.
June 5, 1989	Sporadic murders of civilians by PLA troops continue in Beijing. Around 6:40 a.m., Peng Jun is fatally shot while going out for breakfast. In Chongqing, twenty-eight-year-old factory worker Xu Wanping reacts to the Beijing massacre by forming the China Action Party.
June 6, 1989	More than three thousand protesters attack the 27th Group Army's headquarters in Shijiazhuang. In Shanghai, a train plows into protesters blocking the tracks, killing eight and injuring more than thirty. PLA troops continue killing civilians in Beijing, including a twelve-year-old boy going home from school, as well as two young men in their twenties named Wang Zhengsheng and Yang Ziping.

June 26, 1989	Terrorist bombing of train on the outskirts of Shanghai, killing twenty-four people and injuring fifty-one.
June 28, 1989	Another train explosion, this one in Guizhou, kills five and injures twelve.

Abbreviations

HF   Zhongguo renmin wuzhuang jingcha budui Beijing shi zongdui, 回顾与反思: 1989, 制止动乱平息暴乱主要经验汇编 (Looking back and reflecting: 1989, collected experiences of curbing turmoil and quelling rebellion) (n.p., 1989), reprinted by Service Center for Chinese Publications, "六四" 专题史料丛刊之十一 (Collection of historical materials about "June Fourth," no. 11) (Los Angeles: Service Center for Chinese Publications, 2009).

JY   Zongzheng wenhua bu zhengwen bangongshi, ed., 戒严一日 (A day of martial law) (Beijing: Jiefangjun wenyi chubanshe, 1989).

LP   Zhang Ganghua, 李鹏六四日記真相 (The truth about Li Peng's June Fourth diary) (Hong Kong: Aoya chuban youxian gongsi, 2010).

LSJ   Wu Renhua, 六四事件中的戒嚴部隊 (The martial law troops during the June Fourth incident) (Alhambra, CA: Zhenxiang chubanshe, 2009).

LSQ   Wu Renhua, 六四事件全程實錄 (The full record of the Tiananmen movement) (Alhambra, CA: Zhenxiang chubanshe, 2014).

QZ   公安部总值班室情况摘报 (Ministry of Public Security Duty Office Situation Bulletin).

PS   Bao Pu, Renee Chiang, and Adi Ignatius, trans. and ed., *Prisoner of the State: The Secret Journal of Zhao Ziyang* (New York: Simon and Schuster, 2009).

RMRB   *Renmin ribao* 人民日报 (*People's Daily*).

SCCP   Zhongwen chubanwu fuwu zhongxin, ed., 中共重要历史文献资料汇编 (Collection of the Chinese Communist Party's important historical documents) (Los Angeles: Zhongwen chubanwu fuwu zhongxin, 2005–).

SCPA   Stanford University East Asian Library, Collection of Contemporary Chinese Political Archives.

XF   Ding Zilin, 尋訪六四受難者 (In search of the victims of June Fourth) (Hong Kong: Kaifang zazhi she, 2005).

ZY   Liao Yiwu, 子彈鴉片 : 天安門大屠殺的生死故事 (Bullets and opium: Stories of life and death in the Tiananmen massacre) (Taipei: Yunchen wenhua, 2012).

Part One

China's 1980s

1   Happy

At first glance, Lu Decheng and Chai Ling's trajectories in the 1980s could not have been more different. Lu, who turned eighteen in the summer of 1981, was a bus mechanic in a quiet town in Hunan Province. Volatile and moody, he had gotten in trouble with the police after putting a drop of pesticide in his coworker's thermos.[1] Lu was a skilled mechanic but his prospects seemed limited.

Chai Ling, who was three years younger than Lu Decheng, had a much brighter future. She was an academic superstar from an ordinary town in Shandong Province; in 1983 she tested into Peking University, China's top school. Chai had many opportunities to learn and grow in what she called the "vibrant, dynamic" university atmosphere of the 1980s. She studied psychology, ran track, wrote for the school newspaper, joined student government, worked at a coffee shop, and went to dances on Saturday nights.[2]

China's 1980s offered increased freedom and opportunity for many, but also anxious uncertainty for others. In this environment, Chai Ling was poised to be a winner. Lu Decheng was not. But Chai and Lu had at least one thing in common: their lives would be dramatically thrown off course by the Tiananmen Square protests of 1989. Chai became the face of the student movement in Beijing. She was a motivational speaker who inspired hundreds to join a pivotal hunger strike and who became the self-styled "commander in chief" of the protest site in late May 1989. During the People's Liberation Army's violent crackdown of June 3 and 4, 1989, Chai stayed in the square with the last group of students until the army allowed them to walk away. Chai fled Beijing, eventually escaped China, and started a new life in the United States.

---

[1] Denise Chong, *Egg on Mao: The Story of an Ordinary Man Who Defaced an Icon and Unmasked a Dictatorship* (Toronto: Random House of Canada, 2009), 74.

[2] Chai Ling, *A Heart for Freedom: The Remarkable Journey of a Young Dissident, Her Daring Escape, and Her Quest to Free China's Daughters* (Carol Stream, IL: Tyndale House, 2011), 38.

Lu Decheng also gained prominence in May 1989. Stirred by the students' hunger strike, Lu traveled with friends from Hunan to Beijing, where they planned to attack the symbolic heart of the Communist Party's dictatorship. On May 22, 1989, Lu and his friends threw paint-filled eggs at the official portrait of Mao Zedong overlooking Tiananmen Square. Afraid that the outsiders' vandalism would invite a violent response from the government – or that the egg throwers themselves might be government instigators – students turned Lu and his friends over to the police. Lu was sentenced to sixteen years for the crime of counterrevolutionary sabotage. He was released after nine years in prison; a few years later he fled China and ended up in Canada.

Involvement in the Tiananmen Square protests, however, is not the only thing that connects Lu Decheng and Chai Ling. People like Chai and Lu are useful guides to understanding China's 1980s. Their experiences shed light on what made people in China happy and what annoyed or angered them during the years before 1989. Their happy moments raised their hopes. But like many others, they suffered traumatic setbacks that tempered their high hopes and made them predisposed to plunge into the protests of 1989 when the opportunity presented itself. To understand the Tiananmen protests, we must first explore what made people happy and what made them angry in the preceding decade.

On September 18, 1976, Lu Decheng's middle-school teacher sharply criticized him. Lu was in trouble because he had failed to cry at a mass memorial service for Chairman Mao Zedong. Mao's death did not change everything in China, but the end of the Mao years and the Cultural Revolution (1966–1976) did usher in new personal and political freedoms. During the 1970s, schoolchildren like Lu Decheng had to participate in political rituals – including orchestrated crying – or face criticism. People who dared to openly criticize Mao, and even those who unintentionally defamed the leader, faced prison sentences. During the late 1970s, local courts reexamined these "counterrevolutionaries," set them free, and compensated them for their losses.[3] The crime of counterrevolution remained on the books during the 1980s, but for the most part people in China no longer had to fear that their coworkers, neighbors, or family members might denounce them as a political enemy.

The end of the 1970s also brought freedom from the official class-status label system that had stigmatized millions of families since the

---

[3] Daniel Leese, "Revising Political Verdicts in Post-Mao China: The Case of Beijing's Fengtai District," in *Maoism at the Grassroots: Everyday Life in China's Era of High Socialism*, ed. Jeremy Brown and Matthew D. Johnson (Cambridge, MA: Harvard University Press, 2015), 102–28.

Communists came to power in 1949. Originally intended to monitor and punish landlords and capitalists who had exploited peasants and workers, over the 1950s, 1960s, and 1970s class-status labels evolved into a caste system that limited education and job opportunities for the children of political enemies, who became targets of persecution and violence during the political movements of the Mao years. In 1979, top Communist leaders declared an end to the use of such negative labels as "landlord" and "rich peasant"; all villagers would simply be called "commune member."[4] Modernization, rather than class struggle against the former exploiting classes, became the Party's main focus.

Pursuing modernization was a cause for happiness in the 1980s. For many people, especially students and intellectuals, it meant freedom to seek higher education, debate controversial issues, read foreign articles and books, and travel abroad for academic conferences. This was a major change from the 1970s. The physicist Fang Lizhi, who had been condemned and "reeducated" through hard labor in coal mines during the Mao years, began to challenge classical Marxism in lectures throughout China during the late 1970s and early 1980s. Fang wrote about the experience, "I concluded that the main problem facing modernization in the late 1970s was not that people were ignorant but that they did not even know that they were ignorant."[5] Marxism was still the dominant official ideology in China, but pursuing modernization during the 1980s meant that it was no longer the only game in town.

Professors and students alike found it exhilarating to challenge orthodoxy in what writer Frankie Huang has called

an explosion of expression that served as catharsis for years of repression. In this environment, people felt free to give their own points of view without fear of reprisal. My father recalls testing the waters by saying, "The Communist Party is not sacred" in front of a party secretary at his university. He was not even reprimanded, much less punished.[6]

Students like Chai Ling were deeply affected by this shift. Had she been born a few years earlier, Chai might have been sent to the countryside to toil as a peasant instead of having the opportunity to gain admission to China's most prestigious school during a time of intellectual ferment and

---

[4] Jeremy Brown, "Moving Targets: Changing Class Labels in Rural Hebei and Henan, 1960–1979," in *Maoism at the Grassroots*, 73.

[5] Fang Lizhi, *The Most Wanted Man in China: My Journey from Scientist to Enemy of the State*, trans. Perry Link (New York: Henry Holt, 2016), 186.

[6] Frankie Huang, "China in the 1980s, When People Felt Free to Speak Their Minds," *Goldthread*, August 1, 2019, www.goldthread2.com/culture/china-1980s-censorship/article/3021028.

openness to new ideas. At Peking University during the 1980s, Chai attended lectures introducing American psychological theories. Her mind was blown.[7]

Beijing was a world apart from Hunan's Liuyang. In Hunan, Lu Decheng did not read books for fun, nor did he attend academic lectures. In 1980, however, as an eighteen-year-old, he experienced a different type of freedom: the freedom to fall in love and have sex. The norm in Liuyang was for parents and family friends to arrange relationships for young adults, but Lu and his girlfriend Wang Qiuping became a couple after a chance meeting at a badminton match. Over their parents' objections, Lu and Wang began a sexual relationship and went into hiding, shacking up on the outskirts of town.[8]

Sexual norms had already started changing during the 1970s, when some rural families encouraged young couples to have sex before marriage – as part of a strategy to foster a long-term, stable relationship – and when city kids had clandestine dance parties. These trends continued in the 1980s.[9] Shen Tong was a first-year undergraduate student at Peking University in 1986. Shen recalled that when he and his girlfriend Xiaoying started having sex, "It was very liberating because all my life I had heard that sex was something to be scorned and was done only to have children." Shen linked sexual freedom to a broader sense of personal liberation. He wrote, "Since we lived in a restrictive society, I naturally felt that having sex was somehow an anti-government activity."[10]

Chai Ling also became sexually active as an undergraduate student at Peking University. She got together with a physics student named Qing. Overcoming the logistical challenges of gender-segregated dormitories and restrictions on dating, Chai and Qing became physically intimate. Two years later, Chai and Qing broke up and Chai began a relationship with the intense, politically active Feng Congde. They got married in spring 1988. Couples in love such as Chai Ling and Feng Congde, as well as Lu Decheng and Wang Qiuping, found ways to stay together by circumventing or avoiding state restrictions intended to reduce China's

---

[7] Chai Ling, *Heart*, 36, 38.   [8] Chong, *Egg*, 98–106.
[9] On rural patterns, see Yunxiang Yan, *Private Life under Socialism: Love, Intimacy, and Family Change in a Chinese Village, 1949–1999* (Stanford: Stanford University Press, 2003), 65–66; on city parties, see James Farrer, *Opening Up: Youth Sex Culture and Market Reform* (Chicago: University of Chicago Press, 2002), 66–67; and Paul G. Pickowicz, "High-Rise Counterculture," in *China Tripping: Encountering the Everyday in the People's Republic*, ed. Jeremy Murray, Perry Link, and Paul G. Pickowicz (Lanham, MD: Rowman and Littlefield, 2019), 66–68.
[10] Shen Tong, *Almost a Revolution* (Boston: Houghton Mifflin, 1990), 111–12.

birth rate. When Chai and Feng attempted to register their marriage, they learned that newlyweds had to have a combined age of forty-eight. They were four years short. Undeterred, Feng altered their identification documents and managed to trick the clerk.[11]

One of the most influential changes of China's 1980s was the one-child policy, the repercussions of which would contribute to severe unhappiness for Chai Ling as well as for Lu Decheng and Wang Qiuping, as we shall see in the following chapter. But for rural women who had lived through the 1950s and 1960s, the state's restrictive family planning regime was a cause for celebration. The one-child policy was the result of an intense political debate about how China's population growth hindered economic development.

China's leaders felt troubled by rapid population growth but were not sure how to address it. In 1979, missile scientist Song Jian created complex models and graphs to argue that uncontrolled population growth was a threat to China's national survival and that the only answer was to reduce China's average birth rate to one child per woman by 1985 and to stay at that rate for twenty to forty years. When demographer Liang Zhongtang of the Shanxi Party Academy saw Song Jian's plan, he quickly realized that the only way to implement it was through coercion and violence. Liang argued that the costs were too high and that an excessively low birth rate would lead to adverse consequences such as labor shortages and a rapidly aging society. Liang advocated for capping births at two children per family. But in the end, Song Jian's flashy scientific model, along with his government and military connections, convinced China's top leaders to implement a one-child policy.[12]

Older rural women did not know about the political battle that led to restrictive birth planning, but many supported the policy and worked hard to implement it during the 1980s. According to historian Gail Hershatter, who interviewed women in villages in Shaanxi Province:

As birth planning work intensified in rural areas after 1979, women who had borne many children in the 1950s and 1960s became its strongest supporters, many of them serving as local birth planning cadres. Their personal experience had led them to feel, passionately, that it was difficult to support and care for many children properly.

Feng Sumei was a women's team leader responsible for convincing villagers to restrict births. Feng said that "in most families, women

---

[11] Chai Ling, *Heart*, 80.
[12] Susan Greenhalgh, *Just One Child: Science and Policy in Deng's China* (Berkeley: University of California Press, 2008).

agreed with the family planning, but men did not ... How heavy the housework and sewing burden is for women if they have too many children!"[13] Some rural women during the 1980s saw the state's campaign to limit family size as more of a liberation than a violent intrusion.

* * *

China entered the 1980s with a mostly healthy, mostly literate population. These improvements in life expectancy and education had occurred during the Mao years, and they contributed to rapid economic growth after Mao's death.[14] Other elements associated with China's economic takeoff during the 1980s, including family farming plots, a more mobile workforce, rural markets, and township-and-village enterprises, also had roots in the 1950s, 1960s, and 1970s.

Lai Changxing's family in Fujian Province was uneducated – Lai himself, who was born in 1958, was barely literate – but during the Cultural Revolution Lai's father illicitly appropriated a swamp to use as his own vegetable plot.[15] Privately farming land outside the collective system was a politically risky survival strategy during the Mao years, but many rural families decollectivized before the state told them they were allowed to do so in the 1980s. Families that had farmed for themselves rather than for the collective had a leg up when it became possible to go into business and make money in the 1980s. So did officials, who were advantageously positioned to obtain goods at low prices set by the state, which allowed them to profit by reselling the items at much higher market prices.

Officials also had the power to make life easy or difficult for businesspeople, which encouraged a culture of bribery in which bosses greased the palms of authorities in exchange for permits and tax breaks. Lai Changxing learned this the hard way. After working as an apprentice blacksmith for two years, in 1979 he set up his own auto parts workshop. Lai invested his profits in a shoe factory, clothing shops, and a television import business, among other enterprises.[16] "You could start a business in the morning and make money by the evening," Lai told journalist

---

[13] Gail Hershatter, *The Gender of Memory: Rural Women and China's Collective Past* (Berkeley: University of California Press, 2011), 208–9.

[14] Barry Naughton, *The Chinese Economy: Transitions and Growth* (Cambridge, MA: MIT Press, 2007), 82.

[15] Oliver August, *Inside the Red Mansion: On the Trail of China's Most Wanted Man* (Boston: Houghton Mifflin, 2007), 101.

[16] August, *Red Mansion*, 102.

Hannah Beech. "Everything was so free and open back then that everyone had lots of businesses. You would be stupid not to."[17]

According to his family, Lai's success eventually attracted attention from local officials. Two officials Lai had refused to bribe visited his home to audit his television import business. When Lai's sister rebuffed them, they beat her up, charged Lai with tax fraud, and started investigating his other businesses. Lai suffered so badly from official scrutiny that he liquidated his businesses in Shaocuo, moved to the big city of Xiamen, and started over. He had learned his lesson. In Xiamen, Lai's success in building a massive business empire was matched – and facilitated – by his newfound ability to keep officials happy with favors and gifts.[18] By cultivating officials, Lai was able to make a fortune.

This type of corruption became widespread during the 1980s. The officials who benefited from it felt happy that they could finally milk their positions for privilege instead of constantly being the target of political campaigns, as they had been during the Mao years. A village Party secretary in Guangdong Province named Qingfa appropriated land for his own use, let locals know that he was happy to trade favors for "gifts," and channeled profits from village enterprises to his relatives. Most villagers, who themselves were benefiting from the economic changes of the early 1980s, accepted Qingfa's behavior: "A number of them felt they would do likewise if they were in his shoes," wrote three scholars who did fieldwork in the village near Hong Kong. "Qingfa's abuses seemed in keeping with a widely shared mood of cynical privatism and advantage seeking."[19]

The nexus of corrupt officials and bribe-paying citizens increased incomes for some people during the 1980s, but many others stuck with what they had known during the Mao years: the *danwei* (单位), or work unit, system. After graduating, university students like Chai Ling could expect an assignment to a work unit – usually an office, factory, or school – that would not only pay a salary but also provide housing, health care, child care, and schooling for children, and grant permission to travel or buy rationed goods. There were many downsides to life in a work unit, but Lu Decheng's family celebrated his hiring at the Liuyang bus station because it meant security and stability. Work unit life seemed less risky than going into private business. Even after putting poison in a

---

[17] Hannah Beech, "Smuggler's Blues," *Time*, October 14, 2002, content.time.com/time/world/article/0,8599,2056114,00.html.
[18] August, *Red Mansion*, 105.
[19] Anita Chan, Richard Madsen, and Jonathan Unger, *Chen Village: Revolution to Globalization*, 3rd ed. (Berkeley: University of California Press, 2009), 278–80.

rival's thermos, Lu Decheng kept his job. It would take a far more serious act to get fired.

★ ★ ★

During the 1980s, many people did not spend much time worrying about elite politics. China's top leaders, however, spent hours thinking about how to modernize the country while keeping the Chinese Communist Party in power. Finding the right balance between the benefits of private enterprise and the control and surveillance role of the work unit system was only one of the puzzles that occupied central officials in Beijing.

One major puzzle that top leaders grappled with and that also excited people who had suffered during the oppressive 1970s was how to reform China's political and economic systems. Journalist Yang Jisheng has written that leaders grappled with four different possible paths, each one dependent on a political variable, dictatorship versus democracy, and an economic variable, planned versus market. One path was to continue the Cultural Revolution, combining an authoritarian dictator-ship with the socialist planned economy that had prevailed during the 1960s and 1970s. This meant prioritizing heavy urban and hinterland industry oriented toward national defense, fueled by extracting grain from farmers tied to rural communes while prohibiting private markets and entrepreneurship. In October 1976, Mao's successor Hua Guofeng decisively blocked this path when he ordered the arrests of its primary advocates: Jiang Qing, Wang Hongwen, Yao Wenyuan, and Zhang Chunqiao, who became known as the "Gang of Four."[20]

Another possible path was to continue the Communist Party's dicta-torship alongside a more flexible planned economy akin to that of the pre-1957 period. Chen Yun, who led economic policy during the mid-1950s and who returned to political prominence as a seventy-three-year-old in 1978, was the main proponent of this view. Historian Julian Gewirtz argues that Chen Yun has been "caricatured as an exclusively conservative force in China's reform," but Chen in fact advocated for accepting markets in a "supplementary and secondary" role alongside a socialist planned economy.[21]

Deng Xiaoping, who pushed aside Hua Guofeng to become China's top leader at the age of seventy-four in 1978, ended up pushing for a different path: a market economy open to foreign investment and still

---

[20] Yang Jisheng, 中国改革年代的政治斗争 (Political conflict in China's reform era) (Hong Kong: Excellent Culture Press, 2004), 4.

[21] Julian Gewirtz, *Unlikely Partners: Chinese Reformers, Western Economists, and the Making of Global China* (Cambridge, MA: Harvard University Press, 2017), 46.

overseen by the authoritarian CCP. Deng's central position as the unquestioned boss throughout the 1980s presented a challenge not only for Chen Yun, who Deng repeatedly sidelined by denying him chances to speak at meetings, but also for proponents of a fourth possible path for China: a more open democratic political system plus an open economy.[22] Quashing calls for democracy, while also dealing with those like Chen Yun who feared the ills of market-oriented reforms, meant that even though Deng and his chosen path won out, China's reform journey was not smooth or straightforward. Prospects for economic and political reform seesawed during the 1980s. There was a general – but not absolute – pattern of more openness and promise in even-numbered years, including freely contested elections to local people's congresses in 1980 and public discussions of system change in 1986, often followed by backlash and crackdowns in such odd-numbered years as 1981, 1983, 1987, and, fatefully, 1989.[23]

Deng's willingness to advance his reform path while cracking down on alternatives did not hamper his popularity much during the mid-1980s. By 1984, many people in China felt genuine affection for Deng and his ability to move China away from the worst aspects of the Mao years. *People's Daily* photographer Wang Dong captured this feeling on October 1, 1984, when he snapped a picture of Peking University students unfurling a banner at the PRC's National Day parade that read, "Hello, Xiaoping" (小平，您好), a respectful but decidedly informal way to refer to a top leader. The photo ran in *People's Daily* the next day, and on October 3, 1984, the paper published what would be the first of many articles about the making of the banner and how it represented educated people's favorable opinions about Deng.[24]

The banner's creators originally planned to call Deng "Comrade Xiaoping," but they ran out of space on their cloth. "We all had some misgivings" about omitting "Comrade," said Guo Jianwei, "because this wasn't the way leaders were addressed in China ... But after we continued to discuss it, we felt there was no malice in it; we just wanted to give a friendly greeting to a leader on the part of the college students." Because the banner had not been reviewed and approved by university authorities, Guo Jianwei and his classmates had to sneak it into Tiananmen Square on National Day. They worried that they might get in trouble and that the banner might be deemed counterrevolutionary. Guo even hid at a relative's house after the parade because he feared

---

[22] Yang Jisheng, 中国改革年代的政治斗争 (Political conflict in China's reform era), 18–22.
[23] Yang Jisheng, 中国改革年代的政治斗争 (Political conflict in China's reform era), 19.
[24] *RMRB*, October 2, 1984, 2; *RMRB*, October 3, 1984, 3.

Figure 1.1 Hu Yaobang in 1986. Michel Baret/Gamma-Rapho via Getty Images.

police attention. But in the end, the students' risk taking was rewarded with positive media coverage. Students saying a cheeky hello bolstered Deng's image as a leader who enjoyed broad support.[25]

Retrospective myth making around Deng Xiaoping goes beyond celebrating "Hello Xiaoping" while forgetting Peking University students' fears that using the dictator's given name might get them arrested. The bigger myths relate to the role Deng played in reforming China's economy and opening China up to foreign investment. To be sure, Deng should be at the center of the story – he was the ultimate decider and the unapologetic dictator during the 1980s, after all. But giving Deng credit for everything erases the contributions of Hua Guofeng, General Secretary Hu Yaobang, Premier Zhao Ziyang, and even foreign economists. Mao's designated successor Hua Guofeng agreed with Deng Xiaoping about the need for economic reforms during the late 1970s, including setting up special economic zones that allowed foreign

[25] Joel Martinson, "Celebrating National Day, 1984," *Danwei*, October 1, 2008, web .archive.org/web/20160413235414/http://www.danwei.org/festivals/national_day.php.

investment, before Deng sidelined Hua and labeled him an opponent of reform.[26]

Hu Yaobang became general secretary of the Communist Party in 1982 and had a reputation as an approachable, honest official who – while still a proponent of a single-party system – pushed for tolerance rather than dictatorial methods.[27] In spring 1980, before Hu moved to the Party's central leadership compound in Zhongnanhai, a second-year Peking University student named Wang Juntao, along with a mechanic named Lu Pu, knocked on Hu's door and said they wanted to talk to him about politics. Hu let the two men in and engaged in a four-hour discussion about political reform and democracy. The leader told his visitors to improve China's system gradually rather than overthrowing it, recalling his own revolutionary background and how it took him a while to "learn how to wait and how to compromise."[28] Popular support for Hu's accessible leadership style was genuine throughout the 1980s but has disappeared from the official narrative inside China ever since Hu was purged at the end of 1986.

The presence of such reformers as Hu Yaobang in the central leadership convinced some people that working within a system dominated by the Communist Party was a palatable option. They accepted the logic of gradualism that Hu tried to explain to Wang Juntao and Lu Pu. Physicists Fang Lizhi and Xu Liangying, who had been expelled from the Communist Party during the 1950s, felt intensely critical of the Party but decided to rejoin it after being rehabilitated in 1978. Xu said, "My purpose in going back to the Party will be to change the Party." Fang decided to join his "friends in accepting re-entry into the Party in order to work inside it to change it."[29]

Zhao Ziyang, who was premier during the early 1980s and who took over as the Party's general secretary after the purge of Hu Yaobang, tried to make room for new ideas that would improve Communist Party rule rather than replace it. Roderick MacFarquhar and Julian Gewirtz have shown that Zhao's centrality in achieving reforms during the 1980s cannot be understated. The Communist Party, however, has airbrushed away Zhao's contributions even more thoroughly than those of Hu

---

[26] Frederick C. Teiwes and Warren Sun, "China's New Economic Policy under Hua Guofeng: Party Consensus and Party Myths," *China Journal* 66 (2011): 1–23.

[27] Bao Pu, Renee Chiang, and Adi Ignatius, trans. and ed., *Prisoner of the State: The Secret Journal of Zhao Ziyang*, hereafter abbreviated as *PS* (New York: Simon and Schuster, 2009), 255.

[28] George Black and Robin Munro, *Black Hands of Beijing: Lives of Defiance in China's Democracy Movement* (New York: Wiley, 1993), 54–55.

[29] Fang Lizhi, *Most Wanted*, 189–90.

Yaobang. Zhao had great interest in the theories of foreign economists, many of whom were critics of socialism. Zhao and his aides learned from such economists as Oxford professor Włodzimierz Brus; János Kornai, a Hungarian professor at Harvard; and Ota Šik, who pushed for reforms inside Czechoslovakia before becoming a professor in Switzerland; as well as American Nobel laureates Milton Friedman and James Tobin. Brus, Friedman, Kornai, Šik, and Tobin all visited China during the 1980s, exchanging ideas with Chinese economists and giving suggestions about how to make enterprises profitable, relax state-mandated price controls, and limit inflation. Zhao Ziyang's personal meetings with visiting economists received prominent coverage in *People's Daily*, and the foreign experts' language even made it into Zhao's own speeches.[30]

Roderick MacFarquhar has pointed out that in retrospect, Zhao recognized that in the mid-1980s he was an "economic reformer and a political conservative."[31] By the second half of the 1980s, Zhao's exclusive emphasis on economic reform, based on adapting foreigners' recommendations to China's unique circumstances, started to shift. Zhao realized that economic and political change could not be separated. Until about 1985 or 1986, Zhao recalled, "I'd believed that political reform in China should neither be exceedingly progressive, nor lag far behind economic reform. As economic reform deepened, the resistance from conservative forces within the Party grew more intense. Yet without political reform it would have been difficult to sustain economic reform."[32]

In 1986 and 1987, Zhao spoke of "genuinely doing a bit of democracy" and criticized the overconcentration of power in China's top leadership, saying that the country's current system was well suited for armed struggle and mass movements but not for modern economic development.[33] His proposed solutions included implementing a clear separation between the Communist Party and the state, as well as moving toward intra-Party democracy. Zhao was not talking about introducing multiparty elections or questioning the notion that the Communist Party should continue to dominate. In November 1986 he said, "Discussing reforming the political system is not discussing whether the Communist Party should govern, it is discussing how the Communist Party should govern."[34] Zhao later said that he wanted to make the Party's internal

---

[30] Gewirtz, *Unlikely Partners*.   [31] Roderick MacFarquhar, "Foreword," in *PS*, xxiv.
[32] *PS*, 257.
[33] Zhao Ziyang wenji bianji bu, ed., 趙紫陽文集 (Collected works of Zhao Ziyang) (Hong Kong: Chinese University Press, 2016), 3:472, 491.
[34] 趙紫陽文集 (Collected works of Zhao Ziyang), 3:468.

decision making transparent, increase dialogue with social groups that represented group interests rather than only serving the Party, offer more choices in People's Congress elections, and allow "greater press freedom, though under management and leadership ... Even if we did not allow full press freedom, we should allow the airing of public opinions."[35]

The changes of the 1980s, including major economic reforms and talk of increased political openness, caused happiness for many people in China. But for some people, the things that made them angry and frustrated about everyday life overwhelmed any sense of optimism they may have felt about the future.

[35] *PS*, 259.

2 Angry

New freedoms and economic opportunities made people in China happy during the 1980s. Fresh ideas from the country's top leaders also raised hopes. The flip side of this story, however, is that restrictions and repression, economic stress and unfairness, along with a geriatric dictatorship run by "old-man politics" rather than institutions or rules, caused great anger. People's frustrations predisposed them to hit the streets and demand change in 1989. This chapter mirrors the previous one in discussing how political restrictions, economic problems, and elite politics made people angry.

In August 1980, Deng Xiaoping told Italian journalist Oriana Fallaci that Cultural Revolution-style political movements were a thing of the past. Deng said that people were "fed up with large-scale movements," which harmed many individuals and got in the way of economic development.[1] Even though Deng was careful to not launch anything called a "movement" or "campaign" (运动), local officials still resorted to campaign-style methods at the grassroots during the 1980s in their efforts to punish criminality and enforce the one-child policy. The extralegal methods of the Strike Hard anticrime campaign that began in 1983, as well as the coercive and violent enforcement of the one-child policy, caused grave injustices and sparked grievances against Communist Party rule throughout China.

In August 1983, Deng Xiaoping told Minister of Public Security Liu Fuzhi to launch a "movement that won't be called a movement" to round up and punish murderers, robbers, gang members, human traffickers, and other criminals. Deng had started to pay closer attention to crime after visiting Wuxi in Jiangsu Province in February 1983. In Wuxi, Deng met with Jiang Weiqing, a member of the Central Advisory Commission.

---

[1] Deng Xiaoping, "Answers to the Italian Journalist Oriana Fallaci," August 21 and 23, 1980, in *Selected Works of Deng Xiaoping (1975–1982)*, trans. Bureau for the Compilation of Works of Marx, Engels, Lenin and Stalin under the Central Committee of the Communist Party of China (Beijing: Foreign Languages Press, 1984), 330.

Jiang told Deng that the economy was doing well but that people were feeling unsafe: "women are scared to go to work and good people fear bad people; it can't go on like this! The only way to solve this is for you, Elder Deng, to commit to it."

Deng asked Jiang what specific action he recommended. Jiang recommended a military-style campaign, saying, "arrest those who should be arrested, kill those who should be killed," and also deport some criminals to border zones. Jiang justified his call for extreme measures, saying that criminals feared only the death penalty or the cancelation of their urban residency permits.[2] Over the course of late 1983 and early 1984, police officers set arrest quotas, rounded up large numbers of alleged criminals, and quickly sentenced and punished them.[3] While some urban residents may have been pleased that cities felt safer, friends and relatives of people caught up in Strike Hard sweeps felt aggrieved.

Beijing bus worker Zhao Hongliang saw the human cost of Strike Hard when he traveled to Qinghai Province in 1987. Zhao talked to people who had been sentenced to five to seven years for theft and stripped of urban residency. As George Black and Robin Munro write:

These were the kind of young men Zhao had gone to school with, who had turned from unemployment to petty crime and now found themselves abandoned in Qinghai in the name of an official policy of "opening up the border areas." Zhao found them living in roofless lean-tos, at the mercy of the elements.

The Strike Hard anticrime drive had robbed the men of hope. Zhao felt "sick at heart" at their pitiful circumstances and returned to Beijing, where he would eventually become an activist on behalf of the working class in 1989.[4]

Others in China felt so upset when authorities struck hard against alleged criminals that they tried to exonerate the accused. In Hunan, Lu Decheng and his friend Liu Hongwu could not believe that a high school teacher from their town had been arrested and quickly sentenced to death for the crime of robbing a bank of 240,000 yuan. Liu had met the teacher, Zhang Rongwu, six months before the robbery. Zhang said that he was having trouble supporting his family on his low pay and that he was considering becoming an entrepreneur. Lu and Liu thought that the "police either hadn't got at the truth or they'd arrested the wrong man," according to author Denise Chong. Liu Hongwu wrote a letter

---

[2] Cui Min, "反思八十年代的'严打'" (Revisiting the "Strike Hard" movement of the 1980s), *Yanhuang chunqiu* 5 (May 2012): 16–22.

[3] Harold M. Tanner, *Strike Hard! Anti-crime Campaigns and Chinese Criminal Justice, 1979–1985* (Ithaca, NY: Cornell East Asia Series, 1999).

[4] Black and Munro, *Black Hands*, 119.

pleading for clemency to Hunan's governor and hand-delivered it to a
clerk in Changsha, but when Liu and Lu Decheng returned to Liuyang
that same afternoon, they saw the teacher, bound and gagged, standing
in the back of a truck heading to the execution ground.[5]

A few years later, in May 1989, Lu Decheng stood in front of the
Changsha train station with a banner reading "End one-party dictatorship and build up democratic China." When skeptical passersby spoke to
Lu, he tried to stoke outrage by reminding them of other Strike Hard
excesses. The crowd who gathered around Lu had all heard a story about
two Changsha men who were sentenced to death shortly after being
accused of raping a woman. As the story went, the woman was a sex
worker who had gone to the police to complain that the men had not paid
her. The men claimed that they had indeed paid, but by the time the sex
worker found their money between the mattress and the wall, it was too
late to stop the execution.[6] Lu directly linked the injustices of Strike
Hard to his calls for democracy in 1989.

The other injustice that resonated with the crowd outside the
Changsha train station in May 1989 related to the one-child policy.
When strangers walked by Lu Decheng, he called out, "I want to ask
how you would feel if you came across this situation. Just as a general
example – I'm not speaking for myself. What if your wife was pregnant,
about to deliver, and the planned childbirth people came and dragged
her off to have an abortion." This line of reasoning garnered more
sympathy from onlookers than Lu's banner did.[7] Lu was in fact speaking
from the heart – he and his wife, Wang Qiuping, had suffered deep
trauma because of the repressive tactics of local family planning officials.

Lu Decheng and Wang Qiuping's romance faced obstacles, primarily
because their parents opposed their getting together as teenagers: Lu was
nineteen and Wang was still eighteen. But China's one-child policy
targeted the couple when Wang got pregnant in summer 1982. As
Denise Chong writes:

Her pregnancy was against the law in several ways: only married couples could
apply for a childbirth permit; couples had to apply for the permit, good for one
year, *before* becoming pregnant; and married couples were not eligible for permits
until the wife was twenty-two *and* the couple's combined age was fifty.[8]

When family planning officials heard about Wang's pregnancy, they
confronted Lu and demanded that he show them proof that Wang had
had an abortion.

[5] Chong, *Egg*, 187–90.   [6] Chong, *Egg*, 206–7.   [7] Chong, *Egg*, 207.
[8] Chong, *Egg*, 107, italics in original.

Wang and Lu fled to the countryside outside Liuyang. They did not want to abort the baby. Lu's friend Liu Hongwu approached a doctor on their behalf to ask him to fake an abortion certificate. The doctor refused. Liu Hongwu then found a woman who was already planning on having an abortion. Liu paid her two hundred yuan to pretend to be Wang Qiuping when she went in for the operation. The ruse worked, as did Lu and Wang's sneaky effort to rush a clerk into giving them a marriage certificate during her lunch break – the clerk did not notice that Lu and Wang were too young to marry.

Wang Qiuping gave birth to a boy in January 1983. Baby Jinlong fell ill after a few days. Wang and Lu worried that the main hospital might refuse to treat a child that had been born illegally, so they brought Jinlong to the Chinese Medicine Hospital. A doctor there recommended an incubator and sent them to the main hospital, but it was too late. Jinlong died. Wang and Lu were devastated. According to Denise Chong, Lu Decheng was "haunted by their delay in seeking medical care, their indecision about which hospital to go to, and the precious time lost when they chose the wrong one. 'I blame the authorities,' he told Qiuping. 'They are the ones who forced us into our predicament.'"[9]

Adding to Wang and Lu's grief was guilt about how people who had helped them were punished. Authorities demoted and fined the doctor who had delivered Jinlong in a small clinic without a childbirth permit. The clerk who erroneously registered their marriage was also fined. When Lu Decheng refused to turn over his and Wang's marriage certificate to local family planning officials, they imposed a "social child-raising fee" and docked his pay by one-third. "You had an unauthorized child from a non-marriage," they said. "The child is dead, but don't think the matter is over!"[10] Lu, whose family had previously seen his job as a mechanic in a state-run garage as a ticket to long-term security, now realized that it made him vulnerable to financial penalties. He quit and resolved to open his own repair shop.

Lu Decheng's reaction to his family tragedy is a rare case in which it is possible to draw a direct line from China's repressive birth restrictions to political activism in 1989. Lu blamed China's political system for killing his son, harming kindhearted people who had helped him, and impoverishing a grieving parent. In May 1989, when Lu invoked forced abortions in his attempt to convince passersby at the Changsha train station to join the democracy movement, he hoped that his sense of injustice would resonate with others who had been affected by the one-child policy.

[9] Chong, *Egg*, 144.   [10] Chong, *Egg*, 145.

During the 1980s, campaign-style waves of forced abortions and coercive sterilization surgeries targeted rural women and harmed rural families.[11] Additional research is necessary to determine how many people who experienced reproductive violence behaved as Lu Decheng did and channeled their pain into activism in 1989. Most people, when asked, said that they recognized the need to reduce China's population growth and supported restricting births.[12] But when general support for a national policy clashed with personal preferences, even people whose bodies were not physically traumatized felt wounded. When I talk to friends in China about the joys of parenting my two sons, they often express envy at my freedom to choose my family's size. One professor I spoke to gave a typical response about being the father of an only child: "I am a victim of the birth planning policy." My friend was delighted to have had one daughter but always wished that she could have had a sibling.

In urban China, a different painful reality associated with family planning policy – abortion as birth control – traumatized many women, including such university students as Chai Ling. Many women during the 1980s had multiple abortions – of 1,200 women surveyed at abortion clinics in 1985, almost half had had two abortions and 18 percent had had three or more abortions.[13] Bioethicist Nie Jing-Bao's research uncovered similar numbers: 41 percent of women in a survey had had an abortion; of those who had had one, 37 percent had had two or more. Nie also showed that many women said that they had abortions because of state policy, failed contraception, or a combination of the two. Nie has found that even though abortion was common and widely accepted throughout China, it caused deep and lasting trauma and distress to women.[14]

Chai Ling's experience confirms Nie Jing-Bao's research about pain and trauma. Chai had three abortions before getting involved in the

---

[11] For an account focused on a single village in 1985, see Huang Shu-min, *The Spiral Road: Change in a Chinese Village through the Eyes of a Communist Party Leader*, 2nd ed. (Boulder, CO: Westview, 1998), 175–85; for an overview see Tyrene White, *China's Longest Campaign: Birth Planning in the People's Republic, 1949–2005* (Ithaca, NY: Cornell University Press, 2009). For a revisionist work that questions the assumption that rural families valued girls less than boys, see Kay Ann Johnson, *China's Hidden Children* (Chicago: University of Chicago Press, 2016).

[12] Nie Jing-Bao, *Behind the Silence: Chinese Voices on Abortion* (Lanham, MD: Rowman and Littlefield, 2005), 154.

[13] Virgina C. Li, Glenn C. Wong, Shu-hua Qiu, Fu-ming Cao, Pu-quan Li, and Jing-hua Sun, "Characteristics of Women Having Abortion in China," *Social Science & Medicine* 31, no. 4 (1990): 445–53.

[14] Nie, *Behind the Silence*, 147, 141.

Figure 2.1 Chai Ling. Michael Abramson/The LIFE Images Collection via Getty Images.

Tiananmen protests of 1989. While it is impossible to directly link Chai's three terminated pregnancies to her prominent leadership role in the democracy movement, multiple abortions were a source of anger, pain, and shame for Chai and many other women during the 1980s. In her memoir, Chai explained how abortion, rather than condoms or other contraceptive methods, became a go-to birth control method for young people: "We had no sex education at home, in high school, or in college," Chai wrote:

Even if I had known everything about how reproduction works, there was simply no place to acquire protection. In China, couples could not purchase contraception unless they were married ... Although Chinese society was puritanical in its expectations, it left a vacuum for how to prepare for and deal with our youthful emotions.[15]

Shen Tong's impression of sex and contraception differed from Chai Ling's, probably because Shen was not himself traumatized by multiple abortions. Shen recalled that over time, condoms became easier to buy in pharmacies. He linked the ubiquity of condoms and abortions to the

---

[15] Chai Ling, *Heart*, 46–47.

one-child policy. "Because of the state policy, it was much more convenient for young people to be sexually active. It was convenient because it was easy to have birth control and to have an abortion."[16]

Abortion was widespread during the 1980s not only because some young people did not know about or lacked access to contraceptives but also because restrictive policies made abortion mandatory for unmarried pregnant women. As Chai Ling wrote about getting pregnant as a university student, "there *were* no options" other than abortion.[17] Trauma associated with birth restrictions was a major source of anger throughout China during the 1980s, including on university campuses. University students chafed at other constraints as well.

Wang Yuan, an undergraduate at Peking University between 1984 and 1988, was pleased that she was able to change her major from microelectronics to Chinese literature. The freedom to switch majors affirmed her individuality. Wang and her classmates also debated the meaning of freedom when the university implemented a policy of turning off dormitory lights at 11 p.m. in late 1984. Competing posters appeared on campus, some arguing that "grown men and women should decide for themselves when to brush their teeth, wash their face, and go to bed," while others held that with eight students in each room, reaching consensus about bedtime was impossible. "If our country had a smaller population, direct democracy could work. But in a country as populated as China, only a dictatorship can preserve peace," a poster in favor of a lights-out policy stated.

Wang Yuan was in the shower room when the new lights-out policy suddenly went into effect at 11 p.m. on December 10, 1984. She wiped the soap off of her face, groped her way through a pitch-black hallway, and watched as students yelled, set off firecrackers, and "set fire to broom handles, chair legs, or anything else they could find." After students yelled at the university president's wife and broke a glass display case, the protest fizzled out. "The adrenaline wore off, and exhaustion took its place," Wang recalled. "The next day, the lights-out policy wasn't an issue. Most of us were sound asleep long before that." Wang's schoolmates felt aggrieved about restrictions on their freedom and tried to connect slights in their everyday lives to larger issues of

---

[16] Rowena Xiaoqing He, *Tiananmen Exiles: Voices of the Struggle for Democracy in China* (New York: Palgrave Macmillan, 2014), 100.

[17] Chai Ling, *Heart*, 47, italics in original.

individual rights and democracy, but – at least in 1984 – they lacked focus and direction.[18]

That changed in 1986. Peking University students Li Caian and Zhang Xiaohui set up a "Marxist Youth Faction" and issued a proclamation comparing the Communist Party to a "huge spider that ruled by terror and violence." Li and Zhang were arrested and sentenced for the crime of counterrevolutionary incitement in November 1986.[19] That same month, something even more consequential and disquieting for top leaders in Beijing was taking place in Anhui Province. Students at the University of Science and Technology of China (USTC) in Hefei began pushing to democratize elections for district people's representative. On December 4, 1986, local officials held a forum for candidates and voters. In the words of USTC vice president Fang Lizhi, "this meeting became an almost unheard-of event in China: several thousand students crowded an auditorium for what was essentially a free political convention." In November, Fang had given lectures in Shanghai and Ningbo about democracy, reform, and modernization. Vice Premier Wan Li had followed Fang's tracks and collected recordings of Fang's talks. On November 30, Wan and Fang debated for more than an hour at a roundtable on higher education. Wan Li finally saw that the only way he could beat Fang was by pulling rank. Wan asked when Fang joined the Communist Party. "Thirty years ago," Fang answered. "For me it's fifty," said Wan.[20]

Wan Li had seniority on his side. Fang Lizhi had fresh ideas that garnered support from thousands of young people. His goal at the time, he recalled, was to "support the just demands of the students" while also "trying to show that the Communist Party could still be open-minded." Fang decided to speak his mind at the candidates' forum on December 4. He took the stage and said, "The only reliable democracy is a democracy that is built on popular awareness and won by struggle from below. A thing bestowed from above, after all, can always be taken back from above."[21] Fang's extemporaneous speech at the meeting became an inspiration for bottom-up democratizers and fueled demonstrations on the streets of Hefei and Shanghai, as well as cities in Hubei, Hunan, Shaanxi, and Sichuan provinces.

---

[18] Anna Wang, *Inconvenient Memories: A Personal Account of the Tiananmen Square Incident and the China Before and After* (Foothill Ranch, CA: Purple Pegasus, 2019), 58–59, 60–63.

[19] Chuan Fu, 十年学潮纪实 (Ten-year record of student movements) (Beijing: Beijing chubanshe, 1990), 141.

[20] Fang Lizhi, *Most Wanted*, 258, 254–56.   [21] Fang Lizhi, *Most Wanted*, 263, 258.

Authorities in Hefei gave the student protesters plenty of room and affirmed that their protest was legal. But Shanghai and Beijing officials caused anger by using police to disperse and arrest protesters, sparking new marches. Shanghai students displayed banners reading "Long live democracy" and "Democracy, freedom, equality."[22] Shanghai Jiaotong University students debated Mayor Jiang Zemin in a dialogue session on December 19, 1986; that same day students besieged a Shanghai municipal government building. Students from Shanghai's Tongji University issued four demands to Mayor Jiang: affirm that the democracy movement is justified, patriotic, and legal; acknowledge that students have the right to display posters and march legally; allow newspapers to report accurately on the student movement; and protect the physical safety of student marchers.[23]

In Beijing, Shen Tong marched to Tiananmen Square on January 1, 1987. His father tried to stop Shen from demonstrating, saying, "Blood will be shed." Shen recalled that his dad was "trying to frighten me." He went out anyway. What he saw did scare him. Secret police thrust cameras in the marchers' faces; uniformed officers rushed at students in Tiananmen Square, "grabbing them and throwing them into police vans." Shen ran away and did not get in trouble, but he later learned that twenty-five classmates from Peking University had been arrested; many others had to write self-criticisms after being identified in photographs taken by the authorities.[24]

Cracking down with arrests and other penalties ended the student protests of late 1986 and early 1987. Deng Xiaoping was convinced that this harsh approach, which also included forcing Hu Yaobang to resign as general secretary of the Communist Party and expelling Fang Lizhi from the Party, was appropriate and effective. "When it comes to dictatorial methods," Deng said on December 30, 1986:

we not only need to emphasize them, we need to apply them whenever necessary. Of course, we should be cautious in applying them, trying to not arrest too many and doing our best to avoid bloodshed. But if they want to create bloody incidents, what are you going to do?

The grievances and demands for greater freedom that had sparked the protests remained unaddressed, but Deng was convinced that "if we

---

[22] Jeffrey N. Wasserstrom, *Student Protests in Twentieth-Century China: The View from Shanghai* (Stanford: Stanford University Press, 1991), 298.
[23] Chuan Fu, 十年学潮纪实 (Ten-year record of student movements), 144–45.
[24] Shen Tong, *Almost a Revolution*, 116–19.

retreat, we'll have worse trouble in the future."[25] His unapologetic preference for dictatorial methods would be a recipe for worse trouble in 1989.

Aside from being upset by the repression of their specific demands for
democracy, many people in China were worn down and pissed off by the
arbitrary and corrupt behavior of work unit leaders at the grassroots.
During extensive interviews in 1988, Perry Link observed that leaders of
work units had all-encompassing control over "a worker's rank, salary,
and job description" and also "his or her housing, children's education,
permission to travel, access to rationed goods, and political reputation."
The economic security of a job in a work unit came with a steep price:
loss of control over everyday personal decisions and freedoms. As a
sociologist in Beijing told Link:

Even things that you Westerners take as natural rights – where you live, whether
you can travel, when you can marry, or have a child – are controlled by the unit
leaders in China. Your leader also makes records in your personnel file, which
you are not allowed to see. If you offend him or her, the comments stay with you
forever.[26]

Over the course of the 1980s, people's frustrations mounted as the
indignities of working in repressive conditions were compounded by
economic stress.

★ ★ ★

Economist Steven N. S. Cheung argues that reforms in the countryside
during the 1980s were successful, especially a household responsibility
contract system that distributed land to families who could keep profits
for themselves after fulfilling their obligations to the state.[27] But not
everyone thrived. In the summer of 1986, Bai Hua, a journalism student
at Renmin University in Beijing, traveled to the countryside to investigate
how economic changes were affecting rural China. She noticed that
farmers who had initially been happy with growing prosperity had started
pointing out problems. The price of fertilizer and seed was increasing but
the amount the government paid for crops stagnated. Farmers also
struggled with a two-track economy: the state sold goods at fixed prices,
leading to supply shortages, while private traders had reliable stockpiles
and charged much more. One farmer told Bai Hua, "I spent 2,000 yuan

[25] Deng Xiaoping, 邓小平文选 (Selected works of Deng Xiaoping) (Beijing: Renmin
chubanshe, 1993), 3:196.
[26] Perry Link, *Evening Chats in Beijing: Probing China's Predicament* (New York: Norton,
1992), 61, 64–65.
[27] Steven N. S. Cheung, "The Economic System of China," *Man and the Economy* 1, no. 1
(2014): 15.

on my crops last year, and then made only 2,060 yuan selling them. For a whole year's work I earned almost nothing."[28]

Some farmers struggled. But people in the countryside had more control over their economic lives than industrial workers did during the 1980s, especially after 1986. According to Steven N. S. Cheung, "Applying the responsibility contract to industry was more of a problem." Cheung explains that "in industrial production physical assets depreciate and may get stolen, and state workers could not be discharged under existing laws."[29] One Party history expert I spoke to said that contracting fostered resentment between workers and managers. Factory leaders kept profits for themselves after fulfilling contracts. And because contracts were short term, managers tried to make money quickly rather than maintaining equipment or investing for the future.

Watching factory directors enrich themselves was especially galling for workers who had spent their careers in a single work unit. Sociologist Joel Andreas has found that during the early 1980s, workers' wages increased and work units invested heavily in housing. Workers also had a chance to voice complaints and suggestions in revamped staff and worker congresses (SWC). But as reforms deepened in the mid-1980s, factory directors and other officials increased their authority at the expense of workers, whose role in SWCs diminished. Wages stagnated and what had once seemed like lifetime job security wavered as factories began hiring workers on short-term contracts.[30]

Workers expressed their feelings through song: "We are grateful to Deng Xiaoping for raising wages, but we remember Mao Zedong for not raising prices." By fall 1985, bus drivers and ticket collectors were so fed up that they went on strike. Ticket taker Zhao Hongliang explained that his colleagues' demands for higher pay were not about politics, they were about addressing economic uncertainty. Officials deflected the strike by granting a pay hike and giving new boots and coats to the bus workers, but Zhao's bosses stigmatized him as a troublemaker. Strikes became more widespread in 1987, when there were at least 127, and expanded during the inflation-plagued first ten months of 1988, which saw more than 700 strikes throughout China.[31]

University students and professors also struggled with economic difficulties and substandard living conditions. While they did not go on strike

---

[28] Quoted in Black and Munro, *Black Hands*, 97.
[29] Cheung, "The Economic System of China," 15–16.
[30] Joel Andreas, *Disenfranchised: The Rise and Fall of Industrial Citizenship in China* (New York: Oxford University Press, 2019).
[31] Black and Munro, *Black Hands*, 114–17, 120.

like workers did, they did suffer from low morale. An overexpansion in postsecondary enrollment led to many university students subsisting on paltry stipends and stressing about dismal job prospects after graduation.[32] In Shandong Province, students at a teacher training college languished in "almost complete apathy toward study," knowing that they were on track for careers that offered "low pay, terrible working conditions, no social respect, and no hope of anything better," wrote Andrew J. Spano, who taught at Taian Teachers' College in 1988 and 1989. Spano's students crowded together in dormitories with broken windows, no heat, and frequent electricity and water outages. They urinated in sinks at night because the public toilet was too far away.[33] Professors at elite institutions in Beijing had it better but were still embarrassed and frustrated by their small, crowded homes and insultingly low salaries. One professor of medicine told Perry Link, "We are underpaid, underprivileged, underappreciated, and overworked. That sums it up."[34]

Corruption made people even angrier because they were suffering while they saw others cheating their way toward prosperity. Rumors circulated about how the children of such top officials as Deng Xiaoping, Zhao Ziyang, and others were profiting from corruption. According to sociologist Dingxin Zhao, "The psychological impact of corruption was enormous" during the late 1980s. Public opinion surveys revealed that more than 83 percent of respondents in urban China "believed that most cadres were corrupt"; 63 percent of cadres themselves admitted to corrupt practices.[35] Perry Link learned from his interviews that these practices ranged from "bribery, nepotism, smuggling, trading of favors, eating and drinking on the public dole, taking goods home to 'test' them, 'borrowing' money and not returning it" to *guandao* (官倒, official profiteering) when officials or their family members bought items at low prices fixed by the state and resold them for huge profits.[36]

Rampant inflation in 1988 and early 1989 added to citizens' grievances. People watched corrupt officials being driven around in Mercedes Benzes, then found that their own wages could not cover the skyrocketing costs of food. Official inflation rates were 18.5 percent in 1988 and 28 percent during the first three months of 1989.[37] In August 1988, people reacted to top leaders' plans to relax price controls by rushing to banks to withdraw their savings, which they then used to buy gold and

---

[32] Dingxin Zhao, *The Power of Tiananmen: State–Society Relations and the 1989 Beijing Student Movement* (Chicago: University of Chicago Press, 2001).
[33] Andrew J. Spano, "Death of a Dream in Rural China," in *The Broken Mirror: China after Tiananmen*, ed. George Hicks (Chicago: St James Press), 311–12.
[34] Link, *Evening Chats*, 90–91.   [35] Zhao, *Power of Tiananmen*, 126.
[36] Link, *Evening Chats*, 55.   [37] Zhao, *Power of Tiananmen*, 127.

such items as beds, bicycles, matches, shirts, and toilet paper, hoping that durable goods might retain their value. Press reports about price reforms not only sparked runs on banks and panic buying, they also gave the sense that central leaders lacked the expertise to continue pursuing economic reforms. Although some people had expressed satisfaction with top leaders in the mid-1980s, by the end of 1988 the downsides of a system that historian Chung Yen-lin has labeled "old-man politics" had become clear to many people in China.

★ ★ ★

Rather than explaining elite politics during the 1980s in terms of institutionalization or factionalism, Chung debunks the notion that Deng Xiaoping attempted to institutionalize a system of collective leadership and dismantles the claim that Deng was the arbiter between a reform faction and a conservative, hard-line faction. Instead, revolutionary seniority bestowed political power.[38] Deng was the most senior – he turned eighty-five in August 1989 – and he had credentials as a capable military leader before 1949. According to Frederick Teiwes, Deng's close working relationship with Mao Zedong also bolstered Deng's authority; Mao trusted Deng to accomplish difficult tasks during the 1950s, 1960s, and 1970s, even though Mao had purged Deng twice during the Cultural Revolution.[39] These factors elevated Deng above other politically active octogenarians, including Li Xiannian (eighty years old in 1989), Wang Zhen (eighty-one), Yang Shangkun (eighty-two), Chen Yun (eighty-four), and Peng Zhen (eighty-seven). Deng's claims to revolutionary seniority not only meant that his geriatric colleagues consistently deferred to him as the top decision maker throughout the 1980s. They also meant that political survival for such younger leaders as Hu Yaobang and Zhao Ziyang required successfully interpreting, praising, and amplifying vague signals from Deng and other elders.

Deng may have said that he was systematizing collective leadership, but that does not mean that he was actually doing so. Political scientist Joseph Torigian argues that Deng instead deployed language about institutionalization and consultation to bolster his own position as the ultimate decider behind the scenes.[40] In unguarded moments, Deng and

---

[38] Chung, "The Ousting of General Secretary Hu Yaobang."

[39] Frederick C. Teiwes, "The Paradoxical Post-Mao Transition: From Obeying the Leader to 'Normal Politics'," *China Journal*, no. 34 (1995): 55–94.

[40] Joseph Torigian, "The Shadow of Deng Xiaoping on Chinese Elite Politics," *War on the Rocks*, January 30, 2017, warontherocks.com/2017/01/the-shadow-of-deng-xiaoping-on-chinese-elite-politics.

his colleagues admitted this. Zhao Ziyang recalled hearing that when Deng met with other elders in 1987 to discuss their retirement from formal leadership positions, they agreed that "there should only be one 'mother-in-law'" (婆婆) of the Politburo Standing Committee (PSC) and that "Deng's position was not to change; he was the 'mother-in-law'" of the PSC and no other elders would have the final say on major decisions.[41]

Chen Yun used a different metaphor to acknowledge Deng's dictatorial role. In late May 1989, Chen Yun asked the elders on the Central Advisory Commission to raise their hands to firmly support Deng's position as the "mafia boss" (头子) of Party Center. Chen's secretary Xu Yongyue changed this revealing label to "core" (核心) of Party Center when Chen's remarks were eventually published.[42] In a moment of crisis for the Communist Party, Deng's elderly peers bowed down and kissed the hand of China's godfather.

Serving under a godfather put General Secretary Hu Yaobang (general secretary from 1982 to 1987) and Zhao Ziyang (premier from 1982 to 1987 and general secretary from 1987 to 1989) in an impossible position. The younger leaders in charge of day-to-day leadership lacked autonomy; they often had to guess at what Deng wanted. Deng had poor hearing and a faulty memory, and even in the early 1980s he lacked the stamina to work a full day. One of Frederick Teiwes's interviewees told him that "on one occasion Deng requested a meeting with provincial leaders but when they gathered at his home he demanded to know what they were doing there and sent them away."[43]

Working under a system of old-man politics was difficult not only because Deng, the main old man, was detached; it was especially trying because all the other old men continued to meddle and eventually came together to bring down first Hu Yaobang and then Zhao Ziyang. According to Chung Yen-lin, Hu consistently kissed up to such elders as Peng Zhen by proposing that they "should enjoy the same political treatment and living expenses" that members of the Politburo Standing Committee did. Hu also "directed the Central Propaganda Department to give special prominence to nine veteran revolutionaries," including Chen Yun, Peng Zhen, and Wang Zhen. But elders thought that Hu Yaobang was too weak on attacking "bourgeois liberalization" and

---

[41] *PS*, 209.
[42] Qiao Jun, "晚年陈云与邓小平: 心心相通 – 访国家安全部部长, 原陈云同志秘书许永跃" (Two hearts beat as one: Chen Yun and Deng Xiaoping in old age – an interview with Chen Yun's former secretary and Minister of State Security Xu Yongyue), *Bainianchao* no. 3 (2006): 16–17.
[43] Teiwes, "The Paradoxical Post-Mao Transition," 71.

Figure 2.2 Deng Xiaoping, Zhao Ziyang, and Li Peng. AFP/AFP via Getty Images.

"spiritual pollution." They blamed Hu for the outbreak of protests in 1986. When such elders as Bo Yibo, Peng Zhen, Yang Shangkun, and Wang Zhen sensed that Deng Xiaoping's support for Hu Yaobang was wavering, they circled like sharks and maneuvered to persuade Deng to force Hu to resign. Chung reports that the men went to Deng's home on December 27, 1986, "to express their serious concerns about the student movement. They all attributed the student demonstrations to Hu Yaobang's weak leadership and his excessive indulgence toward outspoken intellectuals."[44] A week later, Hu was out as general secretary.

This was not institutionalized, consensus-driven politics, nor was it a battle between clearly defined reformers and conservatives. It was a system in which elderly men saw themselves as indispensable and irreplaceable guardians. The elders were unwilling to trust younger leaders to get work done or to learn from mistakes. This meant that political survival depended not on taking initiatives or understanding and sympathizing with different social groups. It depended on reading Deng Xiaoping's moods and placating all of the other politically active old men around him. In this regard, Premier Li Peng was second to none.

Li Peng rose to the position of premier in 1987 after Hu Yaobang was forced to resign and Zhao Ziyang ascended to the position of general secretary. After the failed price reforms and the inflation surge of 1988 damaged prospects for further economic openings, Li Peng sensed an opportunity to circle the sharks once again, this time around Zhao

---

[44] Chung, "The Ousting of General Secretary Hu Yaobang," 110.

Ziyang. Ordinary people in China who were paying attention in 1988 and 1989 increasingly linked elders who were unwilling to relinquish power to the many problems bedeviling China during the 1980s. Li Peng's ability to win at old-man politics made Li, along with Deng Xiaoping, a main target of public rage when protests erupted in 1989.

3   China's 1980s
Alternative Paths

What alternative paths might have made more people happy and fewer people angry during the 1980s? What if the old men who pushed aside Hu Yaobang in late 1986 and maneuvered to weaken Zhao Ziyang in 1988 and 1989 had retired and stayed out of politics? Would escaping from old-man politics have led to different outcomes in 1989? Yes. But getting there would have required Deng Xiaoping to depart from his long-standing habits and practices.

Deng has to be at the center of exploring different paths because his revolutionary seniority made big changes possible in the first place. Without support from Deng, younger leaders such as Hu Yaobang and Zhao Ziyang might have found it impossible to implement market-style changes in the economy. Imagine that, starting in the early 1980s, Deng had completely retired and refused to get involved in any major decisions. To prevent Chen Yun and other old men from limiting economic reforms, Deng would have had to persuade Chen and all his other elderly colleagues to retreat, stay silent, and stay completely out of the way as Hu and Zhao pushed a reform agenda.

A scenario empty of meddling old men would not have included the harsh Strike Hard anticrime campaigns that troubled Zhao Hongliang and angered Lu Decheng. It would not have included movements opposing bourgeois liberalization and spiritual pollution, allowing such critical thinkers as Fang Lizhi to openly advocate for bottom-up political reforms and contested elections at the local level. More crucially, Hu Yaobang would have continued as general secretary beyond January 1987. When Hu died in April 1989, some of his mourners speculated that his humiliating dismissal had hastened his death. If Hu had not been purged and had died while still in office, his memorial service would have been an opportunity to celebrate his successors' push for continued reforms instead of becoming a moment for people to vent rage about how the reforms had stalled. The many problems that caused anger in the 1980s, including arbitrary repression by work unit leaders, corruption, and repression, would not have disappeared overnight, but the more consultative and transparent systems that Hu and Zhao favored might have given people hope that solutions and improvements were on the way.

Deng Xiaoping did in fact want to retire and did try to force his elderly colleagues to step aside and stop meddling, but he found no effective way to do so. In May 1986, when Deng told Hu Yaobang about his plan to retire in 1987, Hu's support for the notion became a strike against him among other elders – it was politically incorrect to suggest that Deng was anything but indispensable. After Zhao Ziyang ascended to the position of general secretary, he showed that he had learned this lesson, stating how fortunate the Party was that Deng, Li Xiannian, Chen Yun, Peng Zhen, and other senior revolutionaries were still "alive and well" and available to issue instructions and offer help. On November 2, 1987, Zhao said that even though Deng had given up most of his formal positions,

> his position and role as China's decider on important questions has not changed. We still need Comrade Xiaoping at the helm in pivotal moments. The Politburo Standing Committee thinks that whenever we encounter a major problem, we still must ask Comrade Xiaoping for instructions, and Comrade Xiaoping can still summon us to meet.[1]

Zhao was stuck. Because his position depended not only on Deng's support but also on affirming Deng's seniority, wisdom, and ultimate authority, Zhao had no way to escape from old-man politics.

Just as the depth of China's economic reforms during the 1980s depended on Deng's full support, the hard limits of political change during the decade were set by Deng's unapologetic embrace of single-party dictatorship. Deng differed in this regard from Chiang Ching-kuo, who as leader of the Republic of China in Taiwan tolerated genuine opposition parties in 1986, and from Mikhail Gorbachev, who allowed contested legislative elections in the Soviet Union in 1989. Taiwan and the former Soviet Union have taken strikingly different paths since the 1980s, but in both cases political change came from top leaders willingly loosening their dictatorial powers.

Deng and the elders around him refused to tolerate political opening because it seemed like a betrayal of the revolution that had defined their careers and given their lives meaning since they were young men. Paying proper tribute to that past became more important than China's present or future. This is why, in 1989, such elders as Chen Yun repeatedly referred to the blood shed by revolutionary martyrs as a justification for

---

[1] 趙紫陽文集 (Collected works of Zhao Ziyang), 4:255.

upholding the Communist Party's dictatorship. Chen Yun even quantified it: more than twenty-four million people, including his own bodyguard on the Long March, had died in order to establish socialism in China. Their memories, Chen said, must be "cherished" by upholding Deng's paramount leadership.[2] Deng and Chen did not pause to wonder whether millions of revolutionary martyrs, cut down before their time, would have wanted to be evoked to prop up a system of old-man politics. By refusing to gracefully exit politics, China's elderly power holders had created and worsened a situation that by 1989 had become explosive.

How would the lives of Chai Ling, Lu Decheng, and others have changed if China had followed a different path during the 1980s? Chai Ling dreamed of studying in the United States. In April 1989 she applied to a graduate program in child psychology at Teachers College, Columbia University. A month later, Chai's husband Feng Congde learned that he had been accepted to a PhD program at Boston University; Chai could have joined him regardless of the results of her own application. If Hu Yaobang had stayed in office through 1989, it is unlikely that Chai and Feng would have put aside their "American dream" and thrown themselves into a democracy movement for a "Chinese dream" that "now took priority."[3] They could have continued their academic careers uninterrupted.

What about the traumas that Chai Ling, Lu Decheng, and Wang Qiuping suffered as a result of restrictions on birth that led to widespread abortions in place of contraceptive use and that Lu Decheng believed caused the death of his baby son? What changes might have allowed Chai Ling to avoid multiple unplanned pregnancies or would have allowed Lu and Wang to marry and start a family without being harassed and mistreated by family planning officials?

China's top leaders were committed to controlling population growth – the debate was whether to limit families to one or two children. Even the two-child policy that demographer Liang Zhongtang promoted would have prohibited third births and would have required couples to delay marrying and starting families until they reached a certain age. In 1984, appalled at the violent forced abortions and coercive sterilizations that accompanied the enforcement of the one-child policy in rural China, Liang Zhongtang wrote to Hu Yaobang and Zhao Ziyang advocating for a two-child policy. As early as 1981, Zhao had spoken positively about allowing rural families whose first child had been a girl to have a second

---

[2] Qiao Jun, "晚年陈云与邓小平: 心心相通" (Two hearts beat as one: Chen Yun and Deng Xiaoping in old age), 16–17.
[3] Chai Ling, *Heart*, 90, 181.

baby. Zhao said that to avoid excessive coercion and to prevent rural people from openly resisting, "We need our policy to be based on what farmers can accept."[4] Three years later, both Zhao and Hu Yaobang approved Liang Zhongtang's proposal to permit second births.[5] In practice, the one-child policy became more flexible. Violence and repression continued but were never as awful as the butchery of 1983, which saw 21 million sterilizations and 14 million abortions. But in spite of Zhao and Hu's support, bureaucrats in the National Family Planning Commission prevented the pilot two-child program that Liang promoted in Yicheng County, Shanxi Province from spreading nationwide.[6]

A two-child policy was still quite restrictive. It would not have fundamentally addressed the problems that traumatized Chai Ling, Lu Decheng, and Wang Qiuping. Liang Zhongtang advocated for delaying marriage and birth – under a two-child policy, Lu and Wang would still have been too young and presumably would have had incentives to fraudulently register their marriage and hide Wang's pregnancy. Improved sex education and easier access to contraceptives, including for unmarried teenagers, would have done far more to help Chai Ling, Lu Decheng, and Wang Qiuping. An alternative path that offered these seemingly simple fixes would have required a cultural shift that went far beyond what Hu Yaobang and Zhao Ziyang signed off on in 1984. During the Mao years, normal human sexual behavior sometimes got punished as bourgeois decadence or hooliganism, through extrajudicial violence or even criminal sentences.[7] In the 1980s political environment that "struck hard" at sexual deviance and frowned on "bourgeois liberalization," it would have been risky for political leaders to advocate for changes that appeared to encourage premarital or extramarital sex. But if Zhao Ziyang had been able to continue to push for political reforms as he had begun to do during the second half of the 1980s, a shift in broader cultural norms might have eventually come, albeit too late for Chai, Lu, and Wang.

Urging patience and opting for gradual reform rather than radical, quick action sounded reasonable on an intellectual level and was the

---

[4] 趙紫陽文集 (Collected works of Zhao Ziyang), 1:274.

[5] 趙紫陽文集 (Collected works of Zhao Ziyang), 2:446.

[6] Vanessa Piao, Huang Anwei, and Cao Li, "梁中堂: 一胎是政治特殊階段產" (Liang Zhongtang: The one-child policy was the product of a unique political period), *New York Times* (Chinese web edition), October 30, 2015, cn.nytimes.com/china/20151030/cc30liang/zh-hant.

[7] Neil J. Diamant, *Revolutionizing the Family: Politics, Love, and Divorce in Urban and Rural China, 1949–1968* (Berkeley: University of California Press, 2000); Yang Kuisong, "How a 'Bad Element' Was Made: The Discovery, Accusation, and Punishment of Zang Qiren," in *Maoism at the Grassroots*, 19–50.

most realistic path available to Hu Yaobang and Zhao Ziyang. But gradualism offered scant comfort to people who were hurting and angry because of financial pressures, bad housing, indignities at work, and reproductive traumas. April 1989 offered hope for something better, sooner than many people had imagined.

Part Two

The Tiananmen Protests

4   The Tiananmen Protests as History

A few years ago, I visited a retired couple in China. When I told them that I was working on a book about 1989, their reaction was positive and encouraging. The first thing the woman said was that during the protest movement, people in Beijing were happy, hopeful, and working together. Then her husband got up from his chair, walked over to a bookshelf, and turned around a picture frame that had been facing inward toward the books. It was a photograph of tens of thousands of people waving huge red banners in Tiananmen Square, taken at the height of the hunger strike in May 1989. The photo was normally hidden from view. Casual visitors or snooping neighbors would not have noticed it. When the couple wanted to remember 1989, the image of Tiananmen Square, full of hopeful energy and the potential for meaningful change, became a central part of their living room.

Over the course of our conversation, the couple expressed sadness about the bloody crackdown that ended the protest movement and ushered in an era of cynical corruption and heightened repression. But they mostly focused on the excitement and positivity captured in their secret photo. By remembering the beginning and middle of the Tiananmen protests of 1989, the couple kept hope alive. Few of the hundreds of memoirs, scholarly books, and documentary films about 1989 accomplish this as quickly and effectively as the retired couple's photograph, shining hope into their home with a flick of the wrist. The 1989 protests aimed to change China for the better. For a few weeks in 1989, some aspects of life in China did get better.

In comparison with my hosts' hopeful approach, *Gate of Heavenly Peace* – a must-watch documentary film about the student movement – is grim. I mention it because the film is often the main source through which young people in or outside China contend seriously with the history of the Tiananmen protests of 1989. This is a problem because the viewing experience minimizes hope, maximizes failure, and over-emphasizes students while ignoring other people in Beijing. When I watched *Gate of Heavenly Peace* for the first time in a large auditorium at Portland State University in January 1999 and listened to codirector Carma Hinton lecture about the film, I came away with the same reaction undergraduates have when they see it in the courses I teach at Simon Fraser University. I was crushed and saddened by a sense of unavoidable failure. I was angry about student leaders' mistakes and missteps, each one of which seemed to prod and provoke the Communist Party into harsh responses. I am ashamed to admit now that I loathed Chai Ling, who is the film's central villain, portrayed as someone who purportedly wanted and welcomed bloodshed but who was apparently too scared to stick around for it. Since first watching the documentary, the more I have learned about 1989, the more I have wanted to push back against narratives that dwell on mistakes and failure and that blame activists, participants, and bystanders for things that were not their fault.

It is difficult for printed words to compete with the powerful sights and sounds of documentary films, but memoirs and scholarly books and articles better capture the excitement and positive energy of the protests. Sociologist Craig Calhoun's *Neither Gods nor Emperors* chronicles student leaders' successes, explains how students and bystanders understood democracy, and convincingly argues against the notion that the movement's defeat was inevitable.[1] Sociologist Dingxin Zhao's *The Power of Tiananmen* expertly shows how student leaders' decisions were spontaneous individual acts competing to attract onlookers' attention.[2] Historians Joseph W. Esherick and Jeffrey N. Wasserstrom and political scientist Elizabeth J. Perry, along with other contributors to Wasserstrom and Perry's book about protest and political culture, trace the symbolism of students' petitions, marches, and sit-ins back to earlier moments in Chinese history.[3] And in the recently published *The Last Secret: The Final Documents from the June Fourth Crackdown*, a writer using the pen name Wu Yulun provides the most up-to-date account of how top officials in the Chinese Communist Party handled the protest movement.[4]

The history of the protests in these pages draws on these and other works to argue that university students were important but should not be

---

[1] Craig J. Calhoun, *Neither Gods nor Emperors: Students and the Struggle for Democracy in China* (Berkeley: University of California Press, 1994).

[2] Zhao, *Power of Tiananmen*.

[3] Joseph W. Esherick and Jeffrey N. Wasserstrom, "Acting Out Democracy: Political Theater in Modern China," in *Popular Protest and Political Culture in Modern China*, ed. Jeffrey N. Wasserstrom and Elizabeth J. Perry, 2nd ed. (Boulder, CO: Westview, 1994), 32–69; Elizabeth J. Perry, "Introduction: Chinese Political Culture Revisited," in *Popular Protest and Political Culture in Modern China*, 1–14.

[4] Wu Yulun, "How the Party Decided to Shoot Its People," in Tsoi Wing-Mui, ed., *The Last Secret: The Final Documents from the June Fourth Crackdown* (Hong Kong: New Century, 2019), 70–96.

the sole center of attention or target of blame. They certainly should not be subjected to the hatred and opprobrium that has been dumped on Chai Ling. Student leaders in Beijing were students. They were not career politicians or seasoned organizers, let alone genuine competitors for national leadership. They were smart and savvy but had come of age in a Leninist political culture and had little experience chairing meetings, running organizations, or behaving democratically. When read in isolation, the massive amount of writing produced by and about the student movement since 1989 provides a limited view. It can now be considered alongside the remarkable accounts of Li Peng and Zhao Ziyang, whose memoirs chart their battle about how to handle the protests between mid-April and late May 1989. And to the extent possible, a comprehensive history of the protests must include the voices of people who were neither students nor officials. Factory workers, clerks, businesspeople, and grandparents participated and reacted in diverse ways that reflected the anxiety, confusion, and hope of spring 1989. Their decisions and actions were as momentous as those of students and politicians. Hope is why the movement started and grew. It is why people who experienced it hide a photo of Tiananmen Square on their bookshelf, three decades later.

5   Demands and Responses

After Deng Xiaoping forced Hu Yaobang to resign as general secretary in January 1987, the number of things that made people angry in China, including corruption, inflation, and repression, increased and deepened. Hu himself, however, stuck around as a quiet, diminished member of the Politburo. His continued presence in the Party's top body may have given hope to people that Hu's brand of relatively tolerant politics might make a comeback. When a democracy activist from Anhui Province visited Shen Tong at Peking University in early 1989, the man asked, "Who do we put forward to take over from Deng Xiaoping if we succeed in getting rid of him?" The activist then named Hu Yaobang and Zhao Ziyang as possible candidates. Shen recalled, "We all agreed that Hu Yaobang was probably the better of the two."[1]

It was not to be. During a Politburo meeting about education policy on April 8, 1989, Hu Yaobang felt unwell. Hu stood up, asked Zhao Ziyang to excuse him, and then collapsed. He had suffered a heart attack. Hu was rushed to the Beijing Hospital, where he seemed to be recuperating. According to his son, on the morning of April 15, after drinking watermelon juice and eating breakfast, his heart rate began fluctuating wildly. Hu died a few moments later.[2]

Students, intellectuals, workers, and top Communist Party leaders reacted in different ways to Hu's death. As soon as news spread of Hu's death on April 15, students put pen to paper. At Peking University, Shen Tong and his friends draped a banner outside their dormitory window reading "Yaobang is gone. We mourn." Later that

---

[1] Shen Tong, *Almost a Revolution*, 159–60.

[2] Wu Renhua, 六四事件全程實錄 (The full record of the Tiananmen movement) (hereafter abbreviated as *LSQ*) (Alhambra, CA: Zhenxiang chubanshe, 2014), 6–7. Li Peng, who had visited Hu in the hospital on April 9, felt compelled to tell the world a different story in his memoir: Li recalled that Hu did not like following doctors' orders to constantly stay in bed. Li heard that on April 15, after a doctor refused Hu's request to get out of bed to use the toilet, Hu's attempt to evacuate his bowels while lying in bed strained his heart and killed him. *LP*, 56.

day, Shen bumped into a group of journalism students from Renmin University, telling them: "Hu Yaobang's death has the potential to start a student movement." In fact, the movement had already begun. One of the students from Renmin University told Shen that on their campus, "It's getting exciting ... Someone drew a picture of Li Peng as a pig, and it's on public display."[3]

Wu Renhua, a teacher at China University of Political Science and Law, was part of a memorial march of approximately five hundred people from his campus to Tiananmen Square on April 17, 1989; around four thousand Peking University students also marched to the square that day, chanting "Overthrow corrupt officials," "Long live democracy," "Long live freedom," and "Rejuvenate China."[4] Wu Renhua told me how impressed he was that students and teachers had moved so quickly from campus to the square after Hu's death. Previous student movements had been campus-focused, but in April 1989 students were poised to move into the streets, marching between six and nine miles from universities in the northwest part of the city to Tiananmen in the heart of Beijing.

A small group of workers also gathered at Tiananmen Square on April 17, less interested in talking about Hu Yaobang than in commiserating about inflation, corruption, and workplace grievances. Workers who had a history of complaining and speaking truth to power, such as Zhao Hongliang, were some of the first to appear in the square. Han Dongfang, a twenty-five-year-old worker at a railyard in the Beijing suburbs, stood up and spoke on April 17 about how workers should be allowed to organize themselves instead of relying on the officially sanctioned All-China Federation of Trade Unions (ACFTU). In 1986, Han had been disappointed when he asked his work unit's ACFTU representative for help. He told the official, "As far as I can see, the ACFTU does nothing except organize the occasional film show and hand out soap." Zhao Hongliang liked what he heard from Han Dongfang, as did construction worker Wang Dengyue, cook Xiao Delong, and boilermaker Zhao Pinlu. The men agreed to meet in the square the next day.[5]

Wang Yuan, who had graduated from Peking University and was working for Canon's Beijing office, also went to the square on April 17. Wang listened as a student spoke into a megaphone and claimed that Hu

[3] Shen Tong, *Almost a Revolution*, 167–68.
[4] *LSQ*, 20; He Zhizhou, 血沃中華: 八九年北京學潮資料集 (China awash in blood: Collected material from the Beijing student movement of 1989) (Hong Kong: Xianggang xinyidai wenhua xiehui, 1989), 1.
[5] Black and Munro, *Black Hands*, 153–54, 158–59; Andrew G. Walder and Gong Xiaoxia, "Workers in the Tiananmen Protests: The Politics of the Beijing Workers' Autonomous Federation," *Australian Journal of Chinese Affairs*, no. 29 (January 1993): 1–2.

Yaobang had "died of anger and anxiety" after learning about education budget shortfalls at the Politburo meeting of April 8. The speech implied that public money that should have been going toward education was instead being siphoned off by corrupt officials. The student closed his speech by yelling: "Overthrow the bureaucratic profiteers! Eradicate the corrupt! Education will save the nation! Long live freedom! Long live democracy! Long live law and order!"

After the crowd shouted the slogans in a loud call-and-response, Wang Yuan got caught up in a packed crowd of people. That was when someone tried to steal her expensive Japanese camera. "I screamed 'Help!' and held on firmly. The man let go and disappeared," she recalled. Ten days later, when Wang Yuan was on the campus of Peking University, she had another unpleasant experience. Two young men harassed her, grabbed her camera, and opened it up to expose the film, only giving it back after her company driver intervened.[6] Mourning for Hu Yaobang and demanding democratic reforms did not transform the entire population of Beijing into altruistic angels. When the retired couple showed me their cherished photograph of Tiananmen Square, the woman told me how in spring 1989 she had once absentmindedly left her camera behind on her bicycle near the square. The camera was still there when she returned. Her point was that people in Beijing trusted each other so much during the democracy movement that theft dropped to zero. She cherishes the memory of a utopian moment. This differs from Wang Yuan's darker experience, but neither story is necessarily inaccurate. A number of reports claim that Beijing was so orderly that pickpockets quit stealing in May 1989. Wang Yuan's assailants had not received that memo in April.

While nobody could have predicted that Hu Yaobang would die on April 15 and that mourning him would spark a democracy movement, political activists had already been busy during the first three months of 1989. Hu's death allowed their message to reach a much larger audience. Fang Lizhi had been kicked out of the Communist Party and transferred to a new job at the Beijing Astronomical Observatory. Fang tried and failed to contain his thoughts to astrophysics. On January 6, 1989, Fang sent a letter to Deng Xiaoping. Fang wrote:

1989 is both the fortieth anniversary of the founding of the PRC and the seventieth anniversary of the May 4th Movement.[7] Many activities are expected

---

[6] Wang, *Inconvenient Memories*, 136–37, 165–66.

[7] The May Fourth Movement of 1919 began with student protests against the signing of the Treaty of Versailles and became a part of the broader New Culture Movement against imperialism and traditional Chinese culture. Ever since 1919, intellectuals have

to mark the two anniversaries. However, more people are concerned about the present than about recollections of the past. They are hoping that these important dates will bring new hope.

Fang proposed that Deng commemorate the special year of 1989 by pardoning all political prisoners in China.[8] Inspired by Fang's letter, on February 16, 1989, thirty-three writers and artists issued an open letter urging amnesty for prisoners of conscience. Ten days later, a group of forty-two natural scientists and social scientists wrote a longer open letter calling for democratization, freedom of speech, releasing political prisoners, and better funding for education.

Fang eventually heard that Deng Xiaoping did read his original letter. "True to form, though, he gave no sign of having done so: no acknowledgment, no response," Fang wrote. According to Fang, the Ministry of Justice complained that "writing public letters about prisoners compromises the independence of China's judiciary." Security officials visited the signatories to issue warnings; some were put under surveillance. Fang concluded that even though "public calls for amnesty had failed in their immediate objective ... that they caused such nervousness shows that 'dissidence' had grown into an epidemic that the authorities could not easily be rid of. The regime's absolute power was declining."[9]

The writings and speeches of physicist Li Shuxian and her husband Fang Lizhi inspired Peking University undergraduates Shen Tong and Wang Dan, who had been holding separate reading and discussion groups in 1988 and early 1989. Wang Dan heard Fang Lizhi speak at a Beijing hotel in February 1989. Wang posted an open letter on campus on April 3, 1989, stating that the May Fourth Movement's "legacy of academic freedom and freedom of speech is in danger." Wang also edited an independent magazine called *New May Fourth*, to which Li Shuxian contributed a preface.[10] Li had visited Shen Tong's discussion group in early March 1989. She made a big impression on the students when she described how, on February 26, police officers had blocked her, Fang Lizhi, and Perry Link from attending a Texas barbecue at the

---

emphasized the movement's call for democracy and science, while the Chinese Communist Party, whose founders included such important May Fourth activists as Chen Duxiu and Li Dazhao, eventually deployed May Fourth in the service of patriotism, instructing intellectuals to loyally serve the Party-state. See Fabio Lanza, "The Legacy of May Fourth in China, a Century Later," *Made in China Journal* 4, no. 2 (April–June 2019), madeinchinajournal.com/2019/05/04/the-legacy-of-may-fourth-in-china-a-century-later.

[8] Michel Oksenberg, Lawrence R. Sullivan, and Marc Lambert, eds., *Beijing Spring, 1989: Confrontation and Conflict: The Basic Documents* (Armonk, NY: Sharpe, 1990), 166–67.

[9] Fang Lizhi, *The Most Wanted Man in China*, 275–76.

[10] Black and Munro, *Black Hands*, 140–42.

special invitation of President George Bush, who had been in Beijing for meetings with Deng Xiaoping and Zhao Ziyang. Shen Tong recalled that "Li Shuxian's story of how they had handled themselves when harassed by the police was worth more to us than a thousand lectures on [human] rights."[11]

The small groups of professors and students targeting the seventieth anniversary of the May Fourth Movement as an opportunity to petition the Communist Party for political reforms reacted quickly when they learned of Hu Yaobang's death. They "simply moved the date up," wrote Craig Calhoun, who was teaching in Beijing in 1989.[12] But on April 15, 1989, many people in China were not paying attention to politics and barely reacted to Hu's death. In rural Hunan Province, Lu Decheng had no idea that the former general secretary's death would eventually lead to Lu's own imprisonment and exile. A former classmate of Lu's who had become a high school teacher in 1989 led a small memorial march for Hu, but Lu Decheng did not join in, instead observing from the side-lines. Nor did Lu bother to watch Hu's televised memorial service.[13] Like many working-class people who would eventually get involved in the protests of 1989, Lu did not view Communist Party officials as heroes, symbols of hope, or potential allies.

Chai Ling and her husband Feng Congde saw Hu Yaobang in a positive light, but Chai and Feng did not immediately jump into action in response to Hu's death. After completing her undergraduate studies at Peking University, Chai Ling had entered a graduate program at Beijing Normal University. April 15, 1989, was her twenty-third birthday. She worked on her application to graduate school in the United States, then ate a birthday cake that Feng brought her.[14] Two days later, Feng was shocked to see posters on the Peking University campus that he inter-preted as directly targeting Deng Xiaoping: "He who should die will not die, but he who shouldn't die has left us!" "The sincere person has died but the two-faced person lives on." It was not until three days after Hu Yaobang's death, on April 18, that Chai and Feng first went to Tiananmen Square. They went in a support role, bringing food and water to other students who had been sitting in the square for hours.[15]

Earlier that morning, Wang Dan and another Peking University stu-dent, Guo Haifeng, delivered a list of seven demands to a functionary

[11] Shen Tong, *Almost a Revolution*, 154.   [12] Calhoun, *Neither Gods nor Emperors*, 1.
[13] Chong, *Egg*, 198.   [14] Chai Ling, *Heart*, 82.
[15] Feng Congde, 六四日記: 廣場上的共和國 (June Fourth diary: Republic on the square) (Hong Kong: Zhenzhong shuju, 2009), 75, 77–78.

named Zheng Youmei in the Great Hall of the People next to the square.[16] The seven demands were:

1. Fairly assess Hu Yaobang's achievements, affirm his views on freedom, democracy, and moderation.
2. Thoroughly repudiate the movements to eliminate spiritual pollution and oppose liberalization. Rehabilitate those who suffered unjustly during the movements.
3. Demand that Party-state leaders and their children reveal their property holdings to the people of the nation.
4. Allow independent newspapers; end press censorship.
5. Increase education budgets and raise intellectuals' salaries.
6. Rescind the Beijing People's Congress's unconstitutional "ten articles" restricting demonstrations.
7. Accurately report on this protest in official publications.[17]

Zheng Youmei, who worked for the State Council's Bureau of Letters and Visits, promised to pass the demands on to higher officials and asked the students to return to campus, but the petitioners wanted to speak directly to members of the National People's Congress Standing Committee. Zheng could not make that happen, so the sit-in lasted all day.[18]

Chai Ling and Feng Congde did not know about this – they only knew that their schoolmates were hungry and thirsty – but then something happened on the evening of April 18 that compelled them to join the student movement. After going to Tiananmen Square, the two joined a crowd at Xinhua Gate, the entrance to the top Communist Party leadership compound. Protesters shouting "Li Peng, come out," faced off against guards. Chai and Feng got caught up in a group fleeing police, who were beating people with clubs. "When I finally slowed down to catch my breath," Chai wrote, "I was burning with shame and rage. I had never felt so humiliated in my life, chased down the street like a dog." Chai saw this as a turning point in her life: "My wounded pride and a newfound rage dried up my sorrow. From now on, I would not run away, and neither would Feng."[19] Over the next few days, reports of clashes between protesters and security forces at Xinhua Gate, some purportedly

[16] *LSQ*, 26.   [17] He Zhizhou, 血沃中華 (China awash in blood), 106.
[18] *LSQ*, 26; Han Minzhu, ed., *Cries for Democracy: Writings and Speeches from the 1989 Chinese Democracy Movement* (Princeton: Princeton University Press, 1990), 11–12.
[19] Chai Ling, *Heart*, 87–88; Feng, 六四日記 (June Fourth diary), 84–85.

resulting in bloodied heads, had the same mobilizing effect on other students as Chai Ling's escape had on her.

Feng Congde, Wang Dan, Shen Tong, and others met at Peking University to discuss establishing an independent student organization and boycotting classes. Chai Ling did not join all the meetings or speak very often, but she recalls the crucial role she played in convincing a room full of men to stop cutting each other off and come to a decision:

> As the only girl present, I was the true minority in the room. I sat on the fringe of their debates and listened ... I offered to mediate ... They all listened to what I had to say, probably because I spoke in a soft, feminine voice amid this conclave of males.[20]

That was April 20. The events of the next two days in Beijing – deciding to boycott classes, a big march to Tiananmen Square on April 21, subverting official plans to cordon off the square for Hu Yaobang's memorial service the next day, and then a dramatic sit-in during the service itself – would convince top Communist Party leaders that they needed a plan to deal with the tens of thousands of protesters on the streets and in the square.

★ ★ ★

Li Peng was more worried than Zhao Ziyang was. Li had returned to Beijing from an official visit to Japan on the evening of April 16. When he looked at the front page of *People's Daily* the next morning, he did not like what he saw: a prominently placed photo of a crowd at the Monument to the People's Heroes in Tiananmen Square, gazing mournfully at a memorial wreath dedicated to Hu Yaobang. In spite of Li's claims that he felt sorrow about Hu's death, he did not see *People's Daily*'s coverage as evidence of shared national grief. He interpreted it as an attack on Deng Xiaoping and thought that it would "incite more students to go to Tiananmen Square, resulting in social disorder. This incident made me ponder things and raised my guard."[21] Li viewed students' gathering at Xinhua Gate through a similarly sinister lens, writing in his diary that "thousands of people stormed Xinhua Gate in the deep of night. This is unprecedented in the history of the PRC."[22]

---

[20] Chai Ling, *Heart*, 92. Lee Feigon has analyzed Chai Ling's leadership through a gender lens, writing, "At times it almost appeared she felt more secure when she could think of herself as the traditional, helpless female, although that was clearly not what she was." Lee Feigon, "Gender and the Chinese Student Movement," in *Popular Protest and Political Culture in Modern China*, 132.

[21] *LP*, 60–61.   [22] *LP*, 63.

Zhao Ziyang, however, did not seem bothered by students' mourning or protests. When Li Peng met with Zhao on April 18 to demand a "clear attitude" toward students marching on the streets, Zhao told Li that there was no need to prevent students' spontaneous tributes to Hu Yaobang. As Li recalled in his memoir, Zhao said, "As long as the students are not beating, smashing, or looting, we should not do anything about them. This will avoid intensifying conflict."[23] On April 19, Zhao received a boost of confidence in his approach when he met with Deng Xiaoping to discuss Zhao's upcoming official visit to North Korea. In addition to talking about foreign relations, Zhao recalled that he told Deng "about the student demonstrations, and [gave] him my views on how the situation should be handled. At the time, Deng had expressed support for me."[24] What Zhao omitted from his account was that Deng had not only supported him but had also told him to get ready for a second term as general secretary and to prepare to take over Deng's position as chairman of the Central Military Commission.[25] Zhao knew that his political fortunes depended on Deng's support, but in mid-April 1989 he had no inkling that his leadership position was weakening, let alone that his political career and personal freedom would end in a few short weeks.[26]

As students escalated their protests on April 20, 21, and 22, Zhao Ziyang stayed calm while Li Peng continued to fret. They each saw what they expected to see. Zhao saw spontaneous, patriotic, well-intentioned mourning, recalling that "overall their activities were fairly orderly and nothing excessive took place."[27] Li saw an unprecedented threat to the Communist Party's monopoly on power, writing in his diary that the "nature of the situation" was changing.[28] Neither man was wrong. Past midnight on April 21, the recently formed Peking University Student Preparatory Committee announced that a class boycott would begin at 8 a.m. that day and would continue until "fair news reporting" and "severely punishing the chief culprit" behind police brutality against students at Xinhua Gate had been achieved.[29] Dingxin Zhao's perceptive

---

[23] *LP*, 63.   [24] *PS*, 9.

[25] Bao Tong, director of the Office of Political Reform and Zhao Ziyang's political secretary, heard the details about Deng and Zhao's conversation on April 19, 1989. Dai Qing, who interviewed Bao, believes that Deng's support for Zhao remained genuine when the two met on April 19. Dai Qing, 邓小平在1989 (Deng Xiaoping in 1989) (Hong Kong: New Century, 2019), 63–64.

[26] On this point specifically and for more on how PRC elite politics are a "black box" for scholars and also for Chinese politicians themselves, see Frederick C. Teiwes, "The Study of Elite Political Conflict in the PRC: Politics inside the 'Black Box'," in *Handbook of the Politics of China*, ed. David S. G. Goodman (Northampton, MA: Elgar, 2015), 39.

[27] *PS*, 4.   [28] *LP*, 68.   [29] *LSQ*, 49.

finding that an ever-changing cast of student leaders made "spontaneous and individualistic responses to events rather than conscious decisions arrived at collectively by their organizations" can be seen in the class boycott announcement, which responded to outrage about clashes at Xinhua Gate rather than repeating the seven demands of April 18.[30]

Even more consequential than the class boycott of April 21 was protesters' response to the Beijing Public Security Bureau's announcement that Tiananmen Square would be closed between 8 a.m. and noon on April 22. This edict prohibited people from gathering in the square during Hu's memorial service. But instead of accepting that the square would be closed, approximately forty thousand students and teachers marched from campuses to the square. The front of the parade arrived at the square around 11:15 p.m.; a column extending more than four miles long then filed in, thwarting official plans to keep the square empty during Hu's memorial.[31] Wu Renhua, who led a contingent of around one thousand marchers from his university, told me that the evening march and overnight occupation of the square were a major turning point in the protest movement – in Wu's words, an "unprecedented large-scale united action" coordinated by twenty universities. Wu also felt encouraged that residents along the parade's path had come out to clap, cheer, and give drinks to marchers. Less than a week after Hu Yaobang's death, students and teachers were forming alliances between universities and were also garnering support from Beijing residents.

At 10 a.m. on April 22, the thousands of students who had spent a cold, mostly sleepless night in the square listened to Hu's memorial service broadcast live on loudspeakers. Wang Yuan was watching the service on television with her two Japanese coworkers. Her boss, Mr. Murata, was an avid observer of elite Chinese politics. He told Wang to listen carefully for the word "Marxist." Wang wrote, "Communists believed that after this life, it was Karl Marx that they would meet on the other side. Therefore, it was very important for them to be called a 'Marxist' upon death."[32] When Wang heard Zhao Ziyang say that Hu Yaobang was a Marxist at the opening of his forty-minute eulogy, she interpreted it as a victory for activists who had been calling for a positive appraisal of Hu's life. She did not know that Deng Xiaoping had cut the word "great" before "Marxist" from the eulogy text. According to Li Peng, Deng Xiaoping had approved praising Hu Yaobang's overall life contributions but felt that designating Hu as a "great Marxist" was going

---

[30] Zhao, *Power of Tiananmen*, 146–47.   [31] *LSQ*, 53–54.
[32] Wang, *Inconvenient Memories*, 153.

too far.[33] At the end of the ceremony, Wang Yuan's boss asked her to time the funerary music, telling her that "the length of time indicated the importance of the deceased. The shortest the music had ever played was a mere thirty seconds. The longest was three minutes, thirty-five seconds, at Mao Zedong's memorial service … Hu Yaobang received a minute, seventeen. Not bad."[34]

The thousands of students in the square may have initially shared Wang Yuan's assessment that Hu Yaobang had been properly appreciated. They became restless and upset, however, when no hearse or funeral procession appeared. Students had expected to pay their final respects to Hu and assumed that his hearse would circle the perimeter of Tiananmen Square. But then they learned that the vehicle bearing Hu's body had quietly departed from the west side of the Great Hall of the People, which was not visible from the square. A group of outraged students rushed toward the hall, demanding that Li Peng come out to speak with the students. Three students knelt in front of the hall. One of them, Guo Haifeng of Peking University, lifted above his head a paper scroll on which was written a modified version of the students' seven demands, including properly appraising Hu Yaobang, press freedom, and requiring officials to publicize their incomes and property. The petition had been signed by representatives of nineteen schools. Two staff members from the memorial service organizing committee tried to convince the students to stop kneeling and to let them take the scroll, promising that they would deliver it to Li Peng, but the students refused – they wanted to personally hand it to Li.

The longer the three men knelt on the steps leading from the square to the Great Hall, the more upset the crowd got. Onlookers felt humiliated that the three students had pathetically resorted to a traditional form of supplication, like subjects begging for an emperor's favor, and were outraged that the government seemed to be ignoring them entirely. Pu Zhiqiang of the China University of Political Science and Law was so upset that he hit himself with a megaphone, bloodying his face. Wu Renhua heard bystanders saying, "Those poor students," "Why is nobody paying attention to them, they have been kneeling for such a long time," and "This shows how scared the officials are of the students." After kneeling for thirty minutes, the three supplicants retreated into the crowd of students, carrying the scroll with them.[35] Chai Ling recalled how emotional the moment was: "We felt betrayed. Our government officials had turned a deaf ear to us. The image of students weeping while

[33] *LP*, 71. The text of the eulogy is in *RMRB*, April 23, 1989, 1.
[34] Wang, *Inconvenient Memories*, 153.   [35] *LSQ*, 60.

our petitioners sat on their knees on the steps of the Great Hall before a silent bastion of stone became the symbol to me of our humiliation."[36] The students slowly filed out of the square and resolved to continue and expand their class boycott.

Top Party leaders inside the hall were unaware of the petition or the kneeling. They were taking an elevator down from the memorial service and getting ready to leave the building. On the way out, Zhao Ziyang told his colleagues his ideas about how to handle further protests. The formal version of Zhao's three-point plan proposed that:

1. With the memorial service now over, social activities should return to normal. Students need to be persuaded to discontinue their street demonstrations and return to their classes.
2. According to the principal goal of reducing tensions, dialogue should be conducted at multiple levels, and through various channels and formats to establish mutual understanding and to seek a variety of opinions. Whatever opinions they held, all students, teachers, and intellectuals should be allowed to express themselves freely.
3. Bloodshed must be avoided, no matter what. However, those who engaged in the five kinds of behavior – beating, smashing, looting, burning, and trespassing – should be punished according to law.[37]

If Zhao had been aware of the dramatic events in the square and had communicated the second point promising continued dialogue and freedom of expression before, during, or immediately after the three lone students ritualistically knelt with an uplifted petition, he might have defused the emotional situation. Instead, Zhao and Li Peng had a hasty private conversation and went their separate ways. This would make the coming days and weeks more difficult for both men.

After Li Peng heard Zhao explain his three points, Li was unhappy. The points did not address his main worries. Li asked Zhao, "What if the students want Western-style freedom and democracy?" Zhao said that they could not say yes to that. Li then asked, "What about the illegal student organizations?" Zhao responded that the government could not recognize them. Li wanted to hold a Politburo Standing Committee meeting to discuss these issues, but Zhao said that meeting was unnecessary, got in his car, and took off. Why was Zhao in such a hurry? Two days later, Li Peng ended his diary entry with this nasty note: "According to reliable sources, after the memorial service ended, Zhao went to play golf in the afternoon. He sure can put his worries aside."[38] Li Peng was

---

[36] Chai Ling, *Heart*, 98.   [37] *PS*, 5–6.   [38] *LP*, 72, 81.

not the only person who snarked about Zhao's passion for golf. On April 20, Han Dongfang, Zhao Hongliang, and other workers set up a meeting spot on the western edge of Tiananmen Square because students refused to let them gather in the square itself, saying that they wanted to protect the "purity" of the protest movement. The workers posted "Ten Polite Questions for the Chinese Communist Party." The second question was: "Do Mr. and Mrs. Zhao Ziyang pay the golfing fees when they play every week? Where does the money for the fee come from?"[39]

Activist workers viewed Zhao Ziyang as one among many out-of-touch and corrupt officials. Li Peng saw Zhao's golfing as a political weakness he could exploit. Li was anxious on April 22 because Zhao Ziyang was leaving for North Korea on an official visit the next day, putting Li in charge of implementing what he saw as vague, contradictory principles that failed to address the seriousness of the situation. Li thought that illegal student organizations were asking for Western-style democracy. Craig Calhoun has observed that the emergence of new, independent student groups demanding recognition and concessions "was in fact a basic challenge, for communist China had never recognized the right of people to form independent representative organizations at will."[40] Zhao agreed with Li that the demands and their source were unacceptable, but his answer was to restore normalcy, increase dialogue, and punish looting. Even if Li had liked Zhao's plan, he was uncertain how to implement it.

★ ★ ★

After seeing off Zhao at the train station on April 23, Li Peng met with Yang Shangkun, the eighty-two-year-old elder, to discuss his concerns. Yang suggested that Li ask Deng Xiaoping for instructions. Yang and Li agreed to go together to meet Deng, which they would eventually do in a fateful meeting on the morning of April 25. Beijing municipal Party secretary Li Ximing and Beijing mayor Chen Xitong helped Li Peng craft the message he took to China's godfather. Li Ximing and Chen Xitong were embarrassed that protesters had, with total impunity, flouted Beijing municipal regulations prohibiting unauthorized marches and had subverted city leaders' attempt to keep Tiananmen Square empty during Hu's memorial service. The capital's top officials were also upset that the day after they met on April 23 to tell university

---

[39] Han, *Cries for Democracy*, 277; Black and Munro, *Black Hands*, 161.
[40] Calhoun, *Neither Gods nor Emperors*, 44.

administrators from sixty-seven Beijing schools to get students to stop boycotting classes, more than sixty thousand students refused to attend class.

The two city leaders complained that the growth of the student movement was making it impossible for them to do their jobs. They got the support they wanted when Li Peng convened a Politburo Standing Committee meeting on the evening of April 24. Li agreed with Chen Xitong's claim that plotters had taken advantage of Hu Yaobang's death to try to overthrow the Communist Party.[41] At the meeting, Chen Xitong issued a warning that was certain to get Li Peng's attention and that would spark Deng Xiaoping into action the next day. Chen said, "This student movement is directly targeting Party Center. On the surface it seems to be targeting Premier Li Peng, but in actuality it is targeting Comrade Deng Xiaoping."[42] The meeting ended with a decision to crack the whip against plotters and protesters and to get all officials and news agencies on the same page.

Li Peng and Yang Shangkun went to Deng Xiaoping's house the next morning – this was the meeting that Li and Yang had requested shortly after Zhao Ziyang left for North Korea. Deng's secretary had called Li Peng, telling him to come to see Deng at 10 a.m. on April 25. Li gave Deng an update about the severity of the protests and about the previous evening's decision to take a hard line against them. Li's report sounded compelling to Deng, who agreed with Beijing municipal leaders' description of the severity of the threat to Communist Party rule and to Deng's own position. Deng did not need much persuading on the question of harshly cracking down on student protests. Even though Deng had initially supported Zhao Ziyang's approach of getting back to normal, engaging in dialogue, and punishing vandals, he was inclined to accept Li Peng's portrayal of events. After Zhao found out about Deng's reaction, he was not surprised. Deng "had always tended to prefer tough measures when dealing with student demonstrations because he believed that demonstrations undermined stability." Zhao understood that Deng had sided with Li's version of events because "it coincided more closely with what he had really believed all along."[43]

Deng instructed Li Peng what to do next while also expressing confidence that the Communist Party would emerge victorious against what he saw as a plot to spread turmoil nationwide. Deng said that the Party

[41] *LSQ*, 76–78.
[42] Zhang Wanshu, 歷史的大爆炸: "六四" 事件全景實錄 (Historical explosion: Panoramic record of the "June Fourth" incident) (Hong Kong: Tiandi tushu, 2009), 57.
[43] *PS*, 10.

should issue a strong statement addressing the "turmoil" and should use China's legal system to stop marches and protests. Deng also wanted to build up evidence against the "behind-the-scenes backers and black hands of this turmoil, of whom Fang Lizhi and Li Shuxian are prime examples," telling Li Peng and Yang Shangkun to "deal with them at the appropriate time." Deng expected that a sternly worded public statement, combined with prohibiting demonstrations and arresting people, would "stop the turmoil." Deng said, "All of the workers, farmers, and intellectuals support us. So do the officials ... We also have millions of soldiers. What are we afraid of? Of the sixty thousand students boycotting classes, quite a few have been coerced or prevented from going to class."[44]

Li Peng must have left Deng's house with a spring in his step. He was on the same page as Deng and could now publicize Deng's words. He authorized circulating a transcript of Deng's remarks to officials nationwide and also had it sent to Zhao Ziyang in North Korea. When Zhao read the transcript inside the Chinese consulate in Pyongyang, he felt that he had no choice but to formally respond that he "completely agreed with Comrade Xiaoping's decision on dealing with the current turmoil problem." Maybe the situation had grown worse since he had left Beijing, Zhao thought, and in any case, in late April it was still unthinkable for Zhao to openly split with his boss. Zhao predicted that the student movement would ebb and that he would have to supervise another movement opposing liberalization, as he had had to do in 1987. He was wrong.

On the afternoon of April 25, Li Peng supervised the drafting of the public editorial that Deng had asked for. The editorial, titled "We Must Take a Clear-Cut Stand against Turmoil," was broadcast on television and radio that evening and was published in newspapers nationwide the next day.

Primary Source: The April 26 Editorial (excerpt)

An extremely small number of people were not memorializing Comrade Hu Yaobang, were not promoting socialist democracy in China, and were not merely complaining about minor grievances. Instead, they were flying the false flag of democracy in order to destroy democracy and the rule of law. Their goal is to confuse people's feelings, throw the entire country into

---

[44] *LP*, 86–87.

turmoil, and destroy political stability and unity. This is a premeditated conspiracy. It is turmoil. In essence, it wants to fundamentally negate the Communist Party's leadership and the socialist system.

Source: *RMRB* (*People's Daily*), April 26, 1989, 1.

Reactions to the broadcast and editorial varied. Lu Decheng in Hunan read the newspaper at work, found its language and tactics typical, and shrugged, reckoning that "public opinion didn't count."[45] A good number of people in China may not have paid attention to the broadcast or the editorial, and many of those who did surely had reactions similar to Lu Decheng's, seeing the message as business as usual. This is what Deng Xiaoping, Li Peng, and even Zhao Ziyang in Pyongyang were expecting. But even if Deng had been correct that many workers and farmers were on his side, enough people in China felt so angered and insulted by the tone and contents of Deng's statement that they defied top leaders' expectations. Instead of dying down quietly, the protest movement escalated.

Peking University students, especially those who had taken part in newly formed student associations, felt targeted when they listened to the broadcast on the evening of April 25. It called the new organizations "illegal" and accused them of "seizing power" from Party-approved student groups. Chai Ling recalled that when she heard the broadcast, "Shocked disbelief, fear, and anger were the emotions coursing through my system." Then she heard her schoolmates raging against Deng by smashing glass bottles ("Xiaoping" is a homonym for "little bottle"), banging on tables, yelling, and cursing.[46] That evening, independent student organizations issued statements claiming that they did not oppose the Party. They announced a citywide march from campuses to the square in protest against the "turmoil" label.[47]

Journalists in Beijing also vigorously opposed the editorial. *People's Daily* editor Lu Chaoqi said that on April 26, his colleagues unanimously agreed that the editorial was a mistake – nobody had anything good to say about it. Lu's phone was ringing nonstop; the callers were all reacting to the editorial and had two main complaints: first, they disagreed that students' marching and memorializing Hu Yaobang was "turmoil." Second, they complained that the editorial offered no solutions to the legitimate questions that protesters had raised about democracy and

---

[45] Chong, *Egg*, 200.   [46] Chai Ling, *Heart*, 114.   [47] *LSQ*, 88–89.

corruption.[48] At a meeting for Xinhua News Agency Party members at which someone recited Deng's remarks in their entirety, journalists stood up to take turns denouncing the document. They found it insulting to Hu Yaobang's memory, said it reminded them of the repression of the Anti-Rightist Movement and the Cultural Revolution, and complained that Li Peng and Yang Shangkun, who was not even a member of the Politburo Standing Committee, had gone behind Zhao Ziyang's back while the general secretary was out of the country.[49]

Not everyone in China felt angry like Beijing journalists or indifferent like Lu Decheng in Hunan. Some people interpreted Deng's words as marching orders and tried to implement them faithfully. Beijing municipal leaders made statements warning the "chiefs" of "illegal organizations" that they would suffer "severe consequences" if they did not stop "illegal activities." The Beijing Public Security Bureau issued notices reminding the capital's residents that demonstrations that had not been preapproved were illegal and that giving speeches, collecting donations, and passing out leaflets would be punished according to the law.[50] And university administrators and teachers actually did try to "take a clear-cut stand" against protests by meeting with students on April 26 and trying to convince them not to march the following day.

In some instances, their persuasion was convincing. Örkesh Dölet, an undergraduate at Beijing Normal University better known by his Chinese name Wuerkaixi, went to Peking University on April 26, where he spoke with Shen Tong. Örkesh said that his university's administrators had promised that if he could stop students from marching the next day, "we wouldn't be punished for the organizing we've done so far," and that dialogue between students and officials would follow. Shen Tong could not commit to this, saying that Peking University students had already decided "as a compromise" to "walk part of the way to Tiananmen square and no farther, to show the government that we will cooperate but we can't be intimidated."[51] Örkesh gave up on trying to persuade Shen Tong and went to Tsinghua University nearby to try to convince students there not to march.

Administrators at China University of Political Science and Law put intense pressure on Zhou Yongjun, that school's delegate to the Beijing Students' Autonomous Federation, an alliance of newly formed independent unions at each university. University officials held Zhou in a

[48] Lu Chaoqi, 六四內部日記 (Inside journal of June Fourth) (Hong Kong: Zhuoyue wenhua chubanshe, 2006), 34.
[49] Zhang Wanshu, 歷史的大爆炸 (Historical explosion), 79.   [50] *LSQ*, 96.
[51] Shen Tong, *Almost a Revolution*, 200–1.

Figure 5.1 Student protesters in Beijing on April 27, 1989. Catherine Henriette/AFP via Getty Images.

meeting until 3 a.m. on April 27 until he agreed to sign a slip of paper cancelling the big protest march.[52] Someone pounded on Shen Tong's door at 5 a.m. to show him the cancellation notice; Shen then took it to Feng Congde and other Peking University activists. "We all suspected that Zhou Yongjun had made it by himself, because no other signatures were on the message," Shen wrote, "and we didn't think the federation could have had a meeting in the past couple of hours. In the end we agreed to proceed as planned."[53]

Anger overcame fear on April 27. Approximately one hundred thousand students first broke through university gates that administrators had locked and then pushed through lines of unarmed police officers who were halfheartedly blocking intersections. Once the protesters realized that they would reach the square without facing violence or arrests, the mood turned giddy, and the number of people out on the streets surged to around five hundred thousand. Not wanting to be left out, Örkesh Dölet ended up leading the Beijing Normal University marchers; Feng Congde, Wang Dan, and Shen Tong headed up the Peking University contingent, which decided to march all the way to the square instead of turning around halfway. Chai Ling described the day's "festival" as a

[52] *LSQ*, 96.   [53] Shen Tong, *Almost a Revolution*, 202.

"total victory" for students and Beijing residents.[54] The April 26 editorial had not only failed to stop the student movement, it had emboldened protesters to keep demanding dialogue with the government. It offered hope that they could win recognition and respect.

Why did Deng's harsh approach fail to scare Beijing students into meekly going back to class? Years later, Zhao Ziyang thought that by 1989 something had changed and that the "old ways of political labeling that had worked before were no longer effective." And because almost everyone knew that the April 25 broadcast and April 26 editorial had come directly from Deng Xiaoping's spoken remarks, which had been widely circulated, the protests of April 27 convinced Zhao "that even the symbol of the paramount leader had lost its effectiveness." Not only had threats from the godfather become impotent, Zhao thought, but tough Beijing public security regulations had proven "as good as a piece of wastepaper" when marchers easily pushed through police blockades.[55]

Outwardly, Li Peng and Deng Xiaoping expressed optimism and relief in the immediate aftermath of the April 27 demonstrations. Li wrote in his diary that the *People's Daily* editorial had wielded great power and effectively stabilized the situation.[56] Deng's secretary called Li to say that Deng was pleased because Party Center's attitude had been clear and there was no bloodshed.[57] But in reality, both men were shaken by the events of April 27. Li Peng fielded phone calls from elders, including Deng Yingchao, Li Xiannian, Song Renqiong, and Wang Zhen, urging him to switch course.[58] Li Xiannian and Wang Zhen reportedly called for mass arrests. Peng Zhen made multiple calls to Party Center urging restraint and hoping that force would not be used against protesters.[59]

Li Peng scrambled to try different strategies. He asked State Council spokesperson Yuan Mu to draft a less militant editorial about the importance of maintaining stability. Li also adopted Zhao Ziyang's language about dialogue, instructing officials nationwide to prepare for meetings with student representatives at "multiple levels" and "through various channels" on April 28. But when students who had formed independent organizations and organized huge marches found out about a dialogue session on April 29 between national officials and students who had been vetted by the Party, they reacted with surprise and outrage.

★ ★ ★

[54] Chai Ling, *Heart for Freedom*, 118.   [55] *PS*, 14.   [56] *LP*, 97.   [57] *LSQ*, 107.
[58] *LSQ*, 106.   [59] *PS*, 13.

Dingxin Zhao has argued that the dialogue of April 29 "was not as phony as many have subsequently described it to have been" and that "this was the one where students and government officials had the most substantive discussion."[60] Zhao seems to be admitting that the event was a sham but that it contained a sliver of substance. This is an excessively low bar. The government designed and executed the meeting entirely on its own terms, holding it in the official All-China Students Federation conference room and preselecting forty-one of the forty-five students who attended. When Örkesh Dölet of Beijing Normal University showed up at the door and identified himself as a representative of the independent BSAF, he was not allowed to enter.[61] According to Li Peng himself, during Zhao Ziyang's absence Li set up the dialogue as a "struggle" to be won, not as a solution, conversation, or negotiation. "The PSC was very clear," Li recalled, "dialogue is a struggle, we cannot place hopes of curbing the turmoil on dialogue. Both sides are using dialogue to try to win over undecided people."[62]

By that measure, the selectively edited television broadcast of the dialogue was a victory for Li Peng and Yuan Mu, who chaired the meeting. Yuan was a good talker. He began his long-winded opening speech by saying that "Comrade Li Peng" wanted to clarify that when the April 26 editorial referred to people opposing the Communist Party and opposing socialism, it was not targeting patriotic students but rather a tiny number of lawbreakers. Li had instructed Yuan to say exactly this, and Yuan was careful to give Li credit. Li was happy: "This differentiated the majority of students from a small number of bad people."[63] Li was even happier that most student questions allowed Yuan Mu to speak at length about how the Party was truly committed to eradicating corruption. The format, like a press conference rather than a conversation, played right into Yuan's hands.

Xinhua editor Zhang Wanshu was horrified by stilted exchanges that attacked Zhao Ziyang while allowing Yuan to praise Li Peng.[64] Zhang Wanshu was convinced that the following exchange was preplanned and that the questioner had been planted by the government:

STUDENT: I am Chang Weijun of the Institute of Civil Engineering and Architecture. I want to ask Comrade Yuan Mu a question. Austere times require an air of austerity. We must share joys and hardships together. But bringing one's wife to play golf every week is too far removed from our nation's economic level and from the spirit of overcoming difficulties together (applause). Here

---

[60] Zhao, *Power of Tiananmen*, 157.
[61] Feng Congde, 六四日記 (June Fourth diary), 240.　　[62] *LP*, 100–1.　　[63] *LP*, 104.
[64] Zhang Wanshu, 歷史的大爆炸 (Historical explosion), 90–92.

I have a magazine, it's issue number 2 of this year's *Guide to Health*. On page 48 there is an article and a color photo featuring golfing (while speaking, he holds up a photo of Zhao Ziyang playing golf).

YUAN MU: He plays once a week?

STUDENT: Yes, you are correct, he practices once a week.

YUAN MU: I will pass along this opinion to the leading comrade this student is referring to. It is true that golf is seldom played in China. Do you students think that occasionally playing golf for the sake of international networking is permissible, or is that too much? I'm not clear on the facts of whether he is really golfing every week. If it is true I will pass this along to him. This is one thing. On a related point, I want to tell you that Party Center has considered the masses' complaints, and Comrade Li Peng also spoke about this in his report at the Second Session of the Seventh National People's Congress, saying that each level of government needs to take the lead in austerity to fully gain the masses' sympathy. I fully support this.[65]

Yuan concluded by stating that China would stop importing luxury cars for top leaders' use, garnering a round of applause from the audience. The thousands of students who had marched on April 27 were furious that nobody had mentioned their seven demands and that the independent student associations had been barred from the room. Millions of television viewers throughout China, however, who were totally unaware of the existence of newly formed student organizations or their demands, saw a mature government spokesperson authoritatively handling naive questions from stammering youngsters.

Yuan Mu deftly parried the few punches students were able to swing. Xiang Xiaoji of China University of Political Science and Law questioned the legitimacy of the dialogue meeting, stating that the student representatives present had not been properly elected; that the students had not had a fair opportunity to propose the timing, location, and topics of dialogue; and that they would not consider returning to classes until genuine dialogue started. Yuan Mu managed to evade Xiang Xiaoji's points while appearing magnanimous, stating that he welcomed all types of dialogue big or small, that student-proposed preconditions were unnecessary obstacles to productive conversations, and that holding elections for student representatives would be so difficult that it might make dialogue impossible.[66]

[65] 火與血之真相: 中國大陸民主運動紀實, 1989 (The truth of fire and blood: A documentary on the pro-democracy movement in mainland China in 1989) (Taipei: Institute for the Study of Chinese Communist Problems, 1989), 4.115–16.

[66] 火與血之真相 (The truth of fire and blood), 4.113–14.

In the days after the sham dialogue, students' class boycott continued and Xiang Xiaoji worked together with Shen Tong to organize a democratically elected student dialogue delegation. But on April 30, as Li Peng headed to the train station to welcome Zhao Ziyang home from North Korea, he must have been pleased that the humiliation of April 27 had been followed by a victory on April 29. Zhao had an inkling of the storm he was heading into. In addition to reading Deng Xiaoping's comments about turmoil from Pyongyang, Zhao heard from officials in northeast China on his way home. They told him that "many people were critical of Deng after hearing his remarks." Years later, thinking back on the moment when he arrived in Beijing on April 30, Zhao said that the "situation had grown perilous" and that "large-scale bloodshed had become all too possible."[67] Zhao, Li, many students, and plenty of other people in Beijing were reacting to each other's choices in ways that backed them into corners. But large-scale bloodshed was more than a month away, and while it was always a possibility, it was never inevitable.

[67] *PS*, 14.

6   Backed into Corners

During the first eleven days of May, students held big, festive marches on May 1 to celebrate Labor Day and on May 4 to commemorate the seventieth anniversary of the May Fourth Movement. Hundreds of journalists from *People's Daily*, Xinhua, and other news organizations also marched on May 4, calling for an end to censorship and demanding to report the truth – a sign that the protest movement had expanded to include professionals as well as students.[1] The marches were fun and continued to attract support from Beijing residents, but many participants realized that they were not accomplishing much. Many students who had been boycotting classes began to resume their studies. Every few days, student leaders, including Wang Dan, Xiang Xiaoji, and Wang Chaohua, a graduate student in literature at the Chinese Academy of Social Sciences, presented slightly different petitions to Party and government offices, demanding genuine dialogue on the students' own terms. Each time they were rebuffed, including on May 3, when Yuan Mu said that one petition's threatening tone and unreasonable preconditions were actually provoking turmoil.[2]

Undeterred, the independent dialogue delegation led by Xiang Xiaoji and Shen Tong continued meeting, hoping that by practicing internal democracy and repeatedly asking the government to meet they would be seen as reasonable interlocutors rather than as rabble-rousers. Shen Tong explained the dialogue delegation's long-term goals to reporters on May 11:

We see the movement in three stages. The first is to gain attention so that the people of China understand our concerns. The second is to make our campuses democratic castles and strengthen our own commitment to democratic reform, while giving students in other cities and those in other sectors of society – workers, peasants, and journalists – the time to gain their own political awareness. And third, after this has been achieved, we will probably hold a

---

[1] *LSQ*, 151–52.   [2] *LSQ*, 145.

nationwide prodemocracy movement in the fall, to educate people as to what democratic reform is all about.[3]

Shen Tong and other dialogue delegation members' long game took pains to sound reasonable and even adopted official language about democratic reform. Elizabeth J. Perry has critiqued students "undemocratic style," arguing that, fettered by tradition, they "engaged in an exclusionist style of protest that served to reinforce pre-existing authority relations."[4] Perry's point is perceptive and accurate, but students themselves, including Shen Tong and Wang Chaohua, were aware of this problem and tried to overcome it. Given enough time and space, they could have continued to learn and adjust. But many other students were thinking about the next few days, not the next few months.

Deng Xiaoping was also deeply preoccupied with more immediate concerns, specifically the upcoming visit of Soviet leader Mikhail Gorbachev, who was scheduled to arrive in Beijing on May 15, to normalize diplomatic relations between China and the Soviet Union after decades of tension. Appearing at Hu Yaobang's memorial service had taken its toll on Deng Xiaoping. He felt sick and tired. His number one priority was to rest and recuperate so that he could meet with Gorbachev; he avoided public appearances and even private meetings.[5] Deng's inaccessibility in early May meant that tension between Zhao Ziyang and Li Peng escalated as the two men had to operate with no guidance from above. Deng's absence also caused a diplomatic snafu when Iranian president Ali Khamenei cut off talks with Li Peng on May 9, 1989, because Deng Xiaoping was nowhere to be seen. The Iranian leader knew as well as anyone else that Deng was China's top leader and was scheduled to meet with Gorbachev a few days later; Khamenei demanded the same courtesy. After a series of frantic phone calls, Li promised Khamenei that Deng had agreed to meet. Deng finally emerged from seclusion to spend thirty minutes with Khamenei on May 11.[6]

After returning from North Korea on April 30, Zhao Ziyang was unable to directly contact Deng Xiaoping about how to handle the student movement. When Zhao called Deng's secretary Wang Ruilin to ask for a meeting, the secretary said that Deng was too sick. Zhao then tried to get in touch through intermediaries. The message he received on

---

[3] Shen Tong, *Almost a Revolution*, 234.
[4] Elizabeth J. Perry, "Casting a Chinese 'Democracy' Movement," in *Popular Protest and Political Culture in Modern China*, 88; Perry, "Introduction: Chinese Political Culture Revisited," 7.
[5] Dai Qing, 邓小平在1989 (Deng Xiaoping in 1989), 84, 89.   [6] *LP*, 136, 142.

May 2 from Yang Shangkun, who had spoken with Deng's children and with Wang Ruilin, was that it would be impossible to convince Deng to change his mind about the April 26 editorial. At best, Yang told Zhao, the editorial's harsh tone "could be downplayed by not mentioning it again while gradually turning away from it. They said that if I were to talk to Deng then, only to have him reaffirm his stand, it would make it even more difficult to turn things around in the future."[7]

Zhao's splashiest attempt to downplay the April 26 editorial was his speech to visiting delegates from the Asian Development Bank on May 4. Highlights of Zhao's remarks were published on the front page of *People's Daily* the next day under a prominent headline that lauded Zhao's proposal to "solve problems democratically and legally." Even more notable was this part of Zhao's opening statement: "Major turmoil will not occur in China. I have full confidence in this." Zhao said that people were unhappy and protesting because China's legal system was weak and lacked democratic supervision, and because the political system needed more openness and transparency.[8]

People had varied reactions to Zhao's speech. Some journalists interpreted Zhao's call for openness and transparency as an acceptance of the demands they had issued. On May 5, *People's Daily* editors published an article below Zhao's remarks about how "students and teachers welcomed Zhao Ziyang's speech, hoping that the Party and government will conscientiously strengthen the construction of democracy and the legal system and will increase transparency." In a step toward reporting the truth, a photo of thousands of happy marchers waving banners in Beijing on May 4 appeared at the bottom of the paper's front page. Throughout the rest of May 1989, China's newspapers and broadcast stations, especially those in Beijing, created the most open publishing environment in the history of the People's Republic since autonomous Red Guard organizations had circulated independent newsletters in 1966 and 1967.[9]

While some reporters reacted to Zhao Ziyang's messaging as if they had finally been released from censors' shackles, other journalists felt paralyzed. While working for Canon, Wang Yuan began a relationship with a married journalist named Guo Yan, first hooking up with him at his apartment the day after Hu Yaobang died (unlike Chai Ling, who said she had no access to contraceptives, Wang Yuan was able to obtain condoms in 1989). Wang and Guo traveled to Shanghai in early May,

---

[7] *PS*, 18.   [8] *RMRB*, May 5, 1989, 1.
[9] On the surge in independent publishing at the outset of the Cultural Revolution, see Michael Schoenhals, "China's 'Great Proletarian Information Revolution' of 1966–1967," in *Maoism at the Grassroots*, 230–58.

but after Zhao Ziyang's speech on May 4, Guo told Wang to return to Beijing without him. Guo's father was so anxious when he compared Zhao's words with the April 26 editorial that he forced his son to stay at home in Nantong, upriver from Shanghai. Wang Yuan recalled that Guo's

father just forbade him from going back to work. According to his father, all signs indicated that a schism had formed between Zhao Ziyang and Li Peng, and that the power struggle would continue for a while. If Guo Yan went back to his job, he would be forced to choose a side. Not wanting his son to fall as collateral damage, his father wanted him to wait it out at home.

Wang was less concerned with political analysis than with the sinking feeling that she had been sleeping with a loser. "I couldn't help but groan" when Guo defended his father's wisdom, she wrote. "He was twenty-nine years old, and he still had to listen to his daddy? What had I seen in this man in the first place?"[10]

Guo Yan waited nervously at home, worried that his job might be in jeopardy but not yet realizing that his extramarital affair with Wang was over. Meanwhile, politicians in Beijing did choose sides. Yang Shangkun expressed support for Zhao's speech. Elder Peng Zhen told Yang that he would stand with Zhao if Deng Xiaoping ended up criticizing the general secretary. Peng would be unable to keep this promise. Another elder, Li Xiannian, had a stranger reaction. On May 4, Zhao visited Li in the hospital, where he probably gave him a preview of his message that major turmoil would not occur in China. As soon as Zhao left Li's hospital room, Li was so excited that he jumped out of his bed barefoot and practically danced a jig, shocking a nurse who saw him spinning around. Why was the eighty-year-old former PRC president and current chairman of the Chinese People's Political Consultative Conference so moved? Writer Dai Qing thinks that Li had been looking for a chance to take down Zhao Ziyang and had finally found a way to move against him. Li could now tell Deng Xiaoping that Zhao was actively undermining Deng's orders to strike hard against turmoil.[11]

Dai Qing's interpretation of events is impossible to verify. We do not know for sure why Li jumped out of bed, let alone whether he gleefully went to the godfather to tattle on Zhao. But the elders' maneuvering was probably more consequential for Zhao Ziyang's political future than younger Politburo members' statements were. Of the four members of the Politburo Standing Committee aside from Zhao Ziyang, two – Hu Qili

---

[10] Anna Wang, *Inconvenient Memories*, 178–79.
[11] Dai Qing, 邓小平在1989 (Deng Xiaoping in 1989), 95.

and Qiao Shi – said that they liked Zhao's fresh approach. Two others – Li Peng and Yao Yilin – strongly opposed Zhao's language.[12] When Li Peng and Yao Yilin met for a private talk on the evening of May 4, Yao mused to Li that maybe Zhao Ziyang had incited protests on purpose, to promote himself while trying to overthrow Deng Xiaoping and get rid of Li Peng. Li wrote in his diary that night that he doubted that Zhao was plotting against him and Deng. But looking back on Yao's suspicions years later, Li wrote, they "really make you think."[13]

Li Peng claimed that Zhao's speech on May 4 gave the protest movement a shot of adrenaline, inflaming a situation that had been calming down since April 29.[14] But at the time, activist workers and students were uncertain how to interpret Zhao's remarks and were reluctant to see him or any other Communist Party leader as a potential ally. Such workers as Han Dongfang and Zhao Hongliang were consistently suspicious of Zhao and his motives. Student leaders Chai Ling and Feng Congde were ambivalent toward Zhao and had no reaction to his speech. Feng wrote:

Zhao's speech was obviously a signal, but at the time I did not notice it. If I had, it might have affected my assessment of the situation ... Many students, including me and Chai Ling, did not have especially fond feelings toward Zhao Ziyang until he was purged. I thought he was an opportunist – his going to North Korea to lie low was a prime example.[15]

Feng would later change his mind about Zhao and wish that he had understood what the general secretary was trying to accomplish in May 1989. Older observers had a clearer sense that ending the protests depended on resolving the gap between Zhao's tolerance and Li Peng's intolerance. On May 9, Zhang Wanshu, the editor at Xinhua News Agency, sent a team of junior editors to Beijing's main universities to investigate the state of the protest movement as it related to China's top leaders. Zhang's team discovered two intractable stalemates. The first was between autonomous student organizations and the government. The students were not willing to give up until they got dialogue and recognition. The government refused to grant the new organizations legitimacy, calling them illegal. There was no solution in sight. The second stalemate that the Xinhua editors recognized was between Li Peng and Zhao Ziyang. Zhao had been seeking solutions using legal and democratic channels, while officials allied with Li had showed up on university campuses to tell administrators and teachers that Zhao's

---

[12] *LSQ*, 155.   [13] *LP*, 123.   [14] *LP*, 133.
[15] Feng Congde, 六四日記 (June Fourth diary), 233

speech on May 4 was not a new direction approved by Party Center – instead, the April 26 editorial correctly represented Party Center's view.[16]

On May 8, 9, and 10, Zhao Ziyang acted more like a true general secretary than like Deng's passive underling. Zhao was not completely unshackled – he knew that he could not openly repudiate the April 26 editorial or affirm autonomous student organizations' right to exist – but he pushed as hard as he could within those limits. Knowing that Deng Xiaoping had generally agreed with increasing transparency, Zhao spoke openly about press freedom. This further encouraged journalists to write what they wanted. It also enraged Li Peng, who said that press reports were siding with "turmoil elements" and accused Zhao of "once again inciting turmoil in the news."[17]

Zhao also went out on a limb about how to handle dialogue and student organizations, saying at a PSC meeting on May 8 that dialogue did not have to be mediated by the All-China Students Federation and that it was fine if activist students took over officially approved student unions. Zhao brought up the same points on May 10 at a meeting of the entire Politburo. Li Peng thought that Zhao was openly advocating for student autonomy. "The facts show that Zhao had already departed quite a bit from Party Center's policy," Li wrote in his memoir, retroactively erasing the fact that Zhao himself was a more senior member of Party Center than Li was.[18]

Zhao Ziyang's political authority may have seemed ascendant on the front page of *People's Daily*, which continued to celebrate the general secretary's moderate approach. But the events of May 11 underscored the grim reality that Zhao faced: the elders – above all, Deng Xiaoping – could bring him down at any time. Deng's secretary Wang Ruilin called Li Peng to pass along an encouraging message from Deng. "Without the April 26 editorial, we would not have had the calming of the situation that we see today," Li recalled Wang telling him. "Li Peng should resolutely stand up to the pressure that is coming at him from inside and outside."[19] After this boost from Deng, elder Wang Zhen invited Li to his home for a visit later that evening. Wang wanted Li to hold a new version of the "Seven Thousand Cadres' Conference" of 1962, when the Party had dealt with the fallout of the Great Leap famine. Wang's hope was to gather a large number of officials together to "unify thinking within the Party and solve the turmoil problem." Although Li found

---

[16] Zhang Wanshu, 歷史的大爆炸 (Historical explosion), 146–47.   [17] *LP*, 132.
[18] *LP*, 135.   [19] *LP*, 143.

the "old revolutionary's" plan impractical, he appreciated Wang's support.[20]

By the end of the day on May 11, Li Peng must have felt more confident in trying to block Zhao Ziyang's attempts to behave like a genuine general secretary. But something even more momentous for Zhao's future was brewing. *The Tiananmen Papers*, a compilation of primary sources of questionable provenance, includes an implausibly detailed transcript of a purported private conversation between Deng Xiaoping and Yang Shangkun on May 11. If the two elders indeed met that day, we do not know for sure what they said – *The Tiananmen Papers'* transcripts are not reliable or verifiable. What we do know is that two days later, on May 13, Yang and Zhao went to visit Deng. Zhao recalled that the main point of the visit was to prepare for Gorbachev's visit, but Zhao also advocated for dialogue and increased transparency in handling the protests.[21] Deng was noncommittal, saying that while transparency was good, precisely how to be transparent needed to be investigated further. Later that day, Yang Shangkun told Li Peng that Deng had been grumpy, saying to Zhao, "I'm really tired, my brain isn't working right, and my ears are ringing like the devil. I can't hear what you're saying." Li interpreted Deng's comments about transparency as opposing Zhao's attempts to open up the press.[22] While they were meeting on the morning of May 13, neither Deng, Yang, nor Zhao knew that later that day a group of students would take a dramatic step that would stymie their efforts to end the protests.

★ ★ ★

During the first half of May, such students as Shen Tong, Wang Chaohua, and Xiang Xiaoji tried to set up dialogue meetings that were not stage-managed by the government. Members of autonomous student groups sought to make their organizations more democratic. They discussed possible next steps in the short, medium, and long terms now that marching to Tiananmen Square had become more of a routine than a thrilling breakthrough. A divide emerged between activists who wanted a slower, step-by-step organizing drive and those who felt that the window for change was rapidly closing.

Among those who wanted immediate action were Chai Ling, Örkesh, Wang Dan, and Zhang Boli, a twenty-nine-year-old journalist from northeast China who had entered a writers' training program at Peking University in fall 1988. Zhang recalled that "the time had come for us to

[20] *LP*, 145.   [21] *PS*, 21.   [22] *LP*, 151.

Figure 6.1 Chai Ling, Örkesh Dölet (Wuerkaixi), and Wang Dan in
May 1989. Peter Turnley/Corbis Historical via Getty Images.

step up the pace. A hunger strike appealed to us as being the strongest
action we could take without resorting to violence."[23] Chai Ling remembered that Zhang told her "with great excitement how Gandhi had used
hunger strikes to achieve political goals."[24] On May 12, Wang Dan told
Chai Ling that he and around forty other students at Peking University
had decided to stage a hunger strike, but that he was joining on his own
because student organizations had voted against the move, calling it too
drastic. Chai agreed to join Wang. The two gave speeches that night
announcing their decision.

Chai Ling's speech included two demands: to reverse the "turmoil"
label and to hold dialogue on equal terms. The way she framed her
overall goal, however, was more compelling than her specific demands:

Dear fellow students, when we sacrifice our health, we want to see the true face of
our government. When we were growing up, we were raised to say, "We love our
country, we love our people." Now we want to see if our country loves us and if
our people will stand up for us. We want to know if this country is still worth our
struggle, our sacrifice, our devotion. I want to use the courage to face death to
fight for the right to live life.

[23] Zhang Boli, *Escape from China: The Long Journey from Tiananmen to Freedom*, trans. Kwee
      Kian Low (New York: Washington Square Press, 2002), 39.
[24] Chai Ling, *Heart*, 126.

Chai's powerful language sparked applause and emotional reactions from her audience. After she finished speaking, the number of students who committed to take part in the hunger strike jumped from 40 to 220.[25]

Shen Tong, who was deeply involved in dialogue delegation work, did not think that staging a hunger strike was a good idea. Chai Ling's speech changed his mind. "It touched me as no other speech had," he wrote. "Chai Ling made me understand why students would want to make such a sacrifice." Shen understood that ramping up pressure on the government also raised the stakes of organizing dialogue. As he put it, "The lives of the hunger strikers depended on our success."[26] Feng Congde was equally certain that Chai's appeal had been highly effective, but he differed from Shen in explaining its power. In Feng's view, when Chai said that she wanted to see the government's true face and added, "we want to wake up the conscience of the nation," she was implying that the Chinese government was as authoritarian as it was because people had failed to stand up to it.[27] Chai's focus was as much about getting people to act as it was about demanding a government response.

Act they did. The next afternoon, on May 13, more than three hundred hunger strikers from thirteen Beijing universities, along with more than two thousand supporters, marched to Tiananmen Square to set up a protest camp. A crowd of approximately thirty thousand onlookers surrounded the hunger strikers.[28] Each day over the following week, the crowds grew, as did the number of hunger strikers. People in Beijing were moved by the students' plight and by the wailing sirens of ambulances assisting students who had fainted. On May 15, Wang Yuan's Japanese boss told her to close the doors to their office's balcony because the ambulances were too loud. When Wang went out for lunch, she noticed a change on the streets. Strangers were talking to each other about the fasting students. Even unspoken glances held meaning: "Every pair of eyes I saw were silently screaming to be heard. They radiated anger, worry, even helplessness. The only emotion they didn't communicate was indifference."[29]

The basic message of the hunger strike was that students were willing to die in order to change China. This resonated with the broader population of Beijing, especially as they watched the Communist Party's response, which began with confusion and indifference and ended with martial law. On May 15 and 16, hundreds of thousands of people marched in support of the hunger strikers. On May 17, the number of

---

[25] Chai Ling, *Heart*, 131–32.   [26] Shen Tong, *Almost a Revolution*, 237.
[27] Feng Congde, 六四日記 (June Fourth diary), 281.   [28] *LSQ*, 208.
[29] Wang, *Inconvenient Memories*, 191.

marchers swelled to more than a million, and the number was almost as high on May 18. Hitting the streets to support the students became a popular group activity organized and supported by work units, members of which carried banners and wore uniforms identifying their factory or office. Businesspeople, laborers, journalists, retirees, teachers, and even police officers and soldiers took part. Many of their slogans and petitions praised nonviolent protest while criticizing Deng Xiaoping and the system he oversaw: "Government by old men must end! The dictator must resign!"[30]

The students forgoing food in Tiananmen Square, whose numbers had grown to more than three thousand, had succeeded in mobilizing more than a million people to oppose dictatorship and demand something better. This success in broadening the movement meant that by mid-May, students were no longer the main force of the movement. Of course, students still saw themselves as the most important and newsworthy group in Beijing – in the years since, some scholars, writers, and filmmakers have followed their lead. They were wrong. Students and officials struggled anxiously to find solutions, but few of their ideas addressed or included the hundreds of thousands of people in the streets every day.

Between the middle of May and the early hours of June 4, 1989, students collected donations of money and tents, argued over who was in charge of their rapidly changing organizational structures, and debated whether to withdraw or to continue to occupy the square. Chai Ling took on an even more prominent leadership role, as "commander in chief" of the Hunger Strike Headquarters. Even though Chai occasionally considered scenarios in which students would evacuate the square, the result of each daily debate was to stay. Sociologist Dingxin Zhao explains why:

> While the leaders and organizations that emerged during the movement could usually effectively stage radical movement activities, such leaders and organizations were absolutely unable to exercise effective control over the movement. Whenever movement leaders or organizations wanted to make strategic moves rather than take more radical actions, they were immediately marginalized.[31]

This observation is accurate and perceptive. But Zhao and other analysts, especially the filmmakers of *Gate of Heavenly Peace*, argue that the hunger strike along with student leadership squabbles that led to a prolonged occupation of Tiananmen Square "set the stage for the movement's bloody ending."[32] This is victim blaming. It is also myopic and

---

[30] Han, *Cries for Democracy*, 222.   [31] Zhao, *Power of Tiananmen*, 147.
[32] Zhao, *Power of Tiananmen*, 164.

inaccurate. In an essay written in 1995, Wang Chaohua, who as a leading member of the Beijing Students' Autonomous Federation in 1989 was deeply involved in debates about whether to stage a hunger strike or whether to leave the square, convincingly pushed back against this notion. Wang argued that it is wrong to overemphasize students' decisions, mistakes, and conflicts or to see them as provoking a deadly crackdown. To focus excessively on student leaders' choices after mid-May is to ignore the more than a million Beijing residents who had been inspired to march against dictatorship, to form their own independent organizations, and, eventually, to resist an armed invasion. This demand for change by the broader population of Beijing was not dependent on students' presence in the square. Over the coming days, Beijing residents would make their own choices regardless of students' decision making.[33]

Students and Beijingers were broadly aligned but not in complete agreement. Beginning on May 16, sociologist Craig Calhoun conducted surveys that highlight how students' goals and thinking compared to what other Beijing residents wanted. Calhoun first asked 109 students what they thought were the most important aspects of democracy. The top three answers were "accurate news reporting" (mentioned by 89 percent of respondents), "free expression" (83 percent), and "free elections" (68 percent). Students' understanding of democracy differed from how they stated their goals. Their top three goals were ending corruption, accurate news reporting, and freedom of expression. Only 33 percent of student respondents mentioned free elections as a main goal. Like the students, ordinary Beijing residents said that they supported democracy, but were even more focused on corruption. The most important goals that bystanders hoped that the protests would achieve were ending corruption (82 percent), stopping official profiteering (59 percent), and accurate news reporting (50 percent).[34]

★ ★ ★

The peaceful uprising of millions of people in Beijing, sparked by sympathy with hunger-striking students, meant that the students' numbers were dwarfed by a mass citizens' movement. In the middle of May, the movement suddenly became much more diverse and inclusive, ranging from factory workers to elderly officials, not to mention the tens of thousands of people from hinterland provinces – including Lu

---

[33] Wang Chaohua, 從來就沒有救世主: 六四30週年祭 (There are no saviors: A remembrance on the thirtieth anniversary of June Fourth) (Taipei: Jiangxin wenchuang, 2019), 226–27.
[34] Calhoun, *Neither Gods nor Emperors*, 244–48.

Decheng, the mechanic from Hunan – who took trains to Beijing to join the protests. The broader concerns of nonstudents, focusing on ending corruption and dictatorship, did not bode well for Zhao Ziyang's attempts to resolve the situation by downplaying or repudiating the April 26 editorial and engaging in dialogue with activist students. Students might have liked what they were reading in *People's Daily* about Zhao's approach. Many Beijing residents who were angry about corruption, however, saw him as part of the problem. His golf hobby made him seem out of touch and his sons were rumored to be involved in profiteering. Industrial workers associated Zhao with liberalizing reforms that undermined their job security and weakened their ability to speak up about workplace issues. Zhao's lack of support among protesters did not help him in May 1989, but it did not cause his downfall. Deng Xiaoping did that, with help from Li Peng and others.

Deng, Li, and Zhao's immediate reaction when they learned about the hunger strike on May 13 was not to address students' concerns or solve the problems they had raised. It was to prevent the protests from disrupting Mikhail Gorbachev's visit. Efforts to get the hunger strikers to vacate the square took two forms on May 14, the eve of Gorbachev's arrival: a rushed "dialogue" meeting that ended in disarray, followed by a visit by twelve older intellectuals who pleaded with the students to behave rationally.

On May 13, students demanding dialogue finally got the planning discussion they had been asking for. Yan Mingfu initiated the meeting. Yan led the Party's United Front Work Department and was an ally of Zhao Ziyang. He reached out to the Beijing Social and Economic Research Institute (SERI), a private think tank where Bai Hua and Wang Juntao worked, to figure out how to contact student activists. SERI founders Chen Ziming and Wang Juntao had been paying close attention to the student movement but had shied away from getting directly involved. Now that the Party was asking for SERI's help, Chen and Wang felt obligated to say yes.[35] Wang, Bai Hua, and others drove around in vans to gather up student leaders including Chai Ling, Örkesh, Shen Tong, Wang Chaohua, Wang Dan, and Xiang Xiaoji.

When the students and think tank intellectuals arrived at the United Front Department, Shen Tong got the impression that the intellectuals supported the student movement and were pressing for genuine dialogue. The students had never heard of Yan Mingfu. They learned that he seemed to be a reformer associated with Zhao Ziyang and that the

---

[35] Black and Munro, *Black Hands*, 171–72.

government was desperate to get the students to voluntarily leave Tiananmen Square before May 15. Yan said, "Many of you believe that there is a distinction between reformers and conservatives in the government. You are in fact wrong about this, but if you believe it, then you are hurting the reformers by being stubborn." He added, "If the students do not leave the square by May fifteenth, the consequences will be hard to predict. None of us wants to see anything bad happen."[36]

The next morning, May 14, Zhao Ziyang convened a PSC meeting to let his colleagues know that there would be a formal dialogue meeting later that day with students. The goal was to convince them to leave Tiananmen Square in advance of the Soviet delegation's visit. Zhao had managed to arrange a discussion with members of autonomous student organizations, although he did not show up himself. Yan Mingfu and Li Tieying, China's top education official, did most of the talking. The meeting took place at the United Front headquarters, with thirteen chairs on each side of a table: thirteen Party and government officials sitting directly across from thirteen student representatives, thereby achieving the students' goal of "equal dialogue." More students stood behind the table, constantly passing notes to Xiang Xiaoji and Shen Tong, who tried to summarize the dialogue delegation's points. The meeting fell apart when a group of students disrupted the meeting to complain that it was not being broadcast live over loudspeakers in Tiananmen Square. Before the meeting started, Zheng Youmei, the clerk to whom students had been delivering petitions, had agreed to Shen Tong's request for a broadcast, but the loudspeakers remained quiet. Shen Tong thought that conservative officials had sabotaged the broadcast, while Yan Mingfu blamed technical difficulties.[37] Nobody left satisfied.

The student activists who had been in the room with Yan Mingfu on May 13 and 14 had a sense that he was acting on behalf of Zhao Ziyang. But many of the thousands of students in the square had no idea who Yan Mingfu was and had little interest in Zhao Ziyang. Feng Congde had stayed in the square on May 14 to run the students' own broadcast station. Looking back on events, he thought that the conversation with Yan Mingfu had been a "great opportunity" for students to cooperate with "enlightened" Party leaders. Feng later realized that by pointedly reaching out to the leaders of autonomous student organizations, Yan had actually legitimized the newly formed groups. But at the time, Feng and his fellow students did not trust Zhao Ziyang. "Whether it was Zhao Ziyang or Li Peng, everyone thought they were parts of the Party's

---

[36] Shen Tong, *Almost a Revolution*, 242–43.
[37] Shen Tong, *Almost a Revolution*, 247–50.

bureaucratic machinery and did not place any hope on them," Feng wrote.[38]

Students' distrust extended to the twelve older intellectuals who tried to persuade them to leave the square later on the evening of May 14. After the dialogue meeting fell apart, Dai Qing (a journalist at *Guangming Daily*), Su Xiaokang (a lecturer who had written the script of the *River Elegy* television show), and a professor named Wen Yuankai took turns praising the student movement while asking them to be rational and to compromise with the government by temporarily relocating their protest. Some students were distrustful, saying, "the government's lobbyists have arrived; don't let them trick us!"[39] The students decided to stay in the square. Feng Congde was especially disdainful of the intellectuals' attempt at mediation, calling them cowards and elitists.[40]

★ ★ ★

When Mikhail Gorbachev arrived in Beijing on May 15, the official welcoming ceremony was held at the airport instead of at Tiananmen as originally planned. Li Peng reported that during the banquet honoring Gorbachev in the Great Hall of the People that evening, students and workers kept "attacking" the hall. Li was unable to enjoy his meal because of the reports he was hearing: people were planning on setting themselves on fire in front of the hall. "They were using Gorbachev's visit to threaten the government," Li wrote. Beijing municipal authorities put together a rescue team, but the rumored self-immolations never occurred.[41] Over the next two days, Zhao Ziyang's career did go up in flames.

At a PSC meeting on May 16, Zhao Ziyang formally proposed "revising the judgment of the April 26 editorial." He thought that it was the only way to "end the hunger strike and proceed with dialogue." Zhao recalled that Li Peng jumped in to say that the "designation contained in the April 26 editorial was drafted strictly according to Deng Xiaoping's words and therefore could not be changed." Yang Shangkun also opposed revisiting the question, warning that "revising the April 26 editorial would damage Deng Xiaoping's image." Zhao had failed. He decided that he had "no other choice but to express my views to Deng personally."

Zhao asked for a meeting with Deng and was told to go to Deng's home on the afternoon of May 17. Zhao had expected a one-on-one

---

[38] Feng Congde, 六四日記 (June Fourth diary), 305.   [39] *LSQ*, 221–22.
[40] Feng Congde, 六四日記 (June Fourth diary), 310.   [41] *LP*, 156–58.

conversation, but when he showed up, he had company: "All the members of the Politburo Standing Committee plus [Yang] Shangkun were already there ... Since I had asked for a personal meeting with Deng, only to have Deng call for a full standing committee meeting at his home, I realized that things had already taken a bad turn." Instead of asking what was going on or why Li Peng, Hu Qili, Qiao Shi, Yang Shangkun and Yao Yilin were there, Zhao forged ahead with his original plan, saying that the April 26 editorial, "which caused so much misunderstanding, must have been unclear or incorrectly expressed in some way. The only way to bring about some kind of resolution would be to somewhat relax the judgment from this editorial." Zhao recalled that as he was speaking, "Deng appeared very impatient and displeased."[42]

Li Peng spoke next, saying that the editorial had initially calmed the situation, but that Zhao Ziyang's tone on May 4 had fanned the flames and made the situation worse. Li Peng wrote in his diary that Qiao Shi said that the editorial had been correct, Yao Yilin said that "Zhao's mistakes had caused the turmoil," Hu Qili expressed anxiety about how out of touch the PSC was from ordinary people's thinking, and then Yang Shangkun said that there could be no retreat from the editorial – because protesters were directly targeting Deng, the only choice was to "take a clear-cut stand in opposing turmoil."[43] Zhao Ziyang recalled that Yang Shangkun also said that an elderly high-ranking military officer named Liao Hansheng "believes that martial law should be imposed. Perhaps we should consider imposing martial law."[44]

Deng Xiaoping agreed with Yang. The two elders had probably decided on martial law as a solution before meeting with the PSC. According to notes that Li Peng took while Deng was speaking, Deng also agreed with Li Peng's assessment of events, saying that the April 26 editorial had been correct and that "Zhao Ziyang's speech on May 4 was the turning point. It allowed people to see discord within Party Center, riled up the students, and lots of people shifted allegiance to the students." Deng repeatedly emphasized that because events in Beijing were influencing cities nationwide, a solution in Beijing had to come first.

Deng said:

The method I'm thinking of is martial law. Only this method can put down the turmoil within a short period of time ... Martial law means using the army. The army must be told that as long as bad people are not rioting, the army should not fight back. If conflict does arise, injuries will be unavoidable. Beijing does not

[42] *PS*, 27–28.   [43] *LP*, 165–69.   [44] *PS*, 28.

have enough police, so proclaiming martial law is the only way to restore normalcy and order for working and studying.[45]

Li Peng and Yao Yilin supported Deng's idea. So did Qiao Shi. Hu Qili was again noncommittal, only remarking that he was very worried about the situation. Zhao Ziyang opposed martial law, saying that he could not carry it out. Even though there had not been a formal vote of the standing committee, Deng was satisfied that his authority, plus Yang Shangkun's support, carried the room. Deng put Li Peng, Qiao Shi, and Yang Shangkun in charge of implementing martial law.[46]

Zhao had lost. He asked his secretary Bao Tong to draft a resignation letter, but then withdrew it. Zhao and Li visited hunger strikers in the hospital around 5 a.m. on May 18 and made an early morning visit to the square on May 19. Li Peng shook hands, signed some autographs, and left. Zhao stuck around to give an impromptu speech that was printed in *People's Daily* the next day. "You are still young and you have long lives ahead of you," Zhao said into a megaphone:

You should live healthily so that you can see the day when China achieves the Four Modernizations. You are not like us. We are old, it doesn't matter [what happens to us] ... You are teenagers or are in your twenties, are you really going to sacrifice your lives like this? Can't you think a bit rationally?

With tears in his eyes, Zhao wrapped up his remarks by saying that "we" – referring to top Party leaders – had once been young and had marched and lain down on train tracks in protest without considering the consequences.[47]

Years later, Zhao recalled that he was trying to explain that the hunger strike "was no use against the group of elders who had taken a hard-line position," but that the "students did not understand what I meant."[48] Zhao's final public appearance of his life was feeble and pathetic. Once he had opposed Deng's imposition of martial law, Zhao's already limited authority had plummeted to zero. Zhao was on the verge of losing everything, but he did not behave like someone who had nothing to lose. His speech at the square came across as hesitant and fearful, full of confusing code words about old age and youth. It made the sixty-nine-year-old Zhao seem elderly even though he was the young one compared with the men in their eighties who had settled on a military solution.

In contrast to the defeated Zhao, Li Peng swung into action with authority and confidence on May 18 and 19. On May 18, Li met in the Great Hall of the People with hunger strikers including Örkesh, Wang

---

[45] *LP*, 170–72.   [46] *LP*, 172–73.   [47] *RMRB*, May 20, 1989, 1.   [48] *PS*, 31.

Dan, and Wang Chaohua. Wang Dan stated the students' main demand: that the government affirm that the students were engaged in a patriotic democracy movement, not turmoil. Li Peng's response was that while the government had never said that the majority of patriotic students were causing turmoil, Beijing had descended into a "state of anarchy" over the past few days and that the "chaos" was spreading nationwide. He said that it would be "inappropriate and irrational" to stubbornly "quibble" (纠缠) over the specific issues Wang Dan had raised. Li's stated agenda was for the students to stop the hunger strike, leave the square, and get the medical care they needed.[49]

Then, in the most memorable moment of the meeting, Örkesh, who was wearing hospital pajamas and holding an oxygen tube to his nose, confronted Li Peng. Örkesh said, "It is not us student representatives who are quibbling. Another point is that I should not need to repeat what I said at the beginning, but it seems that some leading comrades still don't understand so I'll say it again." He then rephrased what he had said earlier: the students sitting in the hall with Li Peng did not hold the key to solving the problem. In the middle of a sentence, Örkesh dramatically took the oxygen tube out of his nostril, grabbed a green pillow, and threw the tube and pillow on the ground. The "objective reality, the objective fact," he said, was that if "one single person does not leave the square and continues to hunger strike, then it is very difficult for us to guarantee that the remaining thousands of people" will not stay.

When video of the meeting was broadcast on television nationwide, viewers had diverse reactions. Some may have been impressed by Wang Chaohua's statement that it might be possible to persuade hunger strikers to leave Tiananmen Square, and that overemphasizing students' patriotic enthusiasm obscured the movement's "calm, rational, restrained, and orderly" nature.[50] But the pajama-wearing Örkesh's clash with Li Peng made the opposite point and made a more lasting impression.

Watching the televised meeting at home on the evening of May 18, Wang Yuan was at first amused by Li Peng's awkward style: "I couldn't help but laugh. Not only was Li Peng's IQ cause for concern, but he completely lacked charisma." But when Örkesh said that if one student refused to stop their hunger strike, thousands of others would remain by

---

[49] A transcript of the meeting is in 火與血之真相 (The truth of fire and blood), 4.140–45; televised excerpts translated into English can be found in Oksenberg, Sullivan, and Lambert, *Beijing Spring, 1989*, 269–81.
[50] 火與血之真相 (The truth of fire and blood), 4.142.

their side, Wang Yuan's "laughter tapered off. Something was very wrong with that statement." Wang wrote:

Wu'erkaixi's words told a dangerous story. If the students couldn't be accurately represented by their leaders, and the end of the strike depended on the satisfaction of every student, what end could ever be in sight? What was the point of demanding a sit-down with government officials and broadcasting it to every home in the country? Maybe Li Peng was smarter than he seemed.[51]

It is doubtful that Li Peng won many fans after his performance sitting across from the hunger strikers in the Great Hall, but by allowing Örkesh to imply that negotiating with student leaders was pointless, Li had achieved a public-relations victory on the eve of declaring martial law.

The next morning, Li Peng received another boost at a meeting at Deng Xiaoping's house. Elders Chen Yun, Li Xiannian, and Yang Shangkun were there, as were Yao Yilin and Qiao Shi. Hu Qili and Zhao Ziyang had not been invited, but PLA brass Chi Haotian, Zhao Nanqi, and Yang Baibing were there, as well as three other veteran military leaders named Qin Jiwei, Hong Xuezhi, and Liu Huaqing. According to notes that Li Peng took at the meeting, Deng began by saying that the "turmoil" had been caused by a problem within the Party. "There are two headquarters in Party Center. On the surface it is Li Peng versus Zhao Ziyang, but in actuality it is me against Zhao Ziyang." Deng lamented that he had twice mistakenly picked general secretaries who were too weak in opposing liberalization. Hu Yaobang had been too rushed in making reforms, Deng said, while Zhao Ziyang had "said a lot and not accomplished much, always using my name to do his own thing."

Deng declared that Li Peng would continue as premier – Deng had seen enough to decide that Li was a useful servant but would not make a suitable general secretary. He recommended instead that Shanghai's Party secretary Jiang Zemin take over Zhao Ziyang's position as China's top leader on paper. "Turmoil is a bad thing," Deng concluded, "but the bad thing can become something good. If we resolve this well, we can preserve ten or even twenty years of stability and there will be great hope for China."[52]

Everyone at the meeting agreed with Deng's remarks, including his unilateral selection of a new general secretary. Later that evening, Li Peng delivered a stern speech about Beijing's descent into "anarchy," ordering the students to stop the hunger strike and telling people in Beijing to quit marching in support. Continuing to support the hunger

---

[51] Wang, *Inconvenient Memories*, 197.   [52] *LP*, 187–92.

strikers, Li said, would push them into ruin.[53] Yang Shangkun spoke after Li, saying, "To maintain social order in the capital and restore normal routine, we have had no alternative but to move [to Beijing] some troops from the People's Liberation Army."[54] Troops began entering the city on the evening of May 19. This set the stage for the official imposition of martial law at 10 a.m. on May 20, 1989.

[53] *LP*, 193–95.   [54] Han, *Cries for Democracy*, 258.

7 Workers and Citizens

Deng's decision on May 17 to impose martial law and his move on May 19 to remove Zhao Ziyang as general secretary targeted university students as the central threat. Deng said that Zhao's speech on May 4, along with his comment to Mikhail Gorbachev that Deng was the ultimate authority in China, had encouraged students to continue protesting and allowed them to gain support from broader society. The students, Deng argued, would never be satisfied with compromises. Any retreat would inevitably lead to further demands and eventually to the downfall of the Chinese Communist Party. That was why Deng thought that Zhao Ziyang's strategy to negotiate was dead wrong. For Deng, forcefully ending student protests was the only way to save the People's Republic of China, socialism, and the Communist Party.[1] But in blaming Zhao and targeting students, Deng forgot something important: everybody else in Beijing.

Deng's decision to impose martial law expanded the scope of the protests and compelled more nonstudents, especially workers, to get involved. Martial law disrupted everyday life in Beijing by shutting down public transportation and sparking panic buying. Anger at these disruptions and sympathy for students engaged in peaceful civil disobedience pushed thousands of ordinary Beijing residents to resist what they saw as an unnecessary military invasion of their city. During the four days between May 19 and May 23, citizen resistance against martial law blocked troops from entering central Beijing. After that, military units retreated. Nobody knew what would happen next. This gave the movement time to grow and expand far beyond what had begun as a student-led effort. Not only did the Beijing Workers' Autonomous Federation increase its membership and organizing in late May, but a new broader activist organization called the Capital Joint Liaison Group aimed to push the movement in new directions.

---

[1] Deng's remarks on May 17 as recorded by Li Peng in *LP*, 171.

Most accounts of the first four days of martial law focus on Beijing citizens' successful blockade of tens of thousands of unarmed soldiers who, unable to get to their destinations and not allowed to use force, sat stuck in the middle of large crowds. Li Peng could not believe it. "I had not imagined that the army would encounter such massive resistance upon entering the city," Li wrote. "This proves that news of martial law had been leaked ahead of time."[2] Li and Yang Shangkun themselves had telegraphed the army's involvement on May 19, hours ahead of the official imposition of martial law on May 20. According to historian Timothy Brook, the coming of martial law "was common knowledge in the Square" by late afternoon on Friday, May 19. But as Brook writes, a leak was not the main reason the army failed to advance: "because the citizenry was adamant that the Army not enter the city, the soldiers found no place left unguarded ... In almost every case, the incoming columns were stopped midroute not by students but by ordinary citizens who chose to defend their city against a military occupation."[3]

While many Beijingers mounted a successful defense, even more residents of the capital tried to get to work or stock up on supplies. On the morning of May 20, Wang Yuan hurried to catch a bus to her office before martial law went into effect at 10 a.m. Others had the same idea – the bus was more crowded than usual. As Wang was leaving, she told her worried grandmother, "'I'll be home late, but don't worry.' Martial law was a good excuse to come home whenever I pleased." After buses and the subway stopped running, Wang's boss gave her an extra twenty yuan per day for taxi fares. She pocketed the money and walked instead.

Wang Yuan's grandmother recalled what it had been like to live through the civil war between the Communists and Nationalists in the winter of 1948. On Sunday, May 21, she sensed that it was time to stockpile emergency supplies. She gave Wang Yuan a shopping list. As Wang shuttled between shops to buy "heaving sacks of rice, flour, salt, sugar, and ten or so jars of fermented bean curd," she discovered that people in her neighborhood were buying large amounts of food and lining up to fill buckets of water.[4]

Wang Yuan, her grandmother, and their neighbors were like many other people in Beijing living under martial law. They prioritized work and survival, negotiated fraught relationships, and were also curious to watch the protests unfold. Few of them imagined that commuting,

---

[2] *LP*, 199.
[3] Timothy Brook, *Quelling the People: The Military Suppression of the Beijing Democracy Movement* (New York: Oxford University Press, 1992), 69, 52.
[4] Wang, *Inconvenient Memories*, 202, 204.

shopping, or indulging in curiosity would soon become life-threatening activities. Another, more activist group is also worthy of attention: workers who joined independent unions. Their efforts to organize strikes and oppose dictatorship escalated after May 20.

Scholars have disagreed about the size and significance of the worker movement in 1989. Dingxin Zhao dismisses workers' influence, calling the largest autonomous worker organization "basically only an appendage of the student movement." Because Zhao spoke to students and not to workers, it is no surprise that his account exaggerates students' role while denigrating workers as being unable to write their own handbills or make their own decisions.[5] Workers' collaboration with students shows the worker movement's relative inclusivity, not its weakness. Such authors as Andrew Walder, Gong Xiaoxia, George Black, and Robin Munro, who interviewed workers, have discovered a different story in which activists started to build the foundation of a transformative movement.[6]

As Walder and Gong write, "Unlike the student movement, the workers' movement had picked up momentum after martial law and appeared to gain confidence and strength as May turned into June."[7] A few workers formed a core of activists who began to build an independent union. Many more hit the streets to express their disgust and rage about martial law. Wu Wenjian, who worked at the Yanshan Petrochemical Company, was part of this larger group. In April 1989, Wu randomly crossed paths with a group of students carrying Hu Yaobang's portrait around central Beijing. Wu put one yuan into the students' donation bucket. As the protest movement grew, Wu went downtown as often as he could to listen to speeches. "Everything I heard down there was so refreshing," he recalled.

Like many other people in Beijing, Wu transformed into an active participant after the army menaced his city. "Ordinary Beijingers like me didn't join the students until May 20, when that idiot Li Peng declared martial law," Wu explained. Workers from his factory got together and went en masse to the city center. "I stayed with my factory contingent, caught up in the excitement but without any real political motive. Many people were simpleminded like me, just being patriotic and supporting the students," Wu said. Wu attended several

[5] Zhao, *Power of Tiananmen*, 175–76.
[6] Walder and Gong, "Workers in the Tiananmen Protests"; Black and Munro, *Black Hands*.
[7] Walder and Gong, "Workers in the Tiananmen Protests," 3.

Figure 7.1 Workers protest in Beijing on May 18, 1989. Catherine Henriette/AFP via Getty Images.

demonstrations, once maintaining order overnight in a corner of the square with around one hundred of his coworkers from the chemical factory.[8]

Lü Jinghua's path to activism initially paralleled Wu Wenjian's, but Lü ended up becoming a core member of the Beijing Workers' Autonomous Federation (BWAF). The twenty-seven-year-old Lü, who worked in a dress shop, passed by the square every day as part of her commute. The more speeches she heard, the more interested she got. Lü started joining marches and chanting slogans. On May 26, she met Liu Qiang, a worker at a printing factory who was in charge of BWAF's security. Liu seemed discouraged because the government had called BWAF an illegal organization. Undeterred, Lü came back the next day and every day after that. "When I joined the organization, I thought what the students were saying was good," she said. "One part of having a workers' group was to support the students, the other was to raise positive appeals on behalf of workers.

---

[8] Liao Yiwu, *Bullets and Opium: Real-Life Stories of China after the Tiananmen Square Massacre*, trans. David Cowhig, Jessie Cowhig, and Ross Perlin (New York: Signal Press/Atria, 2019 (2012)), 47–48.

This organization could speak for the workers."[9] Lü became the group's broadcaster, reading announcements, open letters, and poems over a generator-powered loudspeaker system that had been funded by sympathetic entrepreneurs and a Hong Kong journalist.[10]

What were the workers broadcasting? They summarized their main grievances like this:

> Official corruption, workers' suffering under a dictatorship of elites enjoying special privileges, the gap between factory workers' and managers' wages, which was growing wider by the day, a lack of democracy within work units, a lack of genuine worker representation in decision making, a decline in the work environment and job security, and a plummeting standard of living in the last year.[11]

Workers' resentment about elitism extended to the way that some student leaders excluded and looked down on them. But during the last part of May, hopes for a broader movement gained steam.

On May 22, Chen Ziming and Wang Juntao of the Beijing Social and Economic Research Institute went to Tiananmen Square and managed to bring together many of the new groups that had spontaneously formed over the past month: BWAF, intellectuals, Beijing residents, and students. The next day, the umbrella organization met at the Chinese Academy of Social Sciences and decided to call themselves the Joint Liaison Group of All Circles in the Capital to Protect and Uphold the Constitution, or Capital Joint Liaison Group (CJLG) for short. George Black and Robin Munro write that for Wang Juntao and Chen Ziming, forming what amounted to an independent political party "must have appeared ... as the culmination of their political careers." But instead of proceeding cautiously toward reform, as Hu Yaobang had once counselled Wang, events had pushed Wang and Chen to act much more quickly than they had planned. The CJLG was the "derailment of all their caution. It was an unplanned child, an unwanted accident of history."[12]

If Chen and Wang had not been prodded into action by the student hunger strike, worker organizing, and citizen resistance to martial law, they probably would never have found themselves in the same room as Chai Ling or Han Dongfang. On May 26, Han attended a CJLG meeting where he explained that BWAF's calls for general strikes and attempts to

---

[9] 工人起來了: 工人自治聯合會運動, 1989 (The workers have risen up: The workers' autonomous federation movement, 1989) (Hong Kong: Xianggang gonghui jiaoyu zhongxin, 1990), 49–50; Black and Munro, *Black Hands*, 226–27.
[10] Zhao, *Power of Tiananmen*, 174.   [11] 工人起來了 (The workers have risen up), 14.
[12] Black and Munro, *Black Hands*, 206–7.

organize within factories had largely failed. He hoped that the CJLG could help shift away from Tiananmen Square toward broader society. "You theoreticians can go on acting as the brains of the movement, and the students can give it its emotional spark," Han said. "But unless the workers are the main force, the struggle for democracy can never succeed."[13]

Han left frustrated and declared that he was done with meetings. He could not have been overly impressed by the CJLG's next major action, a ten-point written appeal issued on May 27. Black and Munro have called the appeal "perhaps the most significant document of the entire 1989 movement" because it began with a declaration of independence from Communist Party factional divides.[14] But point four of the missive criticized Li Peng, Chen Xitong, and Li Ximing, while point five praised Zhao Ziyang. So much for staying away from inner-Party squabbles. The document did not recognize workers as a main force. It barely mentioned them. BWAF, the Beijing Workers' Dare-to-Die Squad and the Beijing Workers' Picket Squad appeared as signatories below the names of student organizations.[15]

Han Dongfang's insistence on thinking beyond an endless occupation of Tiananmen Square put him at odds with students, who continued to argue about whether to stay in the square. But on May 29 and May 30, something happened that drew students out of the square to show solidarity with workers. Police started to crack down on BWAF. On May 29, a plainclothes officer told Lü Jinghua that it was illegal for the workers to maintain an encampment. He posted a notice ordering the workers to leave. Later that night, three BWAF members, Bai Dongping, Qian Yumin, and Shen Yinhan, were arrested. On May 30, Han Dongfang led a group of activists to the Beijing Public Security Bureau headquarters to demand his colleagues' release. Han and other BWAF members had been to the police office before to try to register their organization as a legal entity, always without success. Now hundreds of students walked over from the square to support the workers.[16] The next day, the number of students marching to demand the release of the three BWAF leaders grew to three thousand. Bai, Shen, and Qian were released later that afternoon.[17]

---

[13] Black and Munro, *Black Hands*, 223.   [14] Black and Munro, *Black Hands*, 216.
[15] The entire document is reprinted in Zhang Wanshu, 歷史的大爆炸 (Historical explosion), 299–302.
[16] Black and Munro, *Black Hands*, 229.
[17] Walder and Gong, "Workers in the Tiananmen Protests," 14.

Signs of solidarity among workers, students, and intellectuals were halting and still based on a hierarchy that put workers at the bottom of the list. Nonetheless, in late May the protest movement was slowly getting more inclusive. The gradual growth of solidarity and inclusiveness among different sectors of Beijing society ended violently with shooting, arrests, and jail terms. The movement's final act of worker–student solidarity came on the evening of June 3, when workers and other Beijing residents put their bodies on the line to try to protect students from machine-gun-wielding soldiers.

8 Protests
Alternative Paths

Throughout April and May 1989, people in Beijing often said, "If only," and asked, "What if ...?" Looking back on the events of spring 1989 with hindsight, participants and observers have obsessed over key turning points and moments that could have pushed events in new directions and led to different outcomes. All of these hypothetical scenarios underscore one crucial point: nothing was inevitable. Each turning point was contingent on countless choices and coincidences. From Hu Yaobang's sudden death to the students kneeling after his memorial service, from Zhao Ziyang taking a train to North Korea to Deng Xiaoping seeing "turmoil," from staged dialogue meetings to a hunger strike, from failed martial law to real bullets, many possible paths unfolded. This was as true for China's political future as it was for the individual fates of Chai Ling, Han Dongfang, and other people whose lives were drastically changed. Students might have found ways to form lasting, democratic organizations that continued to push for political changes. BWAF might have sparked a nationwide movement of independent unions. Zhao Ziyang might have managed to satisfy protesters' demands, prevent the publication of the April 26 editorial, and stay in power. Something different might have replaced the Communist Party's dictatorship. Nothing was predetermined.

Imagine if on April 22, 1989, students and professors had been permitted to attend Hu Yaobang's memorial service inside the Great Hall of the People. Imagine if Li Peng and Zhao Ziyang had stepped outside the hall after the service to receive the kneeling students' petition and to tell them that dialogue was a central part of Zhao's three-point plan. Chai Ling did imagine a different outcome:

I believe the way the government treated the students on the day of Hu Yaobang's funeral incited their anger and led directly to the demonstrations on Tiananmen Square ... I have often wondered whether events might have turned out differently if the government had invited a few students to attend the funeral.[1]

---

[1] Chai Ling, *Heart*, 100.

Welcoming students into Hu's memorial service would have sent a conciliatory message. But Deng Xiaoping did not believe in compromise with critics. He thought that a single compromise would lead to escalating demands that could never be satisfied. And which students would have been invited to the memorial service? Random founders of unauthorized associations, or members of officially approved student groups who had already been vetted by the Party? On April 22, not even Zhao Ziyang had good things to say about "illegal" student organizations. Inviting students seen as stooges or lapdogs would have done little to satisfy the crowd in Tiananmen Square.

What if Li Peng or Zhao Ziyang had personally tried to defuse the emotional scene when Guo Haifeng tearfully held a scroll aloft on the steps of the Great Hall? In his memoirs, Li stewed over claims that he had refused to show his face. He felt targeted by students repeatedly calling on him to appear and insisted that he knew nothing about the kneeling students that day. Li wondered why the students were calling his name and not Zhao Ziyang's. As the two men left the Great Hall on April 22, Zhao told Li his three principles (life should go back to normal and students should return to classes, dialogue at multiple levels, avoid bloodshed and punish lawbreakers), while Li pushed Zhao to condemn Western-style democracy and unauthorized organizations. If someone had alerted the men to the tense scene in the square and convinced them to receive the students' petition together, maybe more students would have returned to classes, and maybe the protest movement would not have gained the angry momentum it did when it seemed as if officials were ignoring good-faith appeals.

Li Peng's protests notwithstanding, he was not inclined to mingle with the public, let alone take charge of an unpredictable public scene. According to Zhao Ziyang, later in May 1989, Li only visited hunger strikers in the hospital and in Tiananmen when he heard that Zhao would be visiting them. This suggests that if one man had decided to step out of the Great Hall and receive a petition on April 22, the other man would have been likely to join him. Ironically, competition between Li Peng and Zhao Ziyang could have presented a message of unity in front of the students in the square after Hu's memorial service, if they had only known that their presence would have been helpful. In an era without ubiquitous mobile phone use and in a political environment in which aides would have been reluctant to interrupt high officials eager to leave a stressful event, Li and Zhao's absence from the square on April 22 was more of a communication mishap than a failure of will.

Respectfully receiving a petition might have defused emotions, but it would not have been likely to end the protests entirely. Of the seven demands on the petition that Guo Haifeng held aloft on April 22, Li and Zhao could have easily said yes to many of them on the spot. Fairly assessing Hu Yaobang: Zhao had already called him a Marxist and his funeral music had played for an appropriately long time. Revealing the property holdings of Party-state leaders and their children: easy to agree to, also easy to fabricate. Increasing education budgets and raising budgets: easy to agree to, also easy to stall on. But neither Li nor Zhao could have quickly said yes to repudiating movements against liberalization. Li supported those movements. Zhao had carried them out (reluctantly, he said in retrospect). He could not openly criticize them without breaking with Deng, something he was not willing to do in April 1989. As for students' demands to allow independent newspapers and end censorship, Zhao did end up moving to promote greater transparency in reporting. At the April 29 "dialogue" chaired by Yuan Mu, Yuan denied that press censorship existed in China. On the whole, it is easy to imagine Zhao delivering assured responses to many of the student demands. It is equally difficult to imagine students being satisfied with any official answers. At best, different choices by Li and Zhao could have deflected and delayed, but were not likely to stop, the protest movement.

★ ★ ★

If Li Peng and Zhao Ziyang had successfully calmed students on April 22, Zhao would have had no qualms about getting on the train to Pyongyang the next day. Zhao's decision to leave China on April 23, 1989, and his statement of support for Deng's language about "turmoil" from a secure room inside the Chinese Embassy in North Korea, are two of the most momentous turning points of spring 1989. If Zhao had decided to postpone his trip to North Korea, he could have taken charge of implementing his three-point plan, and presumably Li Peng, Chen Xitong, and Li Ximing would not have been able to take advantage of Zhao's absence to convince Deng Xiaoping to call the protests "turmoil" and to inflame the situation with the April 26 editorial.

At least two officials urged Zhao to postpone his trip. On April 20, Vice Premier Tian Jiyun reportedly told Zhao that perhaps he should consider not going to North Korea during such a politically sensitive time. Zhao replied that he had thought about it but had concluded that it would look bad to cancel a long-planned diplomatic visit.[2] Shortly before Zhao headed to the train station, Beijing Party secretary Li Ximing called Zhao to say that as the top leader of China, Zhao should not leave the

---

[2] *LSQ*, 43.

country in a time of crisis, especially because Li Peng was ill-equipped to handle things in Zhao's absence. In his memoir, Li Peng claims to agree with Li Ximing: "As a technical cadre with only book knowledge, how could I handle such a thorny political situation? I fully supported Ximing's suggestion, but he was unable to convince Zhao Ziyang."[3]

Zhao's recollections do not discuss the question in depth, but he did talk about the upcoming trip to North Korea when he met with Deng Xiaoping on April 19. According to Zhao's secretary Bao Tong, Deng told Zhao that he should go to Pyongyang, and that when he returned Zhao could take over for Deng as chair of the Central Military Commission. In a conversation in 2018, Bao Tong presents this as a plot in which Deng, who had already decided to purge Zhao, tricked the general secretary into leaving China. Bao Tong thinks that Deng saw Zhao's sympathy with students memorializing Hu Yaobang as an attack on his own authority. For Bao Tong, whose career had been ruined by Deng Xiaoping's choices in 1989, Deng's sole concern was protecting his own image and interests.[4]

Wu Guoguang, who was Bao Tong's assistant in 1989, has given a lot of thought to the question of why Zhao did not postpone his trip to North Korea. Wu thinks that refusing to travel to Pyongyang would have meant openly disobeying Deng Xiaoping. Deng told Zhao to go, so he had to go. And at the moment when Zhao's train pulled away from the Beijing station, the protest movement did not seem out of control and Li Peng had agreed to follow Zhao's guidance in handling it. Zhao had no idea what would happen over the next few days.

In the Chinese embassy in Pyongyang, Zhao had another chance to intervene, but he did not do so. According to Wu Guoguang, this was in part because of technical limitations. Today, a top leader traveling in a foreign country would have access to secure communications and would be able to consult in real time with colleagues back home. In 1989 in North Korea, Zhao and his entourage had no access to information about what was happening in Beijing aside from the telegram reporting Deng's remarks about turmoil.[5] They could not have a back-and-forth conversation. And Zhao did not know that Deng's language would be published as an inflammatory article in *People's Daily*, so he did not move to stop it. Once again, all Zhao felt he could do was to obey the godfather.

---

[3] *LP*, 76.
[4] Li Nanyang, "鮑彤再看六四 (一): 鄧小平的一場政變?" (Bao Tong looks back on June Fourth (Part One): Was it Deng Xiaoping's coup?), *New York Times* (Chinese web edition), May 23, 2018, cn.nytimes.com/china/20180523/bao-tong-talks-89-li-nanyang-part1/zh-hant.
[5] Author's email correspondence with Wu Guoguang, April 22, 2020.

"I replied by telegram: 'I completely agree with Comrade Deng Xiaoping's decision regarding the policy toward the current turmoil,'" Zhao recalled.[6] For Zhao, forging a different path, whether by staying in Beijing or voicing objections from Pyongyang, would have required taking a clear-cut stand against old-man politics.

★ ★ ★

By the time Zhao returned to Beijing, Deng had made up his mind about "turmoil" and nothing would convince him otherwise. Tens of thousands of protesters had felt a sense of exhilaration and victory during the unprecedented marches of April 27. Zhao tried to push for dialogue and for democratic, legal solutions to the protests after he got back to China, and until May 13 his efforts had completely changed the message received by readers of *People's Daily*. But everything changed on May 13. The hunger strike that began that day was the next major turning point of the protests. What if Shen Tong, Wang Chaohua, and other students who preferred gradual measures and opposed the hunger strike had persuaded their classmates not to escalate their protests?

Deng Xiaoping had a playbook for dealing with student protests in 1986 and 1987: shut down meetings, apply pressure to activists, and arrest agitators. If a general secretary was too conciliatory toward protesters, push him aside. It is likely that if there had been no hunger strike, the Party's approach toward the protesters would have been similar to what it had done in 1986 and 1987. Activist students would have been frustrated and would have had to decide whether to wait for another opportune moment to protest or to escalate instead. Knowing that no meaningful changes came from the relatively calm protests of 1986 informed the choices of students who pushed for a hunger strike in 1989. They had tried marching, they had tried talking, they had even formed autonomous organizations and were trying to operate them on democratic principles. But the system around them remained the same. It is no wonder that many wanted to try more radical protests.

Another "what-if" scenario that worried students and leaders alike in May 1989 was that hunger strikers would escalate even further. What was more radical than a hunger strike? Self-immolation. How would events have unfolded differently if protesters had set themselves on fire in Tiananmen Square? The idea crossed the minds of people at the time. On May 15, a student from Nanjing named Li Lu, who was one of the few students from outside Beijing who became a protest leader in the

[6] *PS*, 11.

capital, approached Chai Ling. Li was frustrated that the hunger strike seemed to be ineffective. According to Chai, Li said:

If the government is willing to stand by and watch the lives of these students waste away one by one, then we should take more extreme measures. To gain the support of the people, put pressure on the government, and prevent striking students from dying, we need leaders who will rise up and be willing to burn themselves alive, like that student in the Prague Spring.

Li was presumably referring to Jan Palach, who set himself on fire in Prague in January 1969 to inspire Czechoslovakians to resist the Soviet-led military occupation. Chai's immediate reaction to Li Lu's suggestion was horror: her aunt had died in a fire and she did not want to suffer that way. But the more she thought about it, the more she realized that Li Lu "was right. If by dying I could prevent the death of others, then so be it."[7]

Rumors that self-immolations were imminent spread on May 15. Zhang Boli rushed from Peking University to the square "to help quell that fanatical idea."[8] Someone told Feng Congde that "Chai Ling has announced that she will set herself on fire to use one person's death to save a hundred thousand hunger strikers' lives." Feng frantically tried to find his wife. When he tracked her down, Chai laughed and told him not to worry, the moment had passed.[9] But later that day, reports that students might self-immolate reached Li Peng during his banquet with Mikhail Gorbachev.

If Chai Ling or other students had set themselves on fire, what might have changed in Beijing? On April 7, 1989, across the Taiwan Strait in Taipei, publisher Cheng Nan-jung (also known as Nylon Cheng) committed suicide by setting himself on fire in his office. Cheng pushed for freedom of speech during Taiwan's martial law period by publishing unauthorized magazines. Chiang Ching-kuo ended the Republic of China's four decades of martial law in July 1987, showing that it is possible for a dictator to cede power without "turmoil" and for a formerly authoritarian party – the Kuomintang – to become a participant in a multiparty democracy. But democratization in Taiwan was a slow process. Cheng's activism continued to rile authorities during the late 1980s. In 1989, authorities ordered his arrest because he published a draft constitution for an independent "Republic of Taiwan." Cheng reportedly said that he would not allow the ruling Kuomintang to arrest him, only to seize his dead body.[10]

---

[7] Chai Ling, *Heart*, 147.   [8] Zhang Boli, *Escape from China*, 41.
[9] Feng, 六四日記 (June Fourth diary), 312.
[10] Ashley Esaray, "'Struggle for 100% Freedom': The Legacy of Nylon Cheng and Taiwan's Democratization" (lecture, Taiwan Studies Group, Simon Fraser University, November 26, 2018).

Cheng's self-immolation was a key moment in Taiwan's democracy movement. April 7 is commemorated as "Freedom of Expression Day" in Taiwan and visitors can tour Cheng's still-charred office, which is part of the Nylon Cheng Liberty Foundation and Memorial Museum. Even though commemorations of Cheng's death occurred almost simultaneously with Chai Ling and Li Lu's discussion about escalating protests through self-immolation in Beijing, Chai and Li seemed unaware of what was happening in Taiwan, instead looking to the Prague Spring for inspiration. May 19, 1989, the eve of the imposition of martial law in Beijing, was also the day of Cheng's funeral procession in Taipei. As the march neared the presidential office building, a democracy activist named Chan I-hua set himself on fire.[11]

If hunger-striking students had self-immolated in Tiananmen Square, one possible outcome would have been a deepening and broadening of the democracy movement, as would happen in Taiwan. But self-immolation could have had the opposite effect in Beijing, allowing the authorities to depict suicide by fire as dangerous extremism. In fact, in January 2001, during a very different political moment, Communist Party propagandists managed to use the purported self-immolation of five Falun Gong practitioners in Tiananmen Square to convince hundreds of millions of television viewers that Falun Gong was a fanatical cult that needed to be forcibly repressed.[12] If students had escalated by turning to self-immolation in 1989, the act might not have been as effective in garnering public sympathy as their group hunger strike had been.

★ ★ ★

If Chai Ling had set herself on fire on May 15, 1989, it might have changed the course of events. Ever since 1989, people have obsessed over much smaller things that might have led to different outcomes. Louisa Lim told me that one of the people she interviewed while working on *The People's Republic of Amnesia* was convinced that the single most consequential turning point of spring 1989 was Örkesh's decision to wear hospital pajamas when he met Li Peng on May 18. Lim's contact said

---

[11] "詹益樺簡介" (Brief introduction to Chan I-hua), www.nylon.org.tw/main/index.php?option=com_content&view=article&id=56&Itemid=18.
[12] I was a guest in a home in Wuhan when the *Focus Report* (焦点访谈) anti-Falun Gong documentary aired during Chinese New Year in 2001. My host returned from his office that day saying that the authorities had ordered everyone to watch an important show. Before the documentary aired, people I spoke to in China were ambivalent about Falun Gong. Afterward, people's reaction to the religious group was overwhelmingly one of revulsion.

that Örkesh's clothing and tone during the exchange, which was televised throughout China, was simply too disrespectful and gave Li Peng the upper hand in dealing with the protesters. It strains the imagination to think that pajamas caused a massacre. I see this as victim blaming. Örkesh's self-presentation or his and other protesters' statements about staying in the square did not have the power to cause or avert a military crackdown.

In late May 1989, some activists and officials pushed for an unprecedented political intervention that would have been far more significant than deciding to wear pajamas in the Great Hall of the People. They tried to get another occupant of the Great Hall – the National People's Congress (NPC) – to behave as a genuine legislative body and to vote to cancel martial law. What if the NPC had been able to act? In late May and early June, advocates of continued protests wanted to maintain pressure on the government during the lead-up to June 20, when the NPC Standing Committee was scheduled to meet. Their hope, spurred by a joint letter signed by fifty-seven NPC Standing Committee members calling for an emergency meeting "to solve the serious situation through legal and constitutional means," was that the NPC would rescind martial law and sack Li Peng.[13]

On May 21, after Zhao Ziyang was sidelined but before his formal removal, Zhao himself tried a last-ditch effort to activate the NPC. Zhao spoke with Yan Mingfu, NPC vice chairman Peng Chong, PSC member Hu Qili, and Vice Premier Wu Xueqian about a plan to hold an NPC Standing Committee as soon as possible. Wan Li, who chaired the NPC's Standing Committee, was a key ingredient in this plot. But Wan had been away on official visits to Canada and the United States since May 12, 1989. Zhao tried to have a telegram sent to Wan instructing him to cut his trip short, but Li Peng sent a separate telegram telling Wan not to return early.[14] On May 25, Wan Li changed his itinerary and landed in Shanghai – not Beijing – where Jiang Zemin briefed him. On May 27, Wan issued a statement saying that martial law was legal and completely necessary to "resolutely curb the turmoil and quickly restore order."[15]

This dampened protesters' hopes that the NPC or Wan Li could act as a constitutional check on the declaration of martial law or the removal of Zhao Ziyang, both of which had violated Party and state constitutions. The NPC was supposedly the top governing body in the People's Republic, but in reality it was subordinate to Party leadership. As it

---

[13] Brook, *Quelling the People*, 82–83.   [14] *PS*, 33.   [15] *RMRB*, May 28, 1989, 1.

turned out, when it came to the NPC in 1989, the eighty-seven-year-old Peng Zhen, who held no meaningful official positions, was more powerful than Zhao Ziyang. Chung Yen-lin has discovered that Peng originally supported Zhao's moderate approach to the student protests, but after Deng Xiaoping decided on martial law, Peng quickly fell into line. He then pressured NPC Standing Committee members to support martial law.[16] On May 25, Peng met with Xi Zhongxun, Peng Chong, Liao Hansheng, Geng Biao, Chen Muhua, and Wang Hanbin. Peng's message was that bourgeois liberalization was unconstitutional, the marches and demonstrations were "turmoil," and because the NPC represented all 1.1 billion Chinese people, it could not go along with a small number of protesters. Peng's colleagues obeyed him.[17]

Looking ahead to June 20 as a pivotal date for the NPC Standing Committee meeting, or trying to move up the date of the meeting, were desperate dreams that butted up against the hard wall of old-man politics. They overlooked the reality that Deng Xiaoping wielded or ignored institutions and rules whenever it was convenient for him to do so. Elders like Peng Zhen, even if they had initially liked Zhao Ziyang's approach and had shuddered at the thought of martial law, knew that Deng's word was law. Critics in the square who pilloried Deng as an elderly dictator and who decried old-man politics had accurately identified the main obstacles to meaningful political change in China. Without Deng as godfather and without the elders who did his bidding and whipped colleagues into obeying Deng's orders, the NPC might have been part of a nonviolent solution. Finding a way to defeat old-man politics could have averted a massacre.

---

[16] Chung Yen-lin, "彭真在1989年中共'天安門事件'中的角色和活動," *Zhongguo dalu yanjiu* 62, no. 1 (March 2019): 1–33.

[17] *LP*, 222.

Part Three

Massacre

9   The Beijing Massacre as History

The People's Liberation Army massacred unarmed civilians in Beijing on the evening of June 3, 1989, escalating into the early hours of June 4. There were more killings during the day on June 4; sporadic murders in the capital continued on June 5 and June 6. Most of the dead were gunned down in the streets as the army forced its way from Beijing's outskirts toward Tiananmen Square; others were crushed by tanks and armored personnel carriers (APCs); some were stabbed by soldiers' bayonets.

In the days and months that followed, journalists and scholars documenting the basic details of the massacre had the advantage of immediacy. Eyewitnesses' memories were fresh and citizens were so outraged that they wanted to tell the world what they had seen. The most outstanding book to benefit from its proximity to the events of 1989, historian Timothy Brook's *Quelling the People*, still stands the test of time. Brook is correct that those who died were mostly ordinary Beijing citizens attempting to block the army's passage to Tiananmen Square or simply watching the drama unfold.[1] Brook also addresses one of the most pressing questions about the massacre: how many people died? Brook's careful attempt to quantify the death toll using body counts from specific hospitals remains a plausible guess at how many people the PLA killed. Brook found that eleven Beijing hospitals received at least 478 dead bodies on June 3 and 4, suggesting that the Chinese Red Cross's announcement that 2,600 people had died "comes closer than any other estimate to the number that died." In the end, Brook concedes the impossibility of achieving an accurate tally: "The cold facts are that many died, and that we cannot count their number."[2] This part of the book will address how other death toll estimates compare with Brook's and will answer with more specificity the question of who died, where they died, and how they died.

---

[1] Brook, *Quelling the People*, 168.   [2] Brook, *Quelling the People*, 169.

In contrast to Brook's meticulous accounting, other reactions to the massacre spread inaccurate claims. Some observers exaggerated the death toll and focused on Tiananmen Square itself rather than on the routes leading to the square from the west and south, where most of the deaths occurred. These trends stemmed from posttraumatic reactions by participants and bystanders, a desire to combat the Communist Party's own false narrative about "quelling a counterrevolutionary riot," and Tiananmen Square's status as the heart of a nationwide protest movement. Some – including student leaders Chai Ling and Örkesh Dölet (Wuerkaixi) – speculated that hundreds, even thousands, of peaceful students were mowed down by machine-gun fire or crushed by tanks and APCs inside the square.[3] Chai and Örkesh's guesses were wrong. There was indeed violence and death inside the square, making it a key part of the Beijing massacre, but the approach to Tiananmen was far deadlier than the square itself.[4]

If first- and secondhand accounts from the days and months after June 3, 1989, have the advantage of immediacy but the shortcoming of inaccuracy, what can be gained from studying the military crackdown as history? There has been no widespread release of military or Party documents about the massacre. To this day, the Communist Party censors information about the event, surveils and restricts the movement of victims' families, and has shown no sign of offering what some victims and observers have hoped for since 1989: an official reevaluation, affirming the righteousness of the protests and condemning the architects and perpetrators of the violence.

Despite these challenges, it is possible to write an updated, more comprehensive narrative of the massacre. Thanks to the efforts of the Tiananmen Mothers and other activists, we know about 187 individuals who were killed by the PLA and 10 others who went missing in the Beijing massacre.[5] In many cases, the Tiananmen Mothers have

---

[3] On June 8, 1989, Chai Ling said, "Some say more than 200 students died; there are also others who say 4,000 have already died in the Square. Up to now, I still don't know the exact number." See Han, *Cries for Democracy*, 364. In a Japanese newscast, Örkesh estimated that "at least" one thousand people died in the square: youtube.com/watch?v=59ni_sJOBPE#t=165.

[4] For one account from the square, see Robin Munro, "Who Died in Beijing, and Why," *The Nation*, June 11, 1990: 811–22.

[5] Ding Zilin, whose son Jiang Jielian was shot and killed on June 3, 1989, first published a tally of 96 dead in 1994; the number grew to 186 in 2005; the more recent list of 202 victims (which includes deaths, missing people, suicides prompted by June Fourth, and one person killed in Chengdu) was published in Liao Yiwu, 子彈鴉片：天安門大屠殺的生死故事 (Bullets and opium: Stories of life and death in the Tiananmen massacre) (hereafter abbreviated as *ZY*) (Taipei: Yunchen wenhua, 2012), 262–304, and can also be found at www.tiananmenmother.org/index_files/Page480.htm.

uncovered how the victims encountered the army, discovered where they died, and confirmed the gory details of their deaths. Learning about fewer than 200 specific victims falls far short of the Chinese Red Cross's estimate of 2,600, a more recently released claim that a Chinese Red Cross official personally counted 728 bodies,[6] or even Timothy Brook's baseline death toll of 478, but it does provide a fuller picture of the massacre. Details compiled by the Tiananmen Mothers show that PLA soldiers murdered innocent people trying to save and protect others, shot workers going about their daily business in the city, and even killed civilians hiding inside homes. The names and stories of the victims highlight the over-the-top brutality and recklessness of the army's attack on China's capital.

We know more about the victims than we know about the perpetrators. Independent scholar Wu Renhua, a leading expert on the martial law forces, estimates that Deng Xiaoping and Yang Shangkun mobilized between 180,000 and 250,000 PLA soldiers and People's Armed Police (PAP) officers to enforce martial law in Beijing.[7] Almost all of those who took part have stayed silent about what they did. Only a small handful of PLA soldiers have openly spoken about the massacre, described their actions, and expressed regret. Of this small group, none have admitted to personally harming anyone. But a handful of stories, limited as they may be, is better than zero. And just as the Tiananmen Mothers' naming of the victims is a brave commemoration, naming the PLA officers who commanded the crackdown is a public reckoning. Wu Renhua has done just that in his book on the martial law troops by uncovering the identities of approximately three thousand commanders and soldiers. Students of the massacre owe a great debt to the work of Wu, Liao Yiwu, and Ding Zilin.

As for how the CCP, PLA, and PAP described and assessed their own performance in June 1989, new details have emerged in the past decade. These come from retired leaders' memoirs and anonymous publishers who sell or reproduce internal military publications. Leaked collections dating from 1989 and 1990 corroborate and supplement the contents of the PLA's openly published 戒严一日 (A day of martial law), detailing the army's difficulties in infiltrating soldiers into Beijing, stealthily transporting weapons and ammunition in separate vehicles, battling against fiercely determined crowds of civilians who blocked roads and threw bricks, and finally opening fire to force its way into the square.

---

[6] Zhang Wanshu, 歷史的大爆炸 (Historical explosion), 461.
[7] Wu Renhua, 六四事件中的戒嚴部隊 (The martial law troops in the June Fourth incident) (hereafter abbreviated as *LSJ*) (Alhambra, CA: Zhenxiang chubanshe, 2009), 26.

10 Authorized Force
Preparing to Clear the Square

Two separate orders authorized the bloodbath of June 3 and 4. The first, issued on June 1 and 2 by the Central Military Commission, chaired by Deng Xiaoping, told the PLA to "clear the square" (清场), meaning to retake Tiananmen Square from protesters, by June 4. The second command, transmitted orally to PLA officers and soldiers on the evening of June 3, authorized the military to use deadly force as it advanced toward the square. Previous accounts of the military crackdown correctly assumed that these orders existed but were unable to verify their details. If written orders exist, they remain inaccessible to researchers. Nonetheless, Li Peng's diary, along with Wu Renhua's research and testimony from soldiers, confirms that Party and military leaders drew up and formally approved plans that resulted in soldiers and tanks rampaging through the streets of Beijing and massacring unarmed civilians.

Some observers believe that preparations for a deadly military crackdown against protesters began as early as April 23, 1989. In 2003 and 2004, Li Peng annotated his work diary from spring 1989. The result is more of a memoir than a diary. It was never formally approved for publication. In 2010, however, it was leaked on the internet and printed by a publisher in Hong Kong. It sheds light on top Party and military leaders' decision making and mindset in 1989. When Bao Tong read Li's diary, it "entirely changed his understanding," according to journalist Louisa Lim.[1] Bao Tong thinks that Li Peng might have secretly met with Deng Xiaoping and Yang Shangkun on April 23, 1989, setting in motion a plot that used the student movement as a pretext to remove Zhao Ziyang as general secretary of the Communist Party. Ordering the PLA to violently end the protests in June 1989, after the student

---

[1] Louisa Lim, *The People's Republic of Amnesia: Tiananmen Revisited* (New York: Oxford University Press, 2014), 170. Bao Tong elaborates on his theory in an interview with Li Nanyang, "鲍彤再看六四 (一): 邓小平的一场政变?" (Bao Tong looks back on June Fourth (Part One): Was it Deng Xiaoping's Coup?).

movement was already ebbing, Bao surmised, was the final step in this premeditated plan.[2]

My reading of Li Peng's diary differs from Bao Tong's on this point, partly because Li does not clearly indicate whether he was referring to a meeting that day or to a possible future meeting. The context suggests that Yang Shangkun told Li Peng that they *should* meet with Deng Xiaoping together, not that they had already spoken with Deng.[3] Although Li's comments about April 23 are too ambiguous to provide evidence of a long-term plot, his description of late May and early June 1989 reveals how the crackdown unfolded.

Li Peng recalled that he chaired a Politburo Standing Committee meeting on May 29, 1989, to discuss "how to clear Tiananmen Square, which had been occupied" by what he called "turmoil students." Li's diary entry for that day noted that the main challenge in clearing the square was that the "army must come in, and we also must avoid bloodshed."[4] After the imposition of martial law on May 20, the army had mostly avoided violent clashes, but in the face of massive civilian resistance it failed to reach Tiananmen Square. On May 24, troops withdrew and regrouped. By May 29, Li Peng knew that the PLA would be ordered to the square. He and his colleagues never managed to think of a feasible way for the army to get there without inflicting casualties. Li's concern about avoiding bloodshed might have been genuine, but it was as unrealistic (although not nearly as deadly to civilians) as Harry Truman's statement on July 25, 1945, that the atomic bomb's "target will be a purely military one."[5] Ordering the army to clear the square greatly increased the likelihood of bloodshed. As Timothy Brook writes, "The multipronged invasion of Beijing by troops armed with lethal assault weapons was not a plan suited to gaining control of a city of eleven million hostile residents with a minimum of casualties."[6]

---

[2] Lim, *People's Republic of Amnesia*, 172. Ezra Vogel, without citing a source, claims that Li Peng and Yang Shangkun "communicated" with Deng Xiaoping on the evening of April 23. Vogel, *Deng Xiaoping*, 604.

[3] Li's entry from April 23, 1989, reads, "At 8:30 p.m., I went to Comrade Shangkun's place to analyze the situation. He thought the situation was changing and urged me to talk to Xiaoping. I wanted him to come with me, and he agreed." Li's annotation to this entry states that Yang told him to "proactively ask Comrade Xiaoping for instructions and that he would go with me." See *LP*, 75, 79. Li and Yang did eventually meet with Deng on April 25.

[4] *LP*, 264.

[5] "Diary Entry of Harry S. Truman," July 25, 1945, Papers of Harry S. Truman: President's Secretary's File, Harry S. Truman Library and Museum, web.archive.org/web/20180917081831/trumanlibrary.org/flip_books/index.php?tldate=1945-07-25&groupid=3702&titleid=&pagenumber=1&collectionid=ihow.

[6] Brook, *Quelling the People*, 7.

Li Peng recalled that on May 31, 1989, Deng Xiaoping and Yang Shangkun signed off on plans for the PLA to enter Beijing. Martial law headquarters then issued the plans "in the form of an order" to the Beijing, Shenyang, and Jinan Military Regions, and to the Air Force.[7] Zuo Yinsheng, vice commander of the 15th Airborne Corps, was involved in drafting plans to advance on and clear the square. "This," Zuo wrote later in 1989, "was a special plan, the likes of which I had never encountered in my life." Zuo admitted that clashing with "bad people with evil intentions mixed up with masses who had been tricked into radical words and deeds" was completely different from anything he had ever trained for. Zuo, whose unit had flown to Beijing from Hubei on May 20, did not provide many operational details about the 15th Airborne's advance in his retrospective account, but he did record the plan's "guiding ideology," which was to protect the people and students, state property, weapons and military equipment, and the safety of soldiers "to the maximum extent possible." Of course, Zuo conceded, these principles were subordinate to the 15th Airborne's "resolute completion of its mission," which was to clear Tiananmen Square.[8]

The airborne infantry under Zuo Yinsheng's command did not head toward the square until June 3, but according to Li Peng, the multiday invasion of Beijing began with a secret infiltration of troops two days earlier. Li wrote that advance forces moved on Thursday, June 1, proceeding under cover of darkness and through underground air raid tunnels to the Great Hall of the People directly west of Tiananmen Square. By 3 a.m. on June 2, Li wrote, twenty-five thousand soldiers and officers had hidden themselves in the Great Hall of the People, the Ministry of Public Security complex east of the square, and the area near Tiananmen Gate to the north; an additional three thousand troops had mustered to the south. As far as Li was concerned, the army had already effectively surrounded Tiananmen Square.[9]

Not all troops used underground tunnels. Some posed as civilians and entered Beijing on foot or via public transit. At 1:10 a.m. on Friday, June 2, one PLA unit received orders to "enter the city in disguise." Shortly after noon, after a mad rush to buy civilian clothing, the soldiers donned a bizarre mix of ill-fitting "sweatpants, Hong Kong-style shirts, sportswear, big underwear, small vests ... multicolored and multifarious."

[7] *LP*, 272.
[8] Zongzheng wenhua bu zhengwen bangongshi, ed., 戒严一日 (A day of martial law) (hereafter abbreviated as *JY*) (Beijing: Jiefangjun wenyi chubanshe, 1989), 1:187–88. For more details on the 15th Airborne's role in the crackdown, see *LSJ*, 148–56.
[9] *LP*, 286, 288.

As they set off toward the city center along three preset routes, some carried badminton racquets and posed as unemployed youth; others brought tourist maps and lists of sightseeing attractions. The unit's soldiers had prepared answers in case suspicious Beijing residents interrogated them. Some soldiers did get stopped by civilians and others got lost, but by 6 p.m. they all reached their destination.[10]

Many plainclothes soldiers managed to infiltrate Beijing because they carried no weapons. Getting guns to the hidden troops was a separate challenge. Wearing blue pants and a gray shirt, a young soldier with the 65th Group Army named Chen Guang caught a ride on a repurposed public bus full of crates of guns and bullets. Chen arrived at the Great Hall of the People on the west side of Tiananmen Square after 3 p.m. on June 3.[11] Although Chen made it to his destination smoothly, Beijing citizens blocked other buses carrying weapons and ammunition toward Tiananmen.[12] Chen said that after arriving at the Great Hall, he was one of around fifteen thousand soldiers who received orders to head to Xidan to retrieve weapons that Beijingers had "stolen," but huge crowds blocked the troops, who retreated to the Great Hall around 8 p.m.[13] According to an internal account published by the Beijing Division of the PAP, a top leader of the Beijing Military Region (either Commander Zhou Yibing or Political Commissar Liu Zhenhua) ordered more than one thousand PAP soldiers to Xidan on June 3 to help troops and weapons pass through safely. Beijing citizens fought back, forcing the antiriot squad, which had used up all of its tear gas, to take cover in the Nationalities Palace.[14]

---

[10] *JY*, 1: 60–63, also cited in Brook, *Quelling the People*, 94–95.   [11] Lim, *Amnesia*, 15.

[12] Brook, *Quelling the People*, 102.

[13] Andrew Jacobs, "Q. and A.: Chen Guang on the Soldiers Who Retook Tiananmen Square," *New York Times*, June 2, 2014, sinosphere.blogs.nytimes.com/2014/06/02/q-a-chen-guang-on-the-soldiers-who-retook-tiananmen-square.

[14] Zhongguo renmin wuzhuang jingcha budui Beijing shi zongdui, 回顾与反思: 1989, 制止动乱平息暴乱主要经验汇编 (Looking back and reflecting: 1989, collected experiences of curbing turmoil and quelling rebellion) (hereafter cited as *HF*) (n.p., 1989), 27, reprinted by Service Center for Chinese Publications, "六四" 专题史料丛刊之十一 (Collection of historical materials about "June Fourth," no. 11) (Los Angeles: Service Center for Chinese Publications, 2009).

11   Permission to Open Fire

Even though more than twenty-five thousand soldiers had already surrounded Tiananmen Square, the presence of large crowds in the streets preventing weapons, ammunition, and more troops from reaching the city center convinced China's top leaders to approve the use of deadly force on June 3, 1989. In his biography of Deng Xiaoping, sociologist Ezra Vogel writes that at 2:50 p.m. on June 3, Deng told General Chi Haotian that his troops could use all possible methods to meet their objective.[1] Deng meant that lethal force was allowed. At 4 p.m., civilian leaders Li Peng, Qiao Shi, Li Ximing, and Luo Gan met in the Palace of Industrious Government in Zhongnanhai with top military officials, including Chi Haotian and Lieutenant General Zhou Yibing. Yang Shangkun, who was concurrently secretary-general of the Central Military Commission and president of the PRC, was the most senior official present. Li Peng wrote in his diary that at the meeting, "The military and Beijing agreed that we could not give the rioters a chance to catch their breath. We decided that all of the armies would move at double speed at night to Tiananmen Square. If it encounters armed resistance, the army is authorized to protect itself."[2] When Li wrote "authorized to protect itself" in his diary, he was being coy. What he really meant was that the army could use deadly force.

One reason for taking urgent action on Saturday, Li Peng recalled, was that more people were certain to enter the square on Sunday. China had a one-day weekend at the time and Li expected that Beijingers would use their day off to resist the army. To prevent this, troops would force their way into the city center and link up with those who had already hidden near the square. According to Li Peng's recollection, after the meeting, Yang Shangkun conveyed this plan in person to Deng Xiaoping. Deng approved the plan to clear the square. Later that evening, Li Peng, Yang

---

[1] Vogel does not cite a source to support this claim. Vogel, *Deng Xiaoping and the Transformation of China*, 625.

[2] *LP*, 290.

Shangkun, and Qiao Shi gathered in Zhongnanhai to monitor the military's advance, receiving reports from Chi Haotian, who was directing the operation from a military facility in Beijing's western hills, and from Zhou Yibing and Luo Gan, who were based inside the Great Hall of the People.[3]

At 6:30 p.m. on June 3, radio and television broadcast an "urgent notice" from the martial law headquarters, stating:

Nobody is allowed to illegally block military vehicles, block or surround the PLA, or hinder the martial law forces carrying out their duties. The clothing, methods, and timing of movements of the army are all military matters and nobody is allowed to interfere ... martial law troops, police, and the PAP are authorized to use all measures and use force to deal with whoever does not obey this order and defies the law.[4]

This announcement, following quickly on the heels of top leaders' decision to violently clear the square before Sunday morning, was intended as a final warning. Its mention of clothing tacitly acknowledged that troops had been infiltrating Beijing wearing plain clothes, as many protesters had suspected. Its harsh warning about "using all measures" and "using force to deal with" anyone interfering with the army was deadly serious. But few took it seriously. Wu Renhua, who was in Tiananmen Square and heard the announcement, remembered that the student leaders paid it no heed.[5] As Timothy Brook points out, protesters had been hearing similar announcements for weeks and "nothing dire had happened."[6]

Another urgent announcement issued by the martial law headquarters around 9:50 p.m. on June 3 emphasized the gravity of the situation ("rioters" had attacked PLA soldiers, taken their weapons, blocked access to Zhongnanhai, and besieged the Great Hall of the People), and urged the people of Beijing to stay off the streets and not go to Tiananmen Square.[7] A third, longer official notice broadcast at 10:16 p.m. echoed Li Peng's language authorizing deadly force: "martial law troops will use various ways to protect themselves and will use all measures to remove anyone who is obstructing them."[8] According to Wu Renhua, these official announcements convinced some Beijing residents

[3] LP, 292–94.
[4] Wu Renhua, 天安门血腥清场内幕 (The bloody clearing of Tiananmen Square), 2nd ed. (Alhambra, CA: Zhenxiang chubanshe, 2009), 35.
[5] Wu Renhua, 天安门血腥清场内幕 (The bloody clearing of Tiananmen Square), 36.
[6] Brook, *Quelling the People*, 109.
[7] Wu Renhua, 天安门血腥清场内幕 (The bloody clearing of Tiananmen Square), 43.
[8] Wu Renhua, 天安门血腥清场内幕 (The bloody clearing of Tiananmen Square), 57.

to go out to protect the students gathered in the square.[9] Soldiers ordered to reach and clear the square by dawn did encounter many obstacles – buses, traffic barriers, fences, people – in their way. And troops, especially those from the 38th Group Army and the 15th Airborne Corps,[10] did use various strategies – shooting in the air, shooting at the ground, shooting directly, driving over – to get through whatever and whoever stood in their path.

According to Wu Renhua, PLA units and individual soldiers advancing toward Tiananmen Square on the evening of June 3 received spoken orders permitting them to open fire. Some units received the order by radio transmission, others received it in person from messengers.[11] Because of the absence of written sources about the order to shoot, details remain murky, but there is no doubt that there was an order. On June 30, Beijing mayor Chen Xitong delivered (but apparently played no role in writing) the Communist Party's first detailed official report about "curbing turmoil and quelling counterrevolutionary rebellion."[12] Chen said that after repeatedly warning people to stop attacking and blocking troops, the army, "acting under orders, was forced to clear the way by shooting in the air" (迫不得已奉命对空鸣枪).[13] Chen's use of the phrase "acting under orders" confirms that a military order authorized soldiers to shoot. The absence of shooting before the evening of June 3, in spite of soldiers' encountering obstacles and angry citizens throwing bottles and bricks, followed by multiple military units all opening fire after 10 p.m. as they approached Tiananmen from the west and south, also confirms the existence of a specific order authorizing deadly force. Orders had expressly prohibited soldiers from using their guns – a prohibition that none dared to violate – until a new order permitted them to open fire.[14]

Li Xiaoming, who was in charge of the radar station in the antiaircraft regiment of the 116th Division of the 39th Group Army, is one of the few

---

[9] Wu Renhua, 天安门血腥清场内幕 (The bloody clearing of Tiananmen Square), 58.

[10] *LSJ*, 148.　　[11] *LSJ*, 47.

[12] Chen later claimed that he did not write the report or have anything to do with drafting or revising it; he merely read it "without even changing one punctuation mark." Yao Jianfu, 陈希同亲述—众口铄金难铄真 (Conversations with Chen Xitong: Public clamor obscures the truth) (Hong Kong: New Century, 2012), 61, 163.

[13] Chen Xitong, 关于制止动乱和平息反革命暴乱的情况报告 (Report on stopping the turmoil and quelling the counterrevolutionary riot) (Beijing: Renmin chubanshe, 1989), 35. The official English translation of the report omits the words "act under orders" (奉命), stating that martial law troops "were forced to fire in the air." "Mayor Chen Xitong's Report on Putting Down Anti-government Riot," *China Daily*, July 7, 1989, web.archive.org/web/20150817074818/http://www.chinadaily.com.cn/epaper/html/cd/1989/198907/19890707/19890707004_1.html.

[14] Wu Renhua makes this point in *LSJ*, 40.

soldiers who has spoken publicly about his experiences. Li never heard a clear order explicitly telling soldiers to open fire, but two things signaled to him that deadly force was allowed: first, troops received ammunition on the afternoon of June 3, after they had started moving toward the square. They had been carrying guns since May 20 but had no way to shoot them. As soldiers loaded their rifles on June 3, they understood that shooting would be an acceptable option. Second, Li also heard an order to "spare no cost in reaching Tiananmen Square on time to assemble." Li interpreted "spare no cost" as permission to fire: "I think many people – at least I understood it this way – that it included shooting."[15]

A memoir written by Major General Wang Fuyi, political commissar of the 38th Group Army, details how the unit responsible for widespread bloodshed on the main east–west artery between Beijing's western suburbs and Tiananmen Square received and conveyed permission to shoot.[16] The 38th's orders were to gather near the Military Museum by 10 p.m. before continuing toward the square. Wang recalled that shortly after 9:30 p.m., as soldiers were attempting to push east through crowds and barriers, a messenger ran up to the 38th's leaders and told Major General Zhang Meiyuan to report to the Military Museum for a meeting (Zhang had taken over as acting commander of the 38th after Xu Qinxian refused to enforce martial law).[17] Wu Renhua surmises that asking Zhang to leave his unit in the middle of a military operation could only mean that he was rushing to receive an urgent, top-priority order. Shortly after, the 38th Group Army began shooting. The first reports of live fire came from Wanshou Road and Wukesong Road (today's Fourth Ring Road), west of the Military Museum, around 10 p.m.[18]

---

[15] Quotes from Andrew Jacobs and Chris Buckley, Li Xiaoming interview notes, 2014; other details from Wang Yu, "Living with the Shame: An Officer's Memories of Martial Law in 1989," *Human Rights in China*, February 16, 2003, hrichina.org/en/content/4772.

[16] The name of the artery changes from east to west: it is Fuxing Road as it passes the Wukesong, Wanshou Road, and Gongzhufen intersections, then becomes Fuxingmen Avenue after the Muxidi intersection, and turns into West Chang'an Avenue east of the Xidan intersection until Tiananmen, when it becomes East Chang'an Avenue.

[17] *JY*, 1:87.   [18] *LSJ*, 47.

12   Where Bullets Flew

The assault commenced with great brutality. The most dangerous part of Beijing was along Fuxing Road, Fuxingmen Avenue, and West Chang'an Avenue between 10 p.m. on June 3 and 1 a.m. on June 4 as the 38th Army forced its way through barriers and crowds on the approach to Tiananmen Square. Around 10:30 p.m., APCs rammed through buses that protesters had used to block the Gongzhufen intersection. Civilians were crushed by the APCs and mowed down by machine-gun fire. Protesters responded to the violence by grabbing and killing two soldiers. As eyewitness Robin Munro writes, "The pattern of the night's conflict, then, was set from the start: Random and brutal killings by the army came first, followed swiftly by a small number of revenge killings of troops by distraught, and increasingly insurgent, citizens."[1] Wang Yongli, who journalists Andrew Jacobs and Chris Buckley say was "riding with the 38th Army," describes the soldiers' mindset as they turned their weapons on the people of Beijing who were resisting their advance: "No one said to shoot, but it was, like, 'We're going to teach them a lesson,' and then those soldiers unleashed their fury. You pulled the trigger and bang, bang, bang, it was like rain, the noise shaking the heavens."[2]

Multiple eyewitnesses reported seeing troops shoot indiscriminately at crowds of civilians; soldiers also strafed high-rises near Fuxingmen Avenue and Muxidi, killing people inside their homes.[3] When the 38th Army began killing along Fuxing Road and Fuxingmen Avenue, an area full of housing compounds for officials and their families, news quickly reached protesters gathered in Tiananmen Square. Workers affiliated

[1] Robin Munro, "Remembering Tiananmen Square," *The Nation*, June 2, 2009, thenation .com/article/remembering-tiananmen-square.
[2] Andrew Jacobs and Chris Buckley, "Tales of Army Discord Show Tiananmen Square in a New Light," *New York Times*, June 3, 2014, A1.
[3] Eyewitness accounts are compiled in Brook, *Quelling the People*, 120–23; Wu Renhua, 天安门血腥清场内幕 (The bloody clearing of Tiananmen Square); and Munro, "Remembering."

with the Beijing Workers' Autonomous Federation grabbed kitchen knives, as well as daggers that had been confiscated from martial law troops earlier in the day, and headed west to help block the army's advance. Many students also left the square and proceeded west toward the sound of gunfire.[4] The drama on Beijing's main east–west artery has diverted journalistic and scholarly attention from the 15th Airborne and 54th Group Army's violent assault from the south.[5] Units from the 15th Airborne set out from Dahongmen in Fengtai District, south of Beijing, heading toward Yongdingmen and their final goal: Qianmen, the southern entrance to Tiananmen Square. Vice commander Zuo Yinsheng claimed that his men only fired warning shots, "to avoid mistakenly injuring the masses," and that shooting into the air had "extremely good results" in scattering crowds and clearing the way for the 15th Airborne to arrive at the southern edge of the square at 1:25 a.m.[6] Wu Renhua calls this "pure lies," based on the timing and location of casualty reports from the south of Beijing.[7] CBS cameraman Derek Williams saw the 15th's arrival in the square: "In came the paratroopers … They were real shitkickers."[8] Wu estimates that the 15th Airborne was second only to the 38th Group Army in the casualties it inflicted.[9]

Indiscriminate strafing by the 38th Group Army on West Chang'an and the advance from the south of the 15th Airborne and 54th Group Army made these two areas the bloodiest parts of the Beijing massacre. Soldiers who had already occupied the northeast corner of Tiananmen Square created another killing zone by shooting toward outraged civilians at the Nanchizi intersection, between the Revolutionary Museum and the Beijing Hotel on East Chang'an Avenue.

Two eyewitnesses, one calling himself Xing Cun, the other "common Beijinger," wrote memoirs about the "bloody wall" of Nanchizi. Between 1 a.m. and 7 a.m. on June 4, a crowd of hundreds of angry unarmed citizens faced off against three rows of soldiers, numbering more than one hundred. Why were the civilians there? Wu Renhua thinks that some wanted to get to the square themselves, to protect and rescue the students.[10] Soldiers' willingness to kill unarmed protesters on their way to

---

[4] Wu Renhua, 天安门血腥清场内幕 (The bloody clearing of Tiananmen Square), 63.
[5] Political scientist Andrew Scobell's work is an exception – he identifies Zhushikou (south of the square), Muxidi, Xidan, and Nanchizi as sites of heightened violence in *China's Use of Military Force: Beyond the Great Wall and the Long March* (New York: Cambridge University Press, 2003), 159.
[6] *JY*, 1:188.
[7] *LSJ*, 158. Robin Munro cites four eyewitnesses who described shooting and killing by soldiers who approached the square from the south. Munro, "Remembering."
[8] Munro, "Remembering."   [9] *LSJ*, 148.
[10] Wu Renhua, 天安门血腥清场内幕 (The bloody clearing of Tiananmen Square), 79.

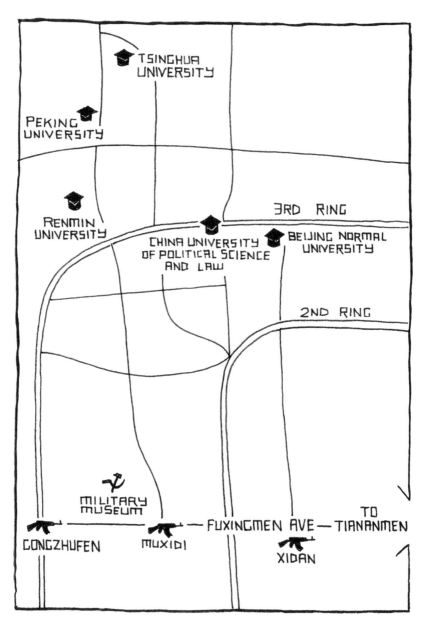

Figure 12.1a Northwest and west Beijing on June 3–4, 1989. Illustrated by Danny Frazier.

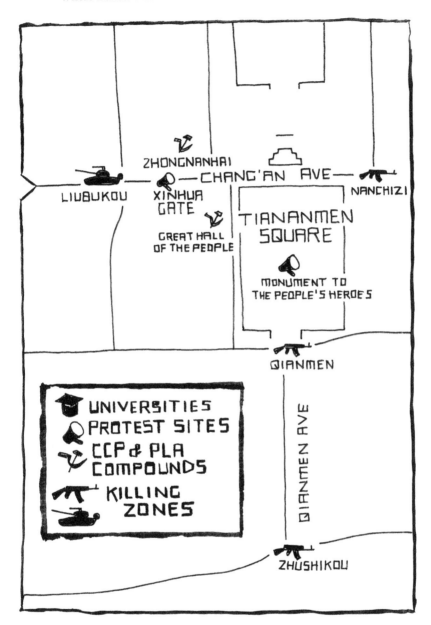

Figure 12.1b Central Beijing on June 3–4, 1989. Illustrated by
Danny Frazier.

Tiananmen gave reason to believe that the massacre might continue inside the square. According to "common Beijinger," some people who faced off against the army wanted to prevent others from the neighborhood from approaching the dangers near the square. They chanted slogans at the troops, yelling, "The PLA doesn't shoot civilians!" "The students are innocent," and "Let the students go, don't clear the square!"[11] The troops were lying on the ground or kneeling, aiming their guns east. They periodically fired toward the crowd. When this happened, the protesters retreated a few feet. Each wave of bullets knocked down several protesters, who others rescued and brought to medical personnel nearby. Even though yelling at the troops seemed to provoke more shooting, people in the crowd, part terrorized, part outraged, continued shouting things like "The martial law forces are murderers," "Where is your conscience?" "Where is your humanity?"[12]

Xing Cun recalled that the most savage moment he observed that night occurred around 3 a.m. Led by a long-haired young woman wearing a white dress, a group of unarmed protesters charged directly at the line of troops. Xing Cun joined the surge. A volley of gunshots hit six or seven civilians. The rest dropped to the ground and retreated. All except the woman in the dress, who continued moving forward by herself until she was several meters from the soldiers. A gunshot rang out and she fell. Medical workers rushed to move the wounded, but Xing Cun never saw what happened to the woman. People around him said she had been shot in the thigh.

---

[11] Putong Beijingren, "回憶南池子的'血牆'" (Remembering the "bloody wall" at Nanchizi), *Liu si dang'an*, June 4, 1999, 64memo.com/b5/2183.htm. Cited in Wu Renhua, 天安门血腥清场内幕 (The bloody clearing of Tiananmen Square), 81–82.

[12] Xing Cun, "她是谁? 她活着吗? 她在哪儿?" (Who was she? Is she alive? Where is she?) *Huaxia wenzhai zengkan*, no. 180 (May 18, 1999), cnd.org/HXWZ/ZK99/zk180-2.hz8.html. Cited in Wu, 天安门血腥清场内幕 (The bloody clearing of Tiananmen Square), 78–81.

13   Inside the Square

The bloodshed at Nanchizi occurred so close to Tiananmen Square – only a few hundred meters away from the square's northeast corner – that it seems pointless, not to mention disrespectful to the victims, to argue about whether the massacre happened inside or outside the square. But the question of whether killings occurred in Tiananmen Square itself has been a contentious issue ever since sunrise on June 4, 1989. In English, "Tiananmen massacre" has become popular shorthand to describe what happened.[1] "Beijing massacre" is a better label for what happened than "Tiananmen massacre" because it more accurately describes the citywide scope of the killing. But is "Tiananmen massacre" wrong?

Not entirely. "Tiananmen massacre" is an appropriate label because the square had been the heart of the protest movement since it began in April. "Clearing the square" was the army's main objective. More crucially, at least two – and possibly ten or more – civilians were killed inside the square, many more were shot or crushed nearby, and martial law troops violently ejected students from the square. Tiananmen Square was an important part of the Beijing massacre.

Previous accounts of what happened inside the square on June 3 and June 4 have centered on debates among the protesters gathered there about whether to resist the assault or to practice nonviolence. During the night, some people left the square to fight back against or witness the army's attack. Many more slipped away to find safety. Those who decided to stay in the square to await the army's arrival huddled near the Monument to the People's Heroes. The dominant narrative of what happened next, based on testimony from protest leaders Feng Congde, pop star Hou Dejian, and Liu Xiaobo, and repeated by the documentary film *Gate of Heavenly Peace*, is that around 3 a.m., Hou Dejian and Zhou Duo negotiated with a martial law officer to secure the students' safe

---

[1] According to Google Books Ngram Viewer, since 1989, the phrase "Tiananmen massacre" has appeared in published books approximately twice as often as "Beijing massacre." See books.google.com/ngrams.

retreat from the square.[2] According to Li Peng, Luo Gan went from the square to Zhongnanhai to relay this proposal to Li, Yang Shangkun, and Qiao Shi. Li Peng wrote that the leaders agreed to the idea of a "peaceful retreat."[3] When protesters learned about this settlement as troops approached the monument an hour later, they argued anxiously about whether to stay or go, finally carrying out a voice vote: "stay" versus "leave." Even though the vote seemed inconclusive, Feng Congde decided that "leave" had won. The students began an orderly retreat, avoiding further bloodshed.

CCP propagandists like this version of the story because it allows them to repeat the lie that nobody was killed during the clearing of the square. Hou Dejian and Liu Xiaobo's statements that they did not see anyone die in the square featured prominently in television reports. Hou, Liu, and other eyewitnesses, such as Robin Munro and a Spanish television team that remained in the square, may not have seen anyone die, but absence of evidence is not evidence of absence. Tiananmen Square is so vast that it was impossible for anyone to see all of it. It is therefore possible to believe Hou, Liu, and Munro while also accepting the validity of other evidence. Credible reports compiled by the Tiananmen Mothers and Wu Renhua suggest not only that people died in the square but also that the protesters' final exit from the square was not peaceful or voluntary. It was violent and coerced.

CCP sources assert that the "clearing of the square" began at 4:30 a.m. At that moment, according to *Five Hundred Questions about Quelling the Counterrevolutionary Rebellion*, martial law forces announced, "The clearing of the square begins now. We agree to the students' appeal to evacuate the square."[4] This official source also corroborates details from eyewitnesses that all the lights in the square went out at 4 a.m. Question 239 of *Five Hundred Questions* is, "How come the lights went out when it was time to clear Tiananmen Square?" PLA official Liu Cunkang answered, "We turned off the lights. We turned them off and then on again because turning them on was the signal for the army to clear the square."[5]

---

[2] Feng Congde, 六四日記 (June Fourth diary), 518–20; *Gate of Heavenly Peace*, directed by Richard Gordon and Carma Hinton (Brookline, MA: Long Bow Group, 1997).

[3] *LP*, 296.

[4] Zhonggong Liaoning shengwei gongchandangyuan zazhi she, 平息反革命暴乱500题 (Five hundred questions about quelling the counterrevolutionary rebellion) (Shenyang: Liaoning daxue chubanshe, 1989), 140.

[5] Zhonggong Liaoning shengwei gongchandangyuan zazhi she, 平息反革命暴乱500题 (Five hundred questions about quelling the counterrevolutionary rebellion), 141.

Wu Renhua argues that the clearing of the square began not at 4:30 a.m. but three hours earlier, when the 38th Army and 15th Airborne arrived. Wu divides the process into three stages: during the first, from 1:30 until 2 a.m., the 38th Army and 15th Airborne attempted to lock down access to the square.[6] The second phase entailed occupying everything except the monument. At some point during these first two phases, Dai Jinping and Li Haocheng were shot inside Tiananmen Square. Both died.

Dai was a twenty-seven-year-old master's student at the Beijing University of Agriculture. On the afternoon of June 3, 1989, Dai met with his supervisor. After dinner, he headed to Tiananmen Square, carrying a camera. After being shot in the chest near the mausoleum of Mao Zedong (which is inside the square), Dai was taken to Friendship Hospital on the back of a flatbed tricycle. He did not survive surgery.[7] Li Haocheng, a twenty-year-old undergraduate at Tianjin Normal University, suffered a similar fate. Li was taking photographs in the southeast corner of the square in the early hours of June 4. After Li's camera flashed he was hit by two bullets. Li was alive when he was rushed to Tongren Hospital, but he died during treatment.[8] Cheng Renxing (a twenty-four-year-old graduate student in Soviet and Eastern European Studies at Renmin University), Zhou Deping (a graduate student in his twenties from Tsinghua University), and Huang Xinhua (a twenty-five-year-old graduate student in physics at Tsinghua) were also reportedly shot and killed in Tiananmen during what Wu Renhua calls the first two phases of "clearing the square."[9] The Beijing massacre was deadliest on West Chang'an, the southern approach to Qianmen, Nanchizi, and – as we shall see – when a tank rampaged at Liubukou on the morning of June 4. But it would be a mistake to exclude Tiananmen Square from the story of the Beijing massacre.

We know the names of five people who died after reportedly being shot inside Tiananmen Square. We do not know for certain who, if anyone, was killed by tanks and APCs that crushed tents and other belongings in the square before dawn on June 4. Wu Renhua watched the tanks as they

---

[6] According to Robin Munro, it was still possible to enter Tiananmen Square from the south until 6 a.m. on June 4. Munro, "Remembering."

[7] You Weijie and Guo Liying, "He Hoped, after Graduation, to Be of Service to His Motherland," *Human Rights in China*, May 16, 2014, hrichina.org/en/china-rights-forum/he-hoped-after-graduation-be-service-his-motherland; Ding Zilin, 尋訪六四受難者 (In search of the victims of June Fourth) (hereafter abbreviated as *XF*) (Hong Kong: Kaifang zazhi she, 2005), 259; Wu Renhua, 天安門血腥清場內幕 (The bloody clearing of Tiananmen Square), 221–24.

[8] *XF*, 61.   [9] *XF*, 227, 249, 264.

advanced toward the monument. Their purpose was to terrify the students, Wu remembers, "When I saw those huge metal tanks easily crushing the iron rods in their way, I felt like my own body was so tiny."[10] Wu is convinced that some students, sleep-deprived, exhausted, and hungry, were resting in the tents when the tanks rolled over them. A Japanese journalist saw students in three of the tents in the early hours of June 4; a Spanish journalist added, "I can assure you that there were not more than five people inside the tents at around 3 a.m."[11] *Five Hundred Questions* confirms that soldiers were aware that some students were so weak that they could not leave the tents on their own. Question 240: "After the students evacuated, was anyone left in the tents?" Answer:

There were a few students in the outer part of the square who were unwilling to leave and a few whose physical condition was extremely poor because they had stayed there so long. They could not move by themselves and were sitting there staring into space. Martial law troops helped them up and moved them to the front door of the mausoleum. Only after inspecting each tent did the APCs drive through.[12]

Robin Munro's testimony casts doubt on the claim that soldiers checked each tent before tanks and APCs destroyed them. "The possibility remains that a handful of students were still in the tents," he writes. "We clearly saw that the advancing infantrymen walked *behind* the tanks."[13]

Whether tanks crushed students as they lay inside tents remains an open question, but the violence that accompanied students' final retreat from the square is beyond dispute. As we know from former soldier Chen Guang's testimony, the 27th Group Army had infiltrated Beijing and gathered inside the Great Hall on June 3 before the 38th Group Army and 15th Airborne began to shoot their way through the city's streets. Contrary to rumors that circulated during and after the massacre that the 27th Army had committed the massacre's worst atrocities[14] – rumors

---

[10] Wu Renhua, 天安门血腥清场内幕 (The bloody clearing of Tiananmen Square), 399.

[11] Munro, "Remembering."

[12] Zhonggong Liaoning shengwei gongchandangyuan zazhi she, 平息反革命暴乱500题 (Five hundred questions about quelling the counterrevolutionary rebellion), 141.

[13] Munro, "Remembering," emphasis in original.

[14] Andrew Scobell was one of the first western scholars to cast doubt on the rumor that the 27th Army rampaged wildly while the 38th exercised restraint (or even helped injured protesters), in *China's Use of Military Force*, 158. Wu Renhua debunks myths about the 27th in *LSJ*, 188–90. Rumors about the 27th Army appear in Brook, *Quelling the People*, 184, 187; and are presented as fact in such books as Frank N. Pieke, *The Ordinary and the Extraordinary: An Anthropological Study of Chinese Reform and the 1989 People's Movement in Beijing* (London and New York: Kegan Paul International, 1996), 226; and Edward Friedman, Paul G. Pickowicz, and Mark Selden, *Revolution, Resistance, and Reform in Village China* (New Haven, CT: Yale University Press, 2005), 269.

that led more than three thousand protesters to attack the 27th's head-quarters in Shijiazhuang on June 6[15] – the 27th's main task was to emerge from the Great Hall, destroy the protest headquarters on the top level of the monument, and arrest student leaders. Special forces from the 27th Army surrounded the monument, disabled the protesters' loudspeakers by shooting at them, menaced students by pointing guns at them, and violently dispersed those who were unwilling to leave voluntarily.

Even though Hou Dejian and Zhou Duo had negotiated with martial law officials to allow protesters to evacuate the square, the final departure from the monument was chaotic and frightening. According to Wu Renhua and Chai Ling, many protesters did not hear or accept the results of the voice vote. Few people were aware that Feng Congde had announced that "leave" had won the vote, because bullets had destroyed the protesters' loudspeakers. Chai writes, "I started grabbing the shoulders of students who were still sitting on the ground as I went down the steps. They looked at me with fatigue and confusion."[16] The number of civilians in the square had shrunk from at least one hundred thousand when the massacre began around 10 p.m. on June 3 to a hard-core group of approximately five or six thousand protesters who remained after the lights went out at 4 a.m. on June 4. Those who stayed in the square had resolved to sacrifice their lives. They did not want to leave. Some got up reluctantly and walked away as soldiers fired guns repeatedly in the air. Others refused to stand up. Wu Renhua saw soldiers trampling, clubbing, and beating protesters.[17]

The CCP's official account confirms that martial law troops used force at the monument. Around 5 a.m., "there were still some students who insisted on not moving." Martial law troops "compelled them to depart the square."[18] Su Zhonghua, a political instructor with the 27th Army, explained that his unit did not carry out its task of arresting protest leaders because the leaders were encircled by lines of departing students holding hands, packed tightly together. "To avoid conflict, we did not strike," Su said.[19]

---

[15] Friedman, Pickowicz, and Selden, *Revolution, Resistance, and Reform*, 269.
[16] Chai Ling, *Heart*, 190–91.
[17] Wu Renhua, 天安门血腥清场内幕 (The bloody clearing of Tiananmen Square), 419–42.
[18] Zhonggong Liaoning shengwei gongchandangyuan zazhi she, 平息反革命暴乱500题 (Five hundred questions about quelling the counterrevolutionary rebellion), 140.
[19] Zhonggong Liaoning shengwei gongchandangyuan zazhi she, 平息反革命暴乱500题 (Five hundred questions about quelling the counterrevolutionary rebellion), 142.

14 Victims

As soon as the massacre began, participants and observers – including students, protesters, top CCP and PLA leaders, and Chinese and foreign journalists – wanted to know how many people had died. On the morning of June 4, while troops were still indiscriminately shooting at crowds, someone from the Chinese Red Cross told foreign media that, based on reports from Beijing hospitals, an estimated 2,600 had been killed.[1] Historian Timothy Brook's own investigation of hospitals' casualty figures in late 1989 confirmed the plausibility of a death toll around 2,600. On June 27, 1989, American diplomats in Beijing wrote to the Department of State that "civilian deaths probably did not reach the figure of 3,000 used in some press accounts," but noted that "the Kyodo News Service reported that the Chinese Red Cross gave a figure of 2,600 military and civilian deaths with 7,000 on both sides wounded, based on a canvass of Beijing hospitals … Beijing based Japanese diplomats find the Kyodo source credible and the estimate convincing."[2]

The figure of 2,600 dead is Brook's extrapolation based on a sample of bodies counted in hospitals. This estimate is as impossible to confirm as Beijing mayor Chen Xitong's claim on June 30, 1989, that "more than 3,000 civilians were injured and more than 200, including 36 university students, were killed."[3] On July 10, 1990, the Ministry of Public Security purportedly issued a higher death toll, stating that 563 civilians had been killed in Beijing, while "more than 11,571" civilians suffered injuries.[4] An educated guess based on statistical sampling seems more plausible

---

[1] Brook, *Quelling the People*, 155.

[2] Cable from US Embassy Beijing to Department of State, Wash DC, What Happened on the Night of June 3/4? (June 22, 1989), in *Tiananmen Square, 1989: The Declassified History*, ed. Jeffrey T. Richelson and Michael L. Evans, National Security Archive Electronic Briefing Book no. 16, June 1, 1999, nsarchive2.gwu.edu/NSAEBB/NSAEBB16/docs/doc32.pdf.

[3] Chen Xitong, 关于制止动乱和平息反革命暴乱的情况报告 (Report on stopping the turmoil and quelling the counterrevolutionary riot).

[4] Zhonggong gongan bu, 有關各地動亂, 暴亂中傷亡情況統計資料匯總 (Summary statistical data on deaths and casualties in the turmoil and riot in various places), July

than these officially approved tallies, but in the absence of actual bodies and death certificates, it is tempting to give up and say that we will never know how many died. In 2009, however, a new claim emerged from Zhang Wanshu, who was the Xinhua News Agency's director of domestic news in 1989. Zhang writes:

Comrade Liu Jiaju, a senior editor of *PLA Art and Literature*, told me that Tan Yunhe, Party secretary and deputy director of the Chinese Red Cross, had conclusively told him that during the entirety of the June Fourth incident the CCP recorded the deaths of 727 people – 14 soldiers and 713 locals (including students and masses). Tan personally inspected each corpse.[5]

Tan Yunhe died in 2014 and Liu Jiaju died in 2017, so it is difficult to dig deeper into this secondhand report. How, when, and where did Tan inspect so many bodies? Were the deaths documented in writing? Why is there such a large gap between Tan's count of 727 and the Red Cross's estimate of 2,600 deaths? There is also the question of who Tan's number excludes. Does it count those who tanks and APCs crushed beyond recognition? Does it count people like the nineteen-year-old Wang Nan, who martial law soldiers buried along with two other nameless victims in a shallow flowerbed abutting West Chang'an on the morning of June 3?[6] What about victims of crackdowns outside Beijing, or those who went missing in Beijing on June 3 and 4? Nonetheless, the odd specificity of a Red Cross official saying that he inspected 727 bodies makes Zhang Wanshu's claim that "this should be the most authoritative and most correct number" impossible to dismiss.[7]

10, 1990. I have not seen the original document and cannot verify the authenticity of the excerpt published by *64 Memo*: 64memo.com/b5/1476.htm#Head5.

[5] Zhang Wanshu, 歷史的大爆炸 (Historical explosion), 461.

[6] Lim, *People's Republic of Amnesia*, 113.

[7] Zhang Wanshu, 歷史的大爆炸 (Historical explosion), 461. A more recent death toll estimate, which received substantial news coverage in late 2017, is much easier to dismiss. In a telegram dated June 5, 1989, Alan Donald, the United Kingdom's ambassador to China, told the Foreign Office, "minimum estimate of civilian dead 10,000." This estimate, presented as a "FACT," came from an informant who had spoken to his friend on China's State Council. Donald's declassified telegram, which also repeats erroneous rumors about the 27th Army, was first revealed in Lao Xianliang, "'六四密檔': 英引中國國務院成員: 27 軍掃射, 學生, 士兵皆中槍" ("Secret June Fourth archives": England cites Chinese State Council member: 27th Army strafes, students and soldiers all shot), *Xianggang 01*, December 20, 2017, web.archive.org/web/20200821035145/hk01.com/社會新聞/140801/六四密檔-英引中國國務院成員-27軍掃射-學生-士兵皆中槍. Anthony Tao convincingly argues that the telegram reveals plenty about divisions among top CCP leaders but says nothing useful about the death toll. Anthony Tao, "No, 10,000 Were Not Killed in China's 1989 Tiananmen Crackdown," *SupChina*, December 20, 2017, supchina.com/2017/12/25/no-10000-not-killed-in-tiananmen-crackdown.

Timothy Brook argues that whatever number we choose to accept, any "death toll is atrocious: the number hardly matters. From close up, however, even one death is too many, and the omission of one in the final count a terrible lie. The quantity of killing matters most to those who died and those who mourn them."[8] In the decades after Brook published his book, the leaders of the Tiananmen Mothers have documented details not only about the number of dead, but about the patterns of a massacre that devastated the parents, children, spouses, siblings, and friends of the victims.

Liao Yiwu's *Bullets and Opium* reprints a list of 202 victims compiled by the Tiananmen Mothers, based on Ding Zilin, Guo Liying, You Weijie, Zhang Xianling, and others' interviews with surviving family members, many of whom provided such documentation as death certificates.[9] The list includes 187 deaths, plus 10 people who went missing on June 3 and 4, 1989, 3 people who committed suicide in the aftermath of the massacre, and 1 person who died of cancer after being released from jail. Each victim deserves their own book about their unique personality, their hopes and dreams, their habits and thoughts. None deserved to die. It is painful and distasteful to only mention them in the context of the worst thing that ever happened to them. It also feels wrong to name only some of the victims to illustrate broader patterns, while omitting the stories of others. Dwelling on the circumstances of certain individual deaths, however, is necessary to achieve a fuller picture of the massacre. Ordinary Beijing residents sacrificed their lives to help others who had been wounded. Many who died were outside on the night of June 3 and the morning of June 4 because they wanted to witness – not block – the army's assault. Even more victims were outside for more prosaic reasons – commuting to or from work, visiting family and friends, getting food – when they randomly encountered rampaging soldiers. Some were killed inside their own homes when bullets penetrated windows and walls. At least eight people were killed after June 4, showing that the massacre continued for several days.

Primary Source: Statement Explaining the Truth

The goal of releasing multiple versions of the *List of Victims of the June Fourth Massacre* is to remember people who sacrificed themselves for

---

[8] Brook, *Quelling the People*, 152.   [9] *ZY*, 262–304.

democracy and freedom in China, as well as innocent people who were deprived of their right to exist during the atrocity. It is also to bring attention to the family members of the dead and to surviving victims who were injured. The Chinese government should be responsible for the work of collecting and publicizing the list of victims, and originally the government promised to do so, but it has not fulfilled its promise. So as members of the group of victims and as a mother who lost a child, we decided to take on the work of compiling a list of the June Fourth dead and injured.

Ding Zilin and Jiang Peikun, "真相說明書" (Statement explaining the truth), 2011. Source: *ZY*, 315–18.

★ ★ ★

The victims of the Beijing massacre were mostly men (the same is true of the killers). Of the 187 dead recorded by the Tiananmen Mothers, 160 were men and 17 were women. When I lecture to undergraduates about the massacre, students often wonder why people went outside and put themselves at risk, ignoring clear warnings from the martial law command. The troubling implication of the question is that the victims should have known better. The reasons Beijingers went outside are varied. Most crucial was their knowledge of what had happened since April – people had been marching, singing, blocking troops, and watching the spectacle in Beijing for weeks; few expected or predicted a massacre. Once they realized that soldiers had begun to shoot, people reacted in diverse ways.

The impulse to help protesters in Tiananmen Square and to witness history drove many people outside, toward the square and toward the sound of gunfire. Children physically overcame terrified parents who tried to prevent them from going outside. When Ding Zilin and Jiang Peikun, professors at Renmin University, heard the urgent official announcements on June 3, they sensed that something bad was going to happen and wanted to stay inside. Their seventeen-year-old son, Jiang Jielian, was agitated. "What should we do? What should we do?" he said. "There are still so many students in Tiananmen Square!" His parents told him that it was too dangerous to go out, but he insisted, so they walked around campus together.

The university gate was crowded with people. A broadcast station urged everyone to go to the square to help. Jielian tried to sneak away but his parents restrained him. Ding Zilin brought Jielian home and locked the front door. When Jielian went to the bathroom, his mother panicked, fearing that he would escape from the window of their ground-floor flat. Jielian came out after she pounded on the door, but then he

Figure 14.1 Jiang Jielian's mother Ding Zilin in 2009. Peter Parks/AFP/
Stringer via Getty Images.

rushed toward the bathroom again. Ding grabbed his shirt to prevent him
from leaving. Jielian kissed her cheek, said goodbye, and pulled away,
barring the bathroom door behind him. He was gone. Near Muxidi,
bullets hit Jielian in his back and left arm. Bystanders rushed him to
Beijing Children's Hospital, but he died before arrival.[10]

In the years after her son's death, testimony that Ding Zilin collected
from other grieving family members shows that people in Beijing shared
her son's sense of obligation to help, support, or protect protesters in
Tiananmen Square. On the streets of Beijing, people put themselves at
great risk to help others. Xiao Bo, a twenty-seven-year-old chemistry
lecturer at Peking University, went out late on the evening of June
3 because he wanted to find his students and escort them back to
campus. Near Muxidi, a bullet pierced Xiao's chest. He was the father

[10] Ding Zilin and Jiang Peikun, "捷连之死" (The death of Jielian), *64 Memo*, April 20, 2004,
web.archive.org/web/20160418195739/http:/www.64memo.com/disp.aspx?Id=12887&
k=蒋捷连; "Testimony of Ding Zilin, Mother of Jiang Jielian," *Human Rights in China*,
January 31, 1999, hrichina.org/en/testimony-ding-zilin-mother-jiang-jielian.

of two-month-old twins.[11] Seven other people whose deaths were documented by the Tiananmen Mothers were trying to help civilians who had already been hurt. Wang Weiping, a twenty-five-year-old obstetrics and gynecology intern, died after she was shot in the head while treating injured people at Muxidi before midnight on June 3.[12] That same night, martial law troops chased Xiong Zhiming, a twenty-year-old economics student from Beijing Normal University, and his female classmate into an alley near Xidan. Xiong's classmate fell after being shot. When Xiong turned back to help her, he was killed.[13]

Curiosity or a desire to witness the atrocity also motivated people to get dangerously close to the army. According to the Tiananmen Mothers' list of victims, at least thirteen people died while trying to watch or document the massacre. Around midnight, Wang Wenming, a thirty-five-year-old worker at a shoe factory, got together with some neighbors and headed in the direction of Zhushikou to watch a "real-life movie." The group's destination put them on a collision course with the 15th Airborne. After Wang encountered soldiers who shot him in the torso, surgeons at Friendship Hospital removed two meters of his intestines but were unable to save his life. Nan Huatong, who worked as a driver at a factory, left home around 5 a.m. on June 4, saying that he was going to see what was happening at the square. His frantic family members finally learned what happened to Nan two days later when they found his body at the Xiehe Hospital. He had been hit in the back by a bullet: there was a hole where the thirty-one-year-old's rib cage used to be.[14]

Holding a camera or binoculars may have exposed observers to additional risk. Wang Nan, whose mother Zhang Xianling would eventually found Tiananmen Mothers alongside Ding Zilin, was carrying a camera when he was shot in the head. Wang was still alive when medical personnel reached him thirty minutes after he was shot, but soldiers refused to allow anyone to take him to a hospital. Wang died within the next ninety minutes.[15] Wu Guofeng, a twenty-year-old student at Renmin University, also had a camera with him when he was shot in the head and then stabbed multiple times with a bayonet. His father, Wu Dingfu, speculates that soldiers targeted Wu when they saw him taking pictures of the massacre.[16] Li Haocheng, the student from Tianjin who

---

[11] *XF*, 226.   [12] *XF*, 228.
[13] *XF*, 240; You Weijie and Guo Liying, "He Lost His Life before Finishing His Studies," *Human Rights in China*, May 21, 2014, hrichina.org/en/china-rights-forum/he-lost-his-life-finishing-his-studies.
[14] *XF*, 239; *ZY*, 279.   [15] Lim, *People's Republic of Amnesia*, 111–12; *XF*, 54–59.
[16] *XF*, 229; Tom Phillips, "Shot and Stabbed as He Tried to Document the Tiananmen Massacre: The 'Unfortunate' Death of Wu Guofeng," *Daily Telegraph*, June 1, 2014,

was killed inside Tiananmen Square, was also taking photographs when he was shot.[17] Observers who tried to watch or take pictures from higher vantage points may have mistakenly assumed that rooftops or top floors offered a safe refuge from the carnage. Wang Tiejun was on the night shift at the Muxidi office of the Beijing Railway. He went to the top of his building and was using binoculars to watch the army's advance when a bullet struck and killed him.[18] A photojournalism major from Renmin University named Chen Laishun climbed on to the roof of a one-story building northeast of the Great Hall of the People to take pictures when a bullet pierced his skull and ended his life.[19]

These victims may not have realized how dangerous it was to help others or observe the events of June 3 and 4. These were all extremely risky behaviors. An even larger group of victims – approximately thirty, by my reading of the Tiananmen Mothers' list – had no desire to have anything to do with the army or the protesters. They were simply doing everyday things when random violence ended their lives. Not everyone was near a radio, television, or loudspeaker to hear the martial law command's urgent announcements on June 3, so they went to work, shopped, or visited family, unaware that they were in a killing zone.

Every morning before dawn, Liu Junhe set up a watermelon stand underneath the Qianmen watchtower. We do not know whether he hesitated before going to work in the early hours of June 4, but Liu decided to sell watermelons in his usual spot and was unable to avoid soldiers shooting their way toward Tiananmen Square. A bullet struck the fifty-six-year-old in the cheek; he died shortly thereafter in the Beijing Friendship Hospital.[20] The following individuals died after randomly encountering the PLA while commuting to or from work: Dai Wei (a cook at a Peking duck restaurant), Zhang Runing (a thirty-two-year-old woman who worked at China Radio International), Wang Hongqi (an employee at a leather research institute), Wang Qingzeng (a driver), Li Chun (a cook), Chen Ziqi (a bus driver), and Wang Junjing (a factory technician).[21] In separate incidents, Wang Gang and Mu Guilan died while getting breakfast on the morning of June 4.[22] Zhang Xianghong

web.archive.org/web/20161224164025/https://www.telegraph.co.uk/news/worldnews/asia/china/10868220/Shot-and-stabbed-as-he-tried-to-document-the-Tiananmen-Massacre-the-unfortunate-death-of-Wu-Guofeng.html.

[17] *XF*, 260.   [18] *XF*, 244.

[19] *ZY*, 280; "Testimony of Zhang Shusen, Mother of Chen Laishun," *Human Rights in China*, January 31, 1999, hrichina.org/en/testimony-zhang-shusen-mother-chen-laishun.

[20] *ZY*, 262–63.

[21] *XF*, 233, 237, 243, 249, 257, 259, 262. Wang Hongqi's name appears as "Wang Hongwei" in *XF*, 243, but appears as Wang Hongqi elsewhere; *ZY*, 282.

[22] *XF*, 238, 240.

and Wang Zhiying each died while trying to return home after family visits.[23] A man was trying to cross the street during the day on June 4 when a military vehicle knocked him down. An APC then ran over him. His unidentifiable remains lay on the pavement until the afternoon of June 5, until someone shoveled them into a plastic bag.[24] The capricious recklessness of some gun-wielding soldiers and army drivers killed civilians going about the most ordinary of urban activities.

Some people decided that their personal circumstances were so urgent that they had to go out on June 3 and 4. Liu Zhenying worked as a technician at the Academy of Military Medical Sciences. He went to buy medicine for his son on the evening of June 3. Around 10 p.m., Liu was chatting with a security guard at the north gate of the PLA General Hospital, near the intersection of Fuxing Road and Wukesong. Liu could not have known that the timing and location of his errand would coincide with the first shots fired by the 38th Group Army. A bullet penetrated Liu's heart. He was treated inside the PLA hospital but died within an hour.[25] Late on June 3, Liu Jinhua and her husband Feng Youxiang also went out to get medicine for their child. Liu, who worked for the PLA's General Political Department, was shot in the head and killed; her husband was hit in the leg and survived.[26] Employees of the army like Liu Jinhua and Liu Zhenying were as vulnerable as anyone else in Beijing during the massacre.

Even people who heeded the martial law command's warnings and stayed at home were at risk. *People's Daily* editor Lu Chaoqi remembers that the newspaper's phones started ringing nonstop shortly after 10 p.m. on June 3 with reports that soldiers were shooting at civilians. One call came from a family member of former deputy chief procurator Guan Shanfu. Guan's son-in-law, Yin Jing, had been shot and killed inside the kitchen of his eighth-floor apartment in a high-rise near Muxidi that housed the families of top officials.[27] "Everyone was shocked," Lu writes:

Weren't the authorities continuously saying that the army's advance was not aimed at students and Beijing residents? Were people living in the ministerial apartments the "tiny tiny minority [of rioters]"? Could this son-in-law of the Guan family be the "tiny tiny minority"? Even if he were, this guy in his kitchen was doing nothing to impede the army.[28]

Yin Jing's death received immediate notice because of his father-in-law's prominence, but other victims died under similar circumstances.

---

[23] *XF*, 227, 242.   [24] *XF*, 257.   [25] *XF*, 249.
[26] *XF*, 217–19; "Testimony of Youxiang, Husband of Liu Jinhua," *Human Rights in China*, January 31, 1999, hrichina.org/en/testimony-youxiang-husband-liu-jinhua.
[27] *XF*, 250.   [28] Lu Chaoqi, 六四內部日記 (Inside journal of June Fourth), 157.

A nanny who worked on the fourteenth floor of the building where Yin lived was shot and killed at the same time.[29]

A mother, father, and child peeked out of their window when they heard gunshots. When they saw soldiers pointing guns toward their building, the father pushed his child's head down but the mother was shot in the head and killed. Her name was Zhou Yuzhen. Before she died, Zhou worked as a secretary at the State Planning Commission. Another woman, a sixty-one-year-old retired official named Zhang Jiamei, was shot and killed when she looked out of her window on June 3. And a former Beijing People's Congress representative and model worker named Song Baosheng was shot in the stomach and killed while trying to close his window. Song had been unable to fall asleep because it was too noisy outside.[30]

---

[29] *ZY*, 289.

[30] *XF*, 252, 256, 253; John Gittings, "Beijing Tank Tracks Crushed Students Dead," *The Guardian*, June 2, 1999, theguardian.com/world/1999/jun/02/china.johngittings.

15   The Massacre Continues

The deadliest phase of the Beijing massacre – the army's advance toward the square on the evening of June 3 and in the early hours of June 4 – killed people on the streets and inside their own homes. But even after the army had cleared the square, Beijing remained unsafe. One grisly spasm of violence at 6:20 a.m. on the morning of June 4 seemed especially inexplicable. Tanks sped west on Chang'an Avenue, heading away from Tiananmen Square. One of them, which observers remembered was tank number 106, smashed through a group of students heading back to their campuses after evacuating the square. Eleven students were killed by the rampaging tank at Liubukou (we know the names of five of them: Dong Xiaojun, Gong Jifang, Lin Renfu, Tian Daomin, and Wang Peiwen). Many others were severely injured, including Fang Zheng, a student from the Beijing Institute of Physical Education who lost his legs.[1]

It is difficult to disagree with Timothy Brook when he describes the tank attack as "gratuitous" and "pointless." Wu Renhua, however, by matching the time and location of the atrocity with the testimony of Colonel Luo Gang of the Tianjin Garrison Command 1st Tank Division, has figured out what the tanks were supposed to be doing.[2] According to Luo's own account, after spending four hours crashing through ten blocked intersections east of Tiananmen Square, the tanks under his command arrived at the square at 5:18 a.m. on June 4, slightly more than twenty minutes before their deadline.[3]

---

[1] *LSJ*, 367; Brook, *Quelling the People*, 149–50 (Brook writes that the rampaging vehicle was tank number 100); Jan Wong, "Tiananmen: Exposing China's Big Lie," *Globe and Mail*, June 2, 1999, A1; Fang Zheng, "The Morning of June 4th and Its Long and Insidious Shadow," *China Change*, June 3, 2014, chinachange.org/2014/06/02/the-morning-of-june-4th-and-its-long-and-insidious-shadow-1. The Beijing Institute of Physical Education became Beijing Sports University in 1993.
[2] *LSJ*, 361–68.   [3] *JY*, 1:269.

Luo's regiment had no time to rest or celebrate. At 5:20 a.m., Luo received orders that his tanks were needed to disperse a crowd of "evil-doers and masses who did not understand the truth" who were attacking Xinhua Gate and threatening the safety of top Party leaders inside Zhongnanhai. Luo led eight tanks west, away from the square. As Luo sat in the lead vehicle, sweat pouring down his face, a frantic voice on his radio kept yelling, "Emergency at Xinhua Gate, emergency at Zhongnanhai!" Luo claims that his tanks successfully dispersed crowds and eliminated the threat to Zhongnanhai by firing guns into the air and shooting tear gas. "During the entire process," Luo writes, "my subordinates did not shoot at any groups of people and did not run over anyone."[4] Photographic evidence and eyewitness reports by bystanders and people injured by the tank attack contradict this claim.[5] But his drama-laden account provides a plausible explanation for why the tanks were driving at high speed near Liubukou, and why at least one tank's operators were so anxious that they ran over crowds of people there. They thought they were following orders to protect China's top leaders.

In 2013, Wu Renhua tracked down Wu Yanhui of Hengshui, Hebei Province, who said he was the second gunner of tank 106 and acknowledged that he had taken part in the military operation of June 1989. Wu Yanhui, who Wu Renhua found in an internet chat room for military veterans, stopped answering his phone, so we do not know his version of what happened at Liubukou, nor do we know the names of tank 106's driver or commanding officer.[6] Wu Renhua's research methods, however, show that the answers to these questions may not be out of reach forever.

The Beijing massacre continued during the day on June 4 and also on June 5 and 6. Victims during this later stage of the massacre were doing the same things as those who died on the night of June 3. Some were

---

[4] *JY*, 1:269–71.

[5] Photos of the aftermath of the tank atrocity were given to the *Globe and Mail* in 1999, Jan Wong, "Tiananmen: Exposing China's Big Lie"; a graphic photograph of Fang Zheng immediately after his legs were crushed is reproduced in Fang Zheng, "The Morning of June Fourth."

[6] Wu Renhua, Twitter post, April 4, 2013, twitter.com/wurenhua/status/319844089979867137; "吴仁华公布六四军人姓名 为还原历史保存记录" (Wu Renhua reveals the names of June Fourth soldiers, to restore the historical record), *Radio Free Asia*, May 29, 2012, rfa.org/mandarin/yataibaodao/th-05292012094126.html; Yaxue Cao, "The Historian of the Tiananmen Movement and the June Fourth Massacre: An Interview with Wu Renhua (Part One of Two)," *China Change*, June 3, 2016, chinachange.org/2016/06/03/the-historian-of-the-tiananmen-movement-and-the-june-fourth-massacre-an-interview-with-wu-renhua-part-one-of-two.

going about their daily lives, others were confronting the army. The Nanchizi intersection one block east of the square was again the site of a bloody face-off between civilians and gun-wielding soldiers. Canadian journalist Jan Wong, who was watching from a room in the Beijing Hotel, said that throughout the day on June 4, groups of around fifty Beijingers shouted curses at the soldiers guarding the square, yelling things like, "Blood debts will be repaid by blood!" After a while, a commanding officer ordered the troops to raise their weapons. When the protesters turned and ran away, the soldiers fired a volley into their backs. People who ventured into the killing zone to rescue the wounded were shot, according to Wong. "Soldiers were picking them off," she said. Every forty to sixty minutes, civilians approached the intersection and yelled at the troops, only to be driven back by another wave of bullets. This sequence repeated itself until late afternoon, when it started to drizzle. "The people left," Wong said. "They weren't afraid of dying. They just didn't want to get wet."[7]

Some people were so angry at the martial law forces that they continued to put themselves in harm's way after the army had control of Tiananmen Square. Others were killed or injured while doing normal urban activities. Around 6:40 a.m. on June 5, Peng Jun was on his way to buy breakfast in Chaoyang District when he was fatally shot.[8] Shortly after 3 p.m. on June 6, a twelve-year-old elementary school student was going home from school when soldiers firing from a tank shot him in the lower abdomen and left arm. Soldiers yelled at bystanders to stay back from the boy, so he lay bleeding in the street for more than thirty minutes until military vehicles left the area. The child survived after doctors at Fuxing Hospital removed one of his kidneys and his spleen.[9]

Later on June 6, a group of six young adults were playing mahjong when their friend, thirty-one-year-old magazine editor An Ji, stopped by and said that he heard that martial law had been canceled and the army had withdrawn. The seven friends – five men and two women – went out to take a look. They encountered soldiers near Nanlishi Road, who yelled "Don't move, hands up," and then shot at the group with machine guns. Bullets killed twenty-year-old worker Wang Zhengsheng and twenty-six-year-old worker Yang Ziping and injured Wang Zhengsheng's brother

[7] "Tiananmen Remembered – Jan Wong – 3 June 09," *Al Jazeera English*, June 3, 2009, youtube.com/watch?v=oTWBDMen7bo, 8:53–11:57; "Interview: Jan Wong," *Frontline*, December 7, 2005, pbs.org/wgbh/pages/frontline/tankman/interviews/wong.html.
[8] *XF*, 254. [9] *ZY*, 309.

Wang Zhengqiang and Yang Ziping's brother Yang Ziming. The Wang brothers' girlfriends, Yang Yuemei and Zhang Xuemei, escaped uninjured but must have been severely traumatized by the shooting. Yang Ziming, who had served with the 63rd Group Army, saw a license plate that indicated that the troops who shot him were from the 38th Group Army. After shooting him, soldiers took the watch from his wrist and removed five hundred yuan from his pocket.[10]

---

[10] *XF*, 86–89; *ZY*, 269–70, 309–10. A Beijing Public Security bulletin reported that when a group of six "rioters" attempted to dismantle a security checkpoint at 1 a.m. on June 7, PLA soldiers shot four of them and arrested two. "六月七日北京情况" (The situation in Beijing on June 7), 公安部总值班室情况摘报 (Ministry of Public Security Duty Office situation bulletin) (hereafter abbreviated as *QZ*), zengkan [89], no. 219 (June 7, 1989), http://web.archive.org/web/20190615083313/blog.boxun.com/hero/201304/xsj14/125_1 .shtml.

16 Quiet Reckonings

The Beijing massacre achieved its goal. Martial law troops took control of the city, violently ending the protest movement and preserving the CCP's hold on power. Emphasizing the victims of the atrocity, however, shows how inaccurate and inhumane it is to think of the crackdown as a success. The massacre was a profound failure of governance. In the days and weeks after June 3 and 4, 1989, Deng Xiaoping congratulated martial law troops for having quelled a counterrevolutionary rebellion. Propaganda played up the sacrifices and bravery of soldiers. But at the same time, survivors and observers knew that "certainly some of [the troops'] actions were more characteristic of rampaging rebels than a disciplined infantry," as Andrew Scobell writes,[1] and that "lethal weapons were made more lethal by being placed in the hands of incompetent and badly officered soldiers," as Timothy Brook puts it.[2] Deng Xiaoping himself must have been aware of these facts, as were Yang Shangkun, Li Peng, and martial law commanders Zhou Yibing and Liu Zhenhua. Quiet reckoning with the failures of the military operation accompanied the loud, public celebrations of its supposed success.

The official description of the crackdown Chen Xitong read on June 30, 1989 said that victims included "rioters who got what they deserved" but also "civilians who were mistakenly hurt and medical personnel doing their jobs." Chen said that the government would compensate civilians and others who were wrongfully injured (政府要认真的做好善后工作).[3] On July 8, 1989, Yu Xiaosong, deputy secretary-general of the Beijing municipal government, was quoted in Hong Kong newspapers as promising that the families of people who had been accidentally killed would receive between ten thousand and twenty thousand yuan;

---

[1] Scobell, *China's Use of Military Force*, 162.   [2] Brook, *Quelling the People*, 202.
[3] Chen Xitong, 关于制止动乱和平息反革命暴乱的情况报告 (Report on stopping the turmoil and quelling the counterrevolutionary riot), 35.

children of the dead would receive stipends through their eighteenth birthdays.[4] Promises of reparations were a tacit official admission that the military operation had been bungled.

How much compensation families and victims actually received – if any – varied widely. Under the work unit system that still dominated much of urban life in the 1980s, schools, factories, companies, and bureaucratic organizations were responsible for reparations. Sympathetic university officials paid for some students' funerals and covered injured students' medical bills. The families of Liu Hongtao, Xiong Zhiming, and Dai Jinping received 1,000 yuan, 1,500 yuan, and 2,000 yuan respectively for burial expenses from the Beijing Institute of Technology, Beijing Normal University, and Beijing Agricultural University – amounts worth approximately $250, $375, and $500 in US dollars at the time.[5] The Beijing Institute of Physical Education paid for some of Kong Weizhen's medical expenses after he was shot in the leg near Fuxingmen on June 3. Kong had thirteen operations and still walks with a cane.[6] Chen Yongting's school, the Central Institute for Nationalities, covered Chen's father's travel expenses from Sichuan to Beijing after Chen was killed in the massacre.[7] Documentation stating that the victim had been "mistakenly injured" (误伤) sometimes accompanied these reparations.

The family of Ni Shilian, an engineer who was killed around 11 p.m. on June 3 near Xidan, received a harsher verdict. In 1990, Ni's work unit issued a certificate confirming his "unnatural death" (非正常死亡) but also noting that he was at fault for having violated the martial law order. Compensation for Ni's death was calculated on the basis of ten months of his salary: 835 yuan.[8] Payments offered to nonstudents seemed to

---

[4] 大公報 (Dagong Daily) (Hong Kong), July 8, 1989, 1. I first found reports of Yu Xiaosong's comments in *XF*, 149–50; Ding Zilin visited the father of Zhang Jin, a nineteen-year-old woman who was shot on June 3 and died in the early hours of June 4, 1989. Zhang's father had seen Yu Xiaosong's remarks in the July 8, 1989, edition of *Wen Wei Po.* He wrote three letters to the Beijing government requesting compensation but received no reply.

[5] You Weijie and Guo Liying, "So That He Can Follow the Waves to See the Free World," *Human Rights in China*, May 16, 2014, hrichina.org/en/china-rights-forum/so-he-can-follow-waves-see-free-world; You Weijie and Guo Liying, "He Lost His Life before Finishing His Studies"; You Weijie and Guo Liying, "He Hoped, after Graduation, to Be of Service to His Motherland."

[6] You Weijie and Guo Liying, "Kong Weizhen, Disabled but Unyielding," *Human Rights in China*, May 9, 2014, hrichina.org/en/china-rights-forum/kong-weizhen-disabled-unyielding.

[7] You Weijie, "Chen Yongting, Son of the Earth," April 10, 2014, hrichina.org/en/china-rights-forum/chen-yongting-son-earth.

[8] *XF*, 251.

depend on where the victims had worked. The family of a cook who was shot and killed on his way to work at the Great Hall of the People on June 4 reportedly received ten thousand yuan in compensation.[9] This is the largest sum I have seen associated with a victim of the Beijing massacre (although it pales in comparison with the seventy thousand yuan that journalist Louisa Lim discovered was paid in 2006 to the mother of Tang Deying, who was killed in Chengdu in June 1989).[10] The high profile of the cook's work unit probably helped to overcome the potential stigma of his working-class job, which disadvantaged such victims as Qi Zhiyong, who, like Ni Shilian, also received a piddling payout. Qi was a painter for a construction company in 1989. Both of Qi's legs were amputated after he was shot in the early hours of June 4. According to Qi:

My work unit was reluctant to pay my hospital expenses and delayed paying them. On August 7, two soldiers, a policeman and two people from the hospital took me in a car to my unit, and a doctor said to the director, "Our hospital treated altogether 273 people, and only his expenses and those of one university student are still unpaid." Only then did the unit pay for my medical treatment.

Qi could no longer paint. His work unit had him fill out resignation papers and offered him a monthly stipend of fifty yuan, plus a food subsidy. In 1999 he was making a living as a street peddler.[11]

Details about other reparations remain hidden: how much money did the family of Yin Jing, the son-in-law of retired top official Guan Shanfu, receive? What about the families of Liu Jinhua and Liu Zhenying, who were employees of the army that shot them? The only fleeting details about funeral, medical, and other payments we have are thanks to evidence collected by the Tiananmen Mothers – an organization that demands "truth, compensation, and accountability" from the Chinese government about the massacre.[12] In the same interviews in which they mention that Beijing universities covered funeral or travel expenses, the parents of massacre victims demand compensation, signaling that what they received in 1989 falls far short of what they would consider proper amends for their child's wrongful death. Zhang Xianling, the mother of Wang Nan, told Louisa Lim that in 2009, a policeman spoke to several Tiananmen Mothers "to ask whether it might be possible that the issue of compensation be dealt with on an individual basis, rather than as a group. They turned the offer down flat, seeing it as an attempt to buy their silence."[13] The quiet payouts that have occurred are a meager

[9] *XF*, 257.   [10] Lim, *People's Republic of Amnesia*, 200.
[11] "Testimony of Qi Zhiyong, Wounded," *Human Rights in China*, January 31, 1999, hrichina.org/en/testimony-qi-zhiyong-wounded.
[12] Lim, *People's Republic of Amnesia*, 107.   [13] Lim, *People's Republic of Amnesia*, 127.

official acknowledgment that something went very wrong in Beijing on June 3 and 4, 1989.

Another group received more valuable – but equally quiet – compensation for their role in the crackdown: the military officials who led it. On February 11, 1990, Jiang Zemin, in his role as chairman of the Party's Central Military Commission, signed off on an order bestowing honors and citations on specific units that had enforced martial law in 1989. In stark contrast to the short-lived burst of propaganda that had commemorated dead soldiers in summer 1989,[14] Jiang's order was secret and did not explain why certain units deserved special mention. Even though we have a general sense of what the 38th Group Army and 15th Airborne did as they assaulted China's capital on June 3, we do not know what exactly the Scout Battalion of the 38th's 112th Division or the 2nd Battalion of the 15th's 44th Brigade did to earn the special title "Heroic Protector of the Republic."[15] We can, however, guess why the 1st Company of the 27th Group Army's Scout Battalion earned the same honor, because this was the unit that forced the final group of protesters to leave Tiananmen Square on June 4.

Official honors that nobody outside the military knew about may have been appreciated, but promotions provided more tangible rewards for officers who participated in the crackdown. Wu Renhua's sleuthing in military veterans' invitation-only internet chatrooms not only identified the second gunner of the rampaging tank at Liubukou but also allowed Wu to document the names, unit numbers, and career paths of almost one hundred other men. From the leaders of military regions to low-level unit commanders, involvement in the crackdown of 1989 was no obstacle to promotion – it might have even been cause for it. Colonel Zuo Yinsheng of the 15th Airborne, who was involved in drafting plans to advance on Tiananmen Square, eventually became a lieutenant general and went on to serve as deputy commander of the PAP and the Beijing Military Region after 1989. Luo Gang, whose testimony explained the

---

[14] Wu Renhua has identified fifteen martial law troops who died and were officially honored as "Guardians of the Republic." Of those, seven were killed by civilians after soldiers started shooting on the evening of June 3, 1989. Their names were Liu Guogeng, Cui Guozheng, Ma Guoxuan, Wang Jinwei, Li Guorui, Liu Yanpo, and Zang Lijie. Six others – Wang Qifu, Li Qiang, Du Huaiqing, Li Dongguo, Wang Xiaobing, and Xu Rujun – were soldiers from the 38th Group Army who died after the vehicle they were in took a turn too fast, crashed, and caught fire. By showing that the soldiers' time of death came after the army's order authorizing deadly force, Wu has discovered that the soldiers' deaths were caused by civilians acting in self-defense or fighting back after the deadly assault commenced, not the other way around. *LSJ*, 58–61.

[15] Ben Keiler, *The China 1989 Army Documents*, 3rd ed., vol. 1 (Seattle, WA: Amazon Digital Services, 2018), Kindle edition, location 850–60.

mindset of tank operators at Liubukou on the morning of June 4, rose from colonel to major general and became deputy commander of the Inner Mongolia Military Region.[16]

Whether or not they received promotions of the sort Wu Renhua reveals, military veterans of the crackdown went on with their lives, hiding away the commemorative wristwatches, medals, and books they received and remaining silent. Those who have spoken publicly about their experiences, such as Chen Guang and Li Xiaoming, are outliers. Even Wu Yanhui, the second gunner of tank 106, is atypical. He was active online and initially forthcoming on the phone, not because he wanted to talk about his time inside a tank on June 4, 1989, but because he was working as a salesman for the Hengshui White Lightning Liquor Distillery and did not want to lose out on a sale.[17]

Denial fueled by shame or fear is more typical. After immigrating to Australia in 2001, Li Xiaoming said that he "felt ashamed to be associated with the army ... I still cannot heal the wounds in my heart. I constantly feel the pain." Li, however, also said that he did not dare to speak while he was still in China, and that his wife was afraid that his remarks from Australia "may cause trouble to other people who are in China ... her worries are not groundless."[18] In 2010, Chen Guang tried to interview five former members of his unit for a documentary film, but nobody would say anything on camera.[19]

When soldiers do speak in private settings, their words have failed to comfort victims. Ding Zilin said that occasionally soldiers seek out members of the Tiananmen Mothers asking for forgiveness. "I can't forgive them," she said. A soldier who met with a grieving parent in northeast China said that he had carried a gun but did not shoot it. According to Ding, "The soldier denied that there was shooting at Qianmen but we have a member whose husband died at Qianmen. Having former soldiers trying to talk to us is distasteful."[20] It did not have to be this way. The massacre was not inevitable. The trauma of the atrocity and its aftermath could have been avoided. What alternative paths might have offered different outcomes?

---

[16] *LSJ*, 72–81.   [17] Author conversation with Wu Renhua.
[18] Wang Yu, "Living with the Shame."   [19] Jacobs, "Q. and A.: Chen Guang."
[20] Andrew Jacobs and Chris Buckley, Ding Zilin interview notes, 2014.

17 Massacre
Alternative Paths

Contemplating things that did not happen and imagining paths not taken might seem like a job for fiction writers, not historians. Analyzing alternatives to the Beijing massacre, however, brings what did actually happen into sharper focus. The exercise pushes back against cynical narratives that blame protesters for the army's advance or insist that a violent crackdown was inevitable, necessary, or somehow beneficial or "worth it" in the long run. Imagining alternative paths, based on evidence from historical sources, shows that the massacre itself resulted from a failure of imagination. What if the army had kept bullets in boxes and cleared the square using nonlethal methods? What if China's top leaders had sent troops back to their barracks, canceled martial law, and ignored the protesters? What if more military officials and soldiers had disobeyed orders?

As soon as the Beijing massacre commenced, people started imagining alternative histories. The scenarios I discuss in this chapter were first voiced by people in China in 1989. After the crackdown, top leaders such as Li Peng and Chi Haotian openly speculated about how things might have gone differently. On July 1, 1989, Li Peng met with Daniel Wong, a city council member and former mayor of Cerritos, California. After the meeting, Wong relayed to journalists what Li had told him: the army had had to use lethal force to clear Tiananmen Square because it had run out of tear gas, had no rubber bullets, and could not use water hoses to disperse protesters because hydrants near the square lacked sufficient water pressure.[1] Li was arguing that the army had done everything it could to avoid bloodshed, only using lethal force as a last resort.[2]

Li never publicly elaborated on his conversation with Wong, but in March 1990, General Chi Haotian, who was chief of staff of the PLA and

---

[1] Daniel Southerland, "China Gives New Motive for Assault," *Washington Post*, July 3, 1989, A1.

[2] Reuters, "Lack of Equipment Forced Army to Kill, Li Peng Tells Visitor," *Globe and Mail*, July 3, 1989, A1.

had played a central role in directing the military operation in Beijing, repeated Li's claim that equipment shortages had forced the army to kill, saying that the

PLA had to fire back in self-defense. At that time, the PLA had no equipment such as tear gas and riot shields. In retrospect, we think equipment of this nature is necessary and that lethal force and firearms should be used only in very critical and special circumstances. If we had had this equipment, casualties could have been less.[3]

Li Peng and Chi Haotian's claim that the PLA had no choice but to kill unarmed civilians because it was ill-prepared and underequipped seems absurd and cruel, but it might accurately depict the leaders' own flawed thought process – we've tried everything else, we're out of time, we have no other options. Li and Chi's purported preference for nonlethal force echoes what protesters themselves predicted. After the declaration of martial law in May 1989, and even as gunshots started ringing out on June 3, many protesters expected and prepared to suffer pain from rubber bullets, tear gas, and clubs, but few expected to die.[4] For those who remembered what had happened in Tiananmen Square in April 1976, this seemed like a reasonable assumption. Beijingers might have known that police and worker militias used clubs to violently clear protesters from the square on the evening of April 5, 1976, injuring some but apparently killing none.[5] On June 1, 1989, perhaps thinking of what had happened in April 1976, Politburo members mused that it would be better to use "workers' patrols," rather than martial law troops, to clear the square.[6] But even though 1976 offered a precedent for the nonlethal clearing of Tiananmen Square, the PLA also had a hidden history of forcefully quelling uprisings. Few people in Beijing knew that the PLA had killed thousands of protesters in Tibet in 1959 and again in March 1989, in Guizhou in 1956, and in Yunnan in 1975.[7] The details of these crackdowns were never publicly released, and few people knew about them. Even if people had known that the army had turned its guns on

---

[3] "Why We Cracked Down: Two Conversations," *U.S. News & World Report* 108, no. 10 (March 12, 1990): 54.
[4] Brook, *Quelling the People*, 134, 137.
[5] Frederick C. Teiwes and Warren Sun, "The First Tiananmen Incident Revisited: Elite Politics and Crisis Management at the End of the Maoist Era," *Pacific Affairs* 77, no. 2 (2004): 219, 229.
[6] *LP*, 286.
[7] Wang Haiguang, "Radical Agricultural Collectivization and Ethnic Rebellion: The Communist Encounter with a 'New Emperor' in Guizhou's Mashan Region, 1956," in *Maoism at the Grassroots*, 218–305; Xian Wang, "Islamic Religiosity, Revolution, and State Violence in Southwest China: The 1975 Shadian Massacre" (master's thesis, University of British Columbia, 2013).

civilians in the past, they might have assumed that deadly crackdowns in frontier areas would not be repeated in China's capital.

Insiders who might have been aware of the PLA's history of violently crushing uprisings were not taken seriously when they warned protesters about the likelihood of deadly violence. In the days before the crackdown, Min Buying, a former deputy chief in the Beijing Public Security Bureau who worked for the Beijing branch of the Ministry of State Security in the early 1980s, visited a friend's house and reportedly told the young people there, "Don't go to Tiananmen or Chang'an Avenue. There will be a crackdown and shooting." One young woman asked, "You mean rubber bullets, right?" Min responded, "China has never wasted money on that crap. China uses real bullets."[8] There is no reason to believe that Min Buying had special knowledge of the martial law forces' equipment or planning. Older people who had experienced the traumas of the Mao years issued similar warnings to young protesters in late May and early June 1989. It is likely, however, that Min had never encountered rubber bullets during his long career in policing and intelligence. I have found no credible evidence that any army unit in China possessed or used rubber bullets during the 1980s.[9] Min turned out to be correct that China only had real bullets in 1989. Liu Jinhua, who worked for the army, did not believe it. One of the last things she said to her husband on June 3 before she was shot in the head was, "They won't be real bullets."[10]

Although the PLA used real bullets, not rubber ones, People's Armed Police (PAP) units did carry nonlethal weapons. PAP troops used shields, clubs, and tear gas in their advance on the square on June 3. And before the PLA was authorized to shoot, martial law troops picked up bricks, bottles, and rocks that civilians had hurled at them and threw them back at the protesters.[11] Could PAP and PLA troops have reached and cleared the square without shooting real bullets? What would have happened if the crackdown had been violent but not deadly?

Evidence from an internally published PAP collection of documents, as well as from *A Day of Martial Law*, confirms that antiriot squads from the PAP as well as military units belonging to the PLA experienced

---

[8] Liu Xiaodong, 亂世迷途: 三代叛逆的紅色家庭 (Lost in the chaos: Three generations of a rebellious red family) (Hong Kong: Xiafeier guoji chuban gongsi, 2012), 430.

[9] *The Tiananmen Papers* contains a single mention of an antiriot squad (presumably belonging to the PAP) firing rubber bullets at Gongzhufen after 9:30 p.m. on June 3. Zhang Liang, comp., *The Tiananmen Papers: The Chinese Leadership's Decision to Use Force against Their Own People – In Their Own Words*, ed. Andrew J. Nathan and Perry Link (New York: Public Affairs, 2001), 372.

[10] *XF*, 217.   [11] *JY*, 1:86.

extreme difficulties fighting their way through angry crowds on June 3. A report authored by Beijing PAP officials in December 1989 declared that even though a "decisive victory" had been achieved in "quelling the riot," the PAP had been unprepared for the scale of the protests in May and June. They lacked sufficient troops, which meant that untrained new recruits made up a significant portion of the antiriot squads. Troops who did enter Beijing did not have enough helmets or boots to go around. They had very few electric prods, and those that they possessed were of poor quality, losing their charge after a few uses.[12] Tear gas was sometimes effective in dispersing protesters, but PAP forces quickly used up all of their tear gas canisters, allowing civilians to regroup and fight back.[13] "Please issue us more – and more effective – tear gas canisters, dye bombs, bulletproof vests, and multipurpose knapsacks," the report concludes.[14] There is only a single mention of rubber bullets or fire hoses in the entire collection of PAP documents: a statement that PAP troops would have done better if they had had access to such equipment.[15]

PAP leaders were pleased to hear martial law leaders Zhou Yibing and Liu Zhenhua encourage them and tell them that they were paving the way for the army, but in the end, PAP authorities concluded that antiriot troops would not have been able to fight their way to the square without the army. "Everyone fully realizes: 'Without the backing of the army, there would have been no way for us to complete our task. And we probably would not have returned alive.'"[16] And according to PAP officials, the "most effective" way to clear intersections of protesters on the night of June 3 was not nonlethal weapons but rather the army firing guns when they came within thirty meters of "rioters."[17] The PAP's assessment of its own performance on June 3 and 4 matches Li Peng and Chi Haotian's arguments that troops lacked equipment and that bullets were a last resort, but a necessary one.[18]

PAP leaders noticed that the army's shooting was "effective," but how possible was it for PLA units to reach the square without resorting to lethal force? Reports about some 54th Army divisions claim that thousands of soldiers pushed through violent protesters without shooting. Like the 15th Airborne, the 54th Group Army also approached the square from the south of Beijing and met its goal of reaching Qianmen by 4 a.m. on June 4. Soldiers from the 54th Army battled against groups

---

[12] *HF*, 37.   [13] *HF*, 27, 187, 303.   [14] *HF*, 37.   [15] *HF*, 200.   [16] *HF*, 32.
[17] *HF*, 81.
[18] The PAP source *HF* contradicts Ben Keiler's claim, based on a shorter PAP document, that because antiriot troops based in Beijing knew the city better than PLA soldiers who were outsiders, some PAP units were able to reach the square without killing civilians or sustaining casualties. Keiler, *The China 1989 Army Documents*, 57–58.

of Beijingers throwing bricks and blocking the way, but they also found routes and intersections clear of protesters.

Major General Zhang Kun, vice political commissar of the 54th Army, claimed that "during the advance, our troops did not fire a single gun." Before setting off toward Tiananmen on the afternoon of June 3, Zhang recalled, "higher levels clearly ordered: opening fire is not permitted." The 54th moved north carrying unloaded guns and separate, sealed boxes of bullets. "Of course, it would have been easy to open the boxes and distribute the bullets," Zhang wrote, "but because our communications were cut off, we did not receive any new orders. No one dared to open up the boxes of ammunition."[19]

Martial law officials prohibited live fire before approximately 10 p.m. Then they authorized shooting. Zhang Kun appears to have known in hindsight about "new orders" that would have permitted shooting. But is his claim of being out of touch and never receiving those orders credible? Soldiers from the 54th did suffer severe casualties as they advanced toward the square: one dead, 246 seriously injured, and around 1,500 lightly injured.[20] Zhang Kun himself was among those who were badly hurt. He had multiple broken bones, was knocked out, and lost his shoes.[21] In 2017 someone calling himself Ben Keiler reprinted maps and excerpts of a report from the 54th Group Army's 162nd Division.[22] The report mentions that the soldiers were carrying guns and ammunition. At 11 p.m. on June 3, the division's officers, whose radio was working well enough to convey orders to subordinate regiments, ordered soldiers to "advance on foot, using firm and resolute measures, at any cost."[23] This order came precisely when shooting had begun elsewhere in the city.

Zhang Shijun, a soldier serving with the 54th Army's 162nd Division, spoke out in 2018 to refute reports that the 54th Army never received orders to open fire. "[My unit] did open fire," Zhang told New Tang Dynasty Television (a station founded by Falun Gong practitioners). "We were shooting as we advanced. After arriving next to Tiananmen, we also opened fire. We opened fire a total of four times."[24] Zhang, who

---

[19] *JY*, 2:294.   [20] *JY*, 2:171.   [21] *LSJ*, 259.
[22] The sources appear authentic – their formatting, coloring, font, and written style are identical to similar military documents published in 1989 and 1990 – and in any case would be difficult and pointless to fabricate.
[23] Keiler, *The China 1989 Army Documents*, doc. 32, 79.
[24] Zheng Lu, "六四军人: 戒严军队全接到开枪命令我营开枪4次" (June Fourth soldier: Martial law forces all received order to open fire, my battalion opened fire four times), *New Tang Dynasty Television*, June 6, 2018, web.archive.org/web/20190308214659/ http://ca.ntdtv.com/xtr/gb/2018/06/06/a1378604.html.

was discharged from the army after the massacre and sentenced to "reeducation through labor" in 1992, has repeatedly denounced the crackdown and told varying – and mostly vague – stories about what he saw on June 3 and 4, 1989. Nonetheless, his firsthand testimony about shooting seems more credible than Zhang Kun's claim in *A Day of Martial Law* – a book full of euphemisms meant to obscure the reality of the military assault – about being out of touch and never opening fire.

Military units that did open fire, including the 38th Army, the 15th Airborne, and probably the 54th Army, opened up routes to the square that allowed other units to advance less violently. Li Xiaoming of the 39th Group Army (not to be confused with the 38th) reckoned that his unit could have made it to the square from the east without having to shoot – an APC had pushed through blockades and "there were no more people left to block our march on the streets."[25] But his division commander, Xu Feng, pretended that his radio equipment had failed, "so we never received orders and were wandering around away from Tiananmen Square." Li assumed that many soldiers were like the ones in his unit who did not aggressively shoot their way to the square. Li thought that without such passive resistance as Xu Feng's purported equipment failure, the death toll would have been much higher. "A single soldier could have easily killed four to eight people in one round," Li Xiaoming said, "then with all the soldiers on the streets of Beijing, with such packed crowds then there could have been thousands, more than ten thousand killed, if all the soldiers shot."[26]

Li Xiaoming's sobering analysis suggests that thousands of soldiers and commanders who did not want to shoot at civilians found ways to avoid killing people. Without such restraint, the massacre might have been far worse than it actually was. But even top military officials recognized that some troops who did open fire did so recklessly. According to Li Xiaoming, on July 4, 1989, one month after the crackdown, his unit finally received clear instructions about when they were allowed to shoot at protesters: if a mob came within one hundred meters, soldiers could fire warning shots into the air. If that failed to deter protesters and they were fifty meters from soldiers, shooting into the ground was allowed. Anyone who came closer after those two volleys could be directly targeted.[27] These directives were presumably meant to prevent a repeat of the wild strafing of bystanders and buildings that killed and injured

[25] Wang Yu, "Living with the Shame."
[26] Andrew Jacobs and Chris Buckley, Li Xiaoming interview notes.
[27] Andrew Jacobs and Chris Buckley, Li Xiaoming interview notes.

unarmed civilians who had no plans to threaten or even encounter martial law troops.

If the July 4 order limiting when troops were allowed to fire directly at protesters is analyzed alongside Li Peng and Chi Haotian's laments about insufficient tear gas, rubber bullets, and water hoses, it appears that top Chinese leaders – concerned about their reputations and their hold on power – were ashamed about how much blood was shed during the crackdown. They were glad that the army had "quelled" the "rebellion" but wished that it had not been so deadly. This complicates arguments by such scholars as Perry Link and Timothy Brook that shooting and killing were central, premeditated elements of a plan to terrorize and subdue the people of Beijing. Link writes that Deng felt that the protest movement was so dangerous that "someone needed to crack a whip that would bring a definitive end to all challenges to the ruling authority."[28] Brook dismisses Li Peng's claim that the army used deadly weapons because it had insufficient nonlethal options. Soldiers shot their way to the square, he argues, not because they lacked proper gear "but because of the refusal of citizens to obey the government," Brook writes. "To government leaders, the scale of resistance seemed so vast as to require a full military response."[29] Link and Brook may be correct about Deng's motivation for authorizing deadly force, but some military officials were horrified at the disproportionate scale of the PLA's assault. The overhaul and growth of the PAP after 1989, and the PAP's active role in cracking down on protests during the 1990s and 2000s, shows that PLA leaders had questioned the appropriateness of shooting at civilians.

★ ★ ★

There is no doubt that the military assault ended the protests by force and terror. But if we think back to June 3, the most immediate spark for the massacre was the sense of urgency – false and unnecessary urgency – caused by the order that troops stationed on the outskirts of Beijing absolutely had to clear Tiananmen Square by dawn on June 4, no matter what, at any cost. This arbitrary deadline arose from top leaders' sense that protests had gone on for too long, that military units were finally in place and ready to overcome the barriers that had stymied them in late May, and also from a more practical concern that tens of thousands of Beijingers would flock to the square on Sunday, the only non-workday of

---

[28] Perry Link, "June Fourth: Memory and Ethics," in *The Impact of China's 1989 Tiananmen Massacre*, ed. Jean-Phillipe Béja (New York: Routledge, 2011), 17.
[29] Brook, *Quelling the People*, 7.

the week. The unnecessarily urgent deadline caused anxiety among officers and troops that they could be accused of failing to obey orders if they were unable to reach the square on time.[30] It incentivized violence and sparked outrage and resistance from civilians in the streets.

According to Li Peng, at least twenty-five thousand troops had already surrounded the square by June 2. What if, instead of asking hundreds of thousands of other troops to fight their way from Beijing's suburbs to the square, the military action had been limited to the twenty-five thousand soldiers already hidden in and around the Great Hall of the People? Could those twenty-five thousand soldiers have waited until 3 or 4 a.m. on any given night, when the number of people in the square would have ebbed to its lowest point, to disperse or detain the remaining protesters and then reoccupy the square and secure its entrances? This type of smaller scale operation, taking a page from the playbook of April 5, 1976, might have prevented a massacre. From the position of China's leaders, however, ordering the military to secure and occupy only Tiananmen Square, and not the rest of Beijing, presented risks. We know that hundreds of thousands of civilians thronged the streets after they learned that military units had begun violently advancing toward the square on the evening of June 3. Outraged that the crackdown had finally commenced, people went out to confront the army, protect the students, or witness history. A limited military operation in Tiananmen Square, even if it managed to remove protesters and prevent them from returning, might have forestalled a massacre but would have sparked popular anger and further demonstrations. As student leader Li Lu saw it, "If the authorities repeated their actions in Tiananmen Square of thirteen years ago, in April 1976, they would enrage the entire country and people would rise up in rebellion against them."[31] This may explain why Deng Xiaoping opted for an overwhelming, multipronged assault to subdue an entire city.

★ ★ ★

After purging Zhao Ziyang, seeing several attempts at dialogue fall apart, and watching civilians defy martial law in late May 1989, Deng Xiaoping,

---

[30] This is an example of what Joseph Fewsmith calls the "task-oriented nature" of the Communist Party, in which "in practice the evaluation and promotion of cadres depends more on their ability to complete assigned tasks and display personal loyalty than it does on fulfilling an abstract set of criteria." Joseph Fewsmith and Andrew J. Nathan, "Authoritarian Resilience Revisited: Joseph Fewsmith with Response from Andrew J. Nathan," *Journal of Contemporary China* 28, no. 116 (2019): 170.

[31] Li Lu, *Moving the Mountain: My Life in China from the Cultural Revolution to Tiananmen Square* (London: Macmillan, 1990), 185.

Yang Shangkun, Li Peng, and other top leaders lost patience. Because they saw no immediate end in sight, they set an arbitrary deadline, forced the issue, and became responsible for a terrible massacre. But there might have already been an end in sight, if only leaders had done nothing. By the end of May 1989, many Beijing-based students had quit the square. New arrivals from the provinces wanted to stay, but more outsiders were taking trains out of Beijing than were entering the city. A donation of tents from Hong Kong had improved living conditions in the square, and the installation of a large statue called the Goddess of Democracy had boosted protesters' morale, but what would have happened if the military had not rushed to meet an arbitrary June 4 deadline? What if the government had ignored the protesters and done nothing?

In the week before the massacre, Chai Ling, Li Lu, and other student leaders were exhausted. They decided that they would leave the square, regroup, and refocus the protest movement. Then they changed their minds. Chai Ling recalled that Bai Meng of Peking University "told me that given the deteriorating conditions on the Square, I should consider the plan to withdraw. It was obvious, he said, the government was waiting for the movement to die out on its own."[32] Bai Meng was wrong: authorities were unwilling to wait; preparations for the military assault were already underway. But what if the government had been more patient? Was letting the movement "die out on its own" a realistic way to avoid violence?

Imagine a scenario in which Party leaders acted more patiently and humanely and decided against a military assault in early June 1989. Also imagine that the NPC Standing Committee canceled its meeting, robbing protesters of their rationale to stay in the square until June 20. Bai Meng's prediction about the government waiting out the protesters could have come true. How many weeks could protesters last in Tiananmen Square before getting so tired, sick, bored, and hot that they left on their own? Would students from the provinces continue to travel to Beijing, or might their numbers dwindle if they heard that not much was happening in the square? At what point would Beijing citizens' support for the protesters shift to annoyance? If the protests ebbed, might people have grudgingly decided to give Jiang Zemin a chance as the new general secretary? If Deng Xiaoping, Yang Shangkun, Chen Yun, Li Xiannian, Wang Zhen, and Li Peng had been brave enough to wait, it might have been possible for them to meet their goals of clearing Tiananmen Square

---

[32] Chai Ling, *Heart*, 174.

and disbanding the autonomous student and worker organizations. They could have averted the massacre.[33]

It is not surprising, however, that Deng, Yang, Li, and others lacked the courage and patience to let nature take its course. The exhausted student leaders who contemplated abandoning the square did not want to give up entirely. They hoped to spread the protest movement nationwide. Likewise, BWAF planned to intensify its organizing inside workplaces, even if it had had to abandon its headquarters near the square. Communist Party leaders were unwilling to watch BWAF expand unchecked. In addition, being patient in early June would have seemed like an official admission that civilians had won when they blocked and encircled martial law forces, as tens of thousands had done between May 20 and May 23, 1989. Savvy propaganda, however, could have framed these events as an example of love and mutual understanding between the people and the people's army, which had acted with great restraint. And given enough space and time, creative leadership could have found a way to disband, discredit, coopt, or even work with autonomous student and worker organizations. Bloodshed was not inevitable. Waiting could have opened up new options for China's top leaders rather than pushing them deeper into a corner. Instead, they chose repression and violence.

★ ★ ★

The men who ordered the assault bear primary responsibility for the massacre, but what if the actual perpetrators – military officials and soldiers – had found a way to avert it? General Xu Qinxian, who headed the 38th Group Army, refused to carry out the initial order to impose martial law around May 20, 1989. He was arrested and imprisoned for four years.[34] The most opportune moment for military dissent would have been for other generals to follow Xu's lead in late May and early June 1989 – or for Xu himself to have coordinated, organized, and persuaded his peers to say no instead of privately acting on his conscience. What were the prospects of a military refusal to use deadly force on the evening of June 3, 1989? We already know that only a small

---

[33] Scholars have noted government leaders' strategy to "wait it out" in response to the Hong Kong Umbrella Movement of 2014. Comparing 1989 and 2014, Lagerkvist and Rühlig write, "The CCP has clearly learnt from the Beijing Massacre to be more patient and wait out the protests." Johan Lagerkvist and Tim Rühlig, "The Mobilization of Memory and Tradition: Hong Kong's Umbrella Movement and Beijing's 1989 Tiananmen Movement," *Contemporary Chinese Political Economy and Strategic Relations: An International Journal* 2, no. 2 (September 2016): 761.

[34] *LSJ*, 89–93; Jacobs and Buckley, "Tales of Army Discord Show Tiananmen Square in a New Light."

handful of the more than 180,000 soldiers who made up the martial law forces shot directly at civilians. Many of those who rampaged and strafed were from the 38th Group Army and the 15th Airborne. Soldiers from other units had no opportunity or desire to shoot. For events to have unfolded differently on the evening of June 3, at some point leading up to the distribution of bullets and the order to use lethal force around 10 p.m., leaders of the 38th Army and 15th Airborne would have had to say no. Or all the soldiers facing off against burning buses and stone-throwing crowds on Beijing's main east–west artery would have had to disobey orders to "spare no cost" in reaching and clearing Tiananmen Square by dawn. All of them.

Military resistance did occur after the massacre began. Officers pretended that their communications had been cut off or feigned deafness. In addition to Li Xiaoming's commander, Xu Feng of the 39th Army, who faked an equipment malfunction and led his troops to meander aimlessly instead of advancing toward the square, other officers declined to "spare no cost." On June 3, the 28th Group Army commanded by He Yanran moved slowly from the northwest of Beijing, only arriving at Beijing's main east–west artery on the morning of June 4, well after other units had occupied Tiananmen Square. Blocked by angry crowds shouting about the previous night's massacre, the 28th Army's long convoy of trucks and APCs stopped and made no effort to advance.[35] According to General Liu Yazhou, who mentioned the incident in a speech in 2004, General Liu Huaqing was so incensed at the 28th Army's failure to move that he instructed a helicopter to hover over the scene. A voice from the helicopter's loudspeaker ordered the troops, "Advance, advance! Advance no matter what."[36] Wu Renhua has interpreted the words "no matter what" (不顾一切) as an order to open fire on the crowds.[37] He Yanran ignored the helicopter. He supposedly turned to Zhang Mingchun, the political commissar of the 28th Army, and said, "Do you want to go in front of the military tribunal, or should I go?" By 5 p.m. on June 4, troops belonging to the 28th Army had all dispersed. Many abandoned their vehicles, of which seventy-four were burned and destroyed. Zhang and He were demoted.[38]

[35] *LSJ*, 402–405.
[36] Liu Yazhou, "信念与道德" (Beliefs and morality), speech posted online at *Zhongguo baodao zhoukan*, May 28, 2005, china-week.com/html/2498.htm.
[37] *LSJ*, 404.
[38] *LSJ*, 407; John Garnaut, "How Top Generals Refused to March on Tiananmen Square," *Sydney Morning Herald*, June 4, 2010, smh.com.au/world/how-top-generals-refused-to-march-on-tiananmen-square-20100603-x7f0.html.

He Yanran and Xu Feng's refusals saved lives. Imagine how much worse the death toll would have been if He Yanran had told his troops to "advance no matter what," as the helicopter had ordered him to do. This type of passive resistance might have reduced the death toll, but it was too little and too late to prevent the massacre. By the time He and Xu decided that they wanted no part of killing civilians, soldiers from the 38th Army and 15th Airborne had already murdered hundreds.

Compare the actions of He Yanran with another Xu – Xu Qinxian of the 38th Army. Both group army commanders opted out of the crack-down – Xu in late May, He on June 4. Both failed to stop it. Just as they had no stomach for perpetrating a massacre, they had no desire (or saw no way) to orchestrate a military coup. On May 19 or 20, 1989, Xu Qinxian had no way of knowing that his lonely, individual refusal to enforce martial law might have been counterproductive, in that it convinced his superiors to strictly enforce discipline and warned his replacement about the cost of disloyalty. If Xu Qinxian had stayed on the job, continued to lead the 38th Army until June 3, and behaved like He Yanran, moving slowly and pretending that he had never received orders to shoot, who knows how many lives might have been saved? Just as the killing was not inevitable, the scale and scope of the massacre was not set in stone. It did not have to be as bad as it was.

Part Four

Nationwide

18 Han versus Non-Han

Beijing was the heart of the protest movement in 1989. China's capital was where Hu Yaobang died and was mourned, where dialogue between students and central leaders took place, where a hunger strike escalated tensions, where Mikhail Gorbachev visited, where Deng Xiaoping decided to use force, and where the Beijing massacre began on the night of June 3, 1989. Although Beijing was at the center of the democracy movement and the crackdown, it was not isolated from the rest of China. What happened in Beijing sparked protests in every province and autonomous region in China, creating a nationwide movement unprecedented in twentieth-century Chinese history. Likewise, events outside Beijing affected the rise and fall of the movement inside the capital. In fact, clashes in places as far away as Hunan, Shaanxi, and Tibet were decisive in convincing Deng Xiaoping that "turmoil" was threatening Communist Party rule and that martial law was a viable, even desirable, option.

It is impossible to understand the Tiananmen Square protests and crackdown without an account of what happened beyond Beijing. China's size and diversity meant that provinces experienced differences in how protesters acted, what they demanded, and how local leaders responded. The country's ethnic and religious diversity posed challenges to Communist Party leaders as well as to ethnically Han protesters who operated in a framework that was nationalistic, sometimes to the point of being racist. This framework harmed minority groups. The chance to protest, however, buoyed their hopes.

The flow of information and people in April and early May 1989 can best be described as "outside in" – people from outside Beijing pushed events in the capital in new directions. But in the second half of May, and especially in June, things turned "inside out," as people throughout China reacted to martial law and the Beijing massacre. While local officials in some cities, most notably in Chengdu, forcibly suppressed demonstrations, leading to hundreds of deaths, authorities in other places showed that it was possible to handle protests with patience and moderation instead of violence.

"The people's army does not shoot the people." Beijing residents said this phrase many times as they blocked martial law troops trying to enter the city starting on May 20, and again when they confronted soldiers shooting machine guns on June 3 and 4. The slogan sounded good. It might have even prompted some soldiers to hesitate before pulling the trigger. It was, however, historically inaccurate. Men from the People's Liberation Army and People's Armed Police had shot and killed people inside the borders of the People's Republic of China on a number of occasions before June 1989, including the invasion of Chamdo in 1950, in which the PLA killed at least 180 Tibetans; the violent suppression of the Mashan uprising in Guizhou in 1956; and the July 1975 massacre of Hui Muslims in Shadian, Yunnan, when the PLA used fighter jets and artillery in addition to guns and hand-to-hand combat to kill more than 1,500 villagers.[1]

Beijingers might not have known about the PLA's history of violence inside China's borders. Those who were aware probably had difficulty imagining that the army would treat Han people in China's capital the same way it treated ethnic and ethnoreligious minorities in frontier regions. Racist notions of Han superiority, exacerbated by a Marxist-inspired hierarchy that placed the "civilized" Han above "backward" Miao, Tibetans, Uyghurs, and other minorities, were commonplace in the 1980s.[2] So when Beijing civilians insisted that the people's army did not shoot the people, the people they were talking about were Han. A pervasive culture of Han supremacy allowed Han people to demand freedom for themselves while ignoring – or even supporting – state violence against minorities who were also fighting for freedom.

State violence against Tibetans demanding freedom from Han oppression was front-page news in March 1989. Anyone reading *People's Daily* would have known that PAP soldiers had opened fire on protesters in Lhasa. A front-page article stated that on March 5, 1989, public security and PAP forces "initially adopted an attitude of restraint, but when that was ineffective they were forced to open fire." The next day, another article described more gunfire on March 6: "When rioters insisted on doing things their own way and dissuasion did not work, public security

---

[1] Chen Jian, "The Chinese Communist 'Liberation' of Tibet, 1949–51," in *Dilemmas of Victory: The Early Years of the People's Republic of China*, ed. Jeremy Brown and Paul G. Pickowicz (Cambridge, MA: Harvard University Press, 2007), 130–59; Wang Haiguang, "Radical Agricultural Collectivization and Ethnic Rebellion"; Wang Xian, "Islamic Religiosity, Revolution, and State Violence in Southwest China."

[2] Stevan Harrell, "Introduction: Civilizing Projects and the Reaction to Them," in *Cultural Encounters on China's Ethnic Frontiers*, ed. Harrell (Seattle: University of Washington Press, 1995), 3–36.

Figure 18.1 Protesters in Lhasa on March 6, 1989. AFP via
Getty Images.

police were forced to shoot and took resolute measures to control the
situation from developing further." In addition to learning about shots
being fired in Lhasa, readers of *People's Daily* learned that top
Communist Party leaders' response to "rioting" was to declare martial
law and to deploy thousands of PLA troops to arrest protesters and
restore order. Who formally issued the martial law decree? Li Peng.[3]

The people's soldiers shot people in Lhasa three months before they
shot people in Beijing. Eyewitnesses in Lhasa reported that on March
5 several hundred monks and nuns, gearing up to commemorate the
thirtieth anniversary of the 1959 Tibetan uprising, marched on Barkhor
Street. They were shouting pro-independence slogans. When PAP soldiers lobbed bottles into the crowd, protesters threw rocks at the security
forces. That is when PAP soldiers shot at the demonstrators. When
Tibetan residents of Lhasa heard about the shooting, some hit the
streets to protect fellow citizens, leading to more confrontations and
more killings – and foreshadowing what would occur in Beijing in June
1989. Similarities to the Beijing massacre did not end there. According

---

[3] *RMRB*, March 6, 1989, 1; March 7, 1989, 1; March 8, 1989, 1.

to one report, "Some Tibetans were even shot dead in their houses by gunshot[s] coming from the street; a young Tibetan girl died after being hit by a stray bullet while she was making tea in her home."[4] Tang Daxian, a journalist who was working for the United Front in Lhasa at the time, claimed that he had access to a report authored by the Tibet Autonomous Region Public Security Department and Tibet Military Region stating that the violence had killed "387 Lhasa civilians, of whom most died by gunshot," along with "82 religious people."[5]

The massacre of civilians in their homes, along with state violence provoking resistance rather than quelling it, would link March 5 and 6 in Lhasa with June 3 and 4 in Beijing. But there were also important differences between the two atrocities. According to Steve Marshall, who was in Lhasa at the time, gun-wielding PAP soldiers did most of the killing on March 5, 6, and 7, before the official imposition of martial law and before PLA soldiers entered the city. PAP troops' behavior seemed haphazard and aimless. They repeatedly surged forward and shot into crowds, then fell back and ceded control of the streets to Tibetan protesters. After martial law was announced on the night of March 7 and the PLA took control of Lhasa, mass arrests of Tibetans began, but there were no further reports of widespread shooting.[6]

When Deng Xiaoping decided to impose – and Li Peng officially announced – martial law in Beijing in May 1989, they were not doing something new. They were drawing on what they thought had been a successful attempt to combat "turmoil" in Lhasa two months earlier. This precedent surely informed Deng's preference for, and Li's strong support of, a forceful crackdown against protesters in Beijing. In his government work report to the second session of the 7th National People's Congress on March 20, 1989, Li Peng celebrated the efficacy of martial law in Lhasa and credited "support from the people nation-wide" for the attack on "separatists' reactionary fury."[7]

Li may have been correct about broad Chinese support for shooting Tibetans who shouted pro-independence slogans. Protests against martial law in Lhasa came from foreign governments, not from democracy

---

[4] Tibet Information Network, "'A Struggle of Blood and Fire': The Imposition of Martial Law in 1989 and the Lhasa Uprising of 1959, February 25, 1989," savetibet.org/a-struggle-of-blood-and-fire, 2–3.
[5] Tang Daxian, 刺刀直指拉萨: 八九年拉萨事件纪实 (Bayonets pointing at Lhasa: A record of the Lhasa incident of 1989), web.archive.org/web/20170714231717/https://www.chinesepen.org/blog/archives/69059. See also Robert Barnett, "Zhao 'Organised Police Slaughter of Tibetans'," The Guardian, August 13, 1990.
[6] Tibet Information Network, "A Struggle of Blood and Fire," 5–10.
[7] RMRB, April 6, 1989, 3.

advocates inside China. One open demand to rescind martial law came from Tibetan students in Lanzhou, the capital of Gansu Province, more than 1,300 miles from Lhasa. Protests by Tibetans in Lanzhou began after Tibetan and Han students fought each other with rocks, bricks, and beer bottles on May 1, 1989. According to a Ministry of Public Security internal bulletin, the fight started after Tibetan students demanded to use a table tennis table where Han students were playing. Each side in the fight seized hostages; police intervened to stop the violence and release the captives. On May 4, almost two hundred Tibetan students in Lanzhou marched, chanting, "Ethnic equality without discrimination!"[8] On May 11, Tibetan marchers who had traveled from Qinghai Province to Lanzhou carried a banner reading, "We strongly demand cancelling the martial law proclamation in Tibet." That same day a group of Tibetan student representatives presented a list of demands to the Gansu provincial government: Impose the death penalty on the Han students who had beaten up Tibetans. Immediately rescind martial law in Tibet. Dialogue with provincial officials at or above the vice Party secretary and vice governor level.[9]

Ethnic friction or indifference rather than solidarity characterized Han-dominated protests during the late 1980s. I have seen no evidence that Han people linked their demands for freedom to Tibetans' fight for self-determination.[10] To the contrary, when demonstrations ramped up in Nanjing on April 22, 1989, a middle-aged Chinese man approached Richard Lufrano, an American who was observing a student protest, and began "angrily attacking the U.S. Congress's recent resolution condemning China for its occupation of Tibet."[11] Racism and xenophobia were prominent parts of Chinese nationalism in the 1980s. Both might have been present in the man's remark to Lufrano in Nanjing. His comment linked concerns about China's territorial integrity and freedom from foreign interference to racist views about the inferiority of non-Han

---

[8] "兰州气象学校藏汉学生连续发生互殴事件并先后上街游行" (Tibetan and Han students from the Lanzhou Meteorological School repeatedly fight and successively march on the streets), *QZ* [89] 126 (May 5, 1989), web.archive.org/web/20140908203938/blog.boxun .com/hero/201304/xsj14/27_1.shtml.

[9] "青海省二百余名藏族学生到兰州游行请愿" (More than two hundred Tibetan students from Qinghai Province went to Lanzhou to march and petition), *QZ* [89] 143 (May 12, 1989), web.archive.org/web/20190621032424/blog.boxun.com/hero/201304/xsj14/42_1 .shtml.

[10] One exception came in 2008 from Liu Xiaobo, who proposed that the Dalai Lama serve as China's president, in "Obama's Election, the Republican Factor, and a Proposal for China," in Liu Xiaobo, *No Enemies, No Hatred: Selected Essays and Poems*, ed. Perry Link, Tienchi Martin-Liao, and Liu Xia (Cambridge, MA: Harvard University Press, 2012), 270–74.

[11] Richard Lufrano, "Nanjing Spring: The 1989 Student Movement in a Provincial Capital," *Bulletin of Concerned Asian Scholars* 24, no. 1 (January–March 1992): 22.

people. It helps to explain why Han protesters failed to see shooting in Lhasa as a precursor to killing in Beijing. The protest movement in Chinese cities in April, May, and June 1989 called for freedom from the tyranny of the one-party dictatorship but did not link the fight to non-Han people's struggles.

★ ★ ★

The clash between Han and Tibetan students in Lanzhou was reminiscent of even larger racialized fights and protests in Nanjing in December 1988. The late 1988 marches in Nanjing were sparked by a fight between Chinese and African students at Hehai University on Christmas Eve. African students at Hehai chafed at restrictions against hosting Chinese women in their dormitory. When authorities built a wall around the building, African students tore it down. After the wall went up again, foreign students dismantled it a second time, prompting university officials to deduct construction costs from the students' stipends. But the wall stayed down, and eventually the money was returned. Chinese students saw this as evidence that foreigners were getting special treatment.[12] Influenced by long-standing racist theories about the purported superiority of Europeans and Asians over Africans,[13] Chinese students at Hehai were annoyed that African students had loud parties, dated Chinese women, and enjoyed better housing and larger stipends than domestic students did.[14]

Tensions, therefore, were already running high on Christmas Eve, when a student from Benin and another from Liberia attempted to enter the Hehai campus with two Chinese women they had met at a restaurant earlier that evening. When the security guard at the university gate demanded that the women register their names, the men took offense and scuffled with the guard. Chinese students nearby joined the fight. Dossoumou Boni Lodovic of Benin, Alpha Robinson of Gambia, and Alex Dzabaku Dosoo of Ghana were later accused of being involved in the fighting.[15] According to two American students on campus, news about the fight "spread rapidly among the Chinese students at Hehai,"

---

[12] Richard Lufrano, "The 1988 Nanjing Incident: Notes on Race and Politics in Contemporary China," *Bulletin of Concerned Asian Scholars* 26, nos. 1–2 (January–June 1994): 91.

[13] Yinghong Cheng, "From Campus Racism to Cyber Racism: Discourse of Race and Chinese Nationalism," *China Quarterly* 207 (2011): 563–64.

[14] Michael J. Sullivan, "The 1988–89 Nanjing Anti-African Protests: Racial Nationalism or National Racism?", *China Quarterly* 138 (1994): 438.

[15] Jim Abrams, "Expelled African Says He Was Beaten by Police," *Associated Press*, January 15, 1989, apnews.com/c52f50960f115bc1b3fbcb60bab918bf.

and the "foreign dormitory complex was soon surrounded by thousands of angry Chinese students throwing bricks and rocks."[16] The siege continued the next day, punctuated by Chinese students yelling racial slurs and circulating the claim that an African student had killed a Chinese person. The besieged African students feared for their lives. Hoping to flee the city and to secure support from their embassies in Beijing, they managed to walk to the Nanjing train station, but they were not allowed to board a train. Demonstrations and marches by Chinese students over the course of three days centered on the train station and also the provincial government compound, where, according to Lufrano, the "students demanded the punishment of guilty Africans and the equal treatment of foreigners and Chinese under the law, couching these demands in calls for human rights and equal justice."[17] Political scientist Sam Crane argues that some Chinese student organizers of the marches genuinely wanted to push for legal reforms. According to Crane, "Democracy advocates had to try to make something of the situation, since mobilization opportunities are few and far between, but their call for human rights was overwhelmed by racist rhetoric."[18] Human rights activists could not find a way to channel the anger of crowds who menaced the African students by besieging the foreign student dormitory and train station. Protesters seemed more interested in anti-Black vigilantism than in legal procedure.

Eventually, Chinese officials forcibly evacuated foreign students from the train station to a military guesthouse. Protests waned after the targets of racist rage left the city. A Jiangsu Ministry of Education official debunked the rumor that someone had died, and by December 30, 1988, there were no further demonstrations.[19] In the end, three African students were expelled from China for having "instigated" fighting on December 24 and 25. The two Chinese women who refused to show identification at the university gate were sentenced to two years of reeducation through labor, while two of the Hehai University students who had organized the anti-African protests went on to lead the student movement of spring 1989.[20]

Like the anti-Japan protests that roiled multiple Chinese cities in 1985 after Prime Minister Yasuhiro Nakasone paid tribute to Japan's

[16] Lufrano, "The 1988 Nanjing Incident," 87.
[17] Lufrano, "The 1988 Nanjing Incident," 89.
[18] George T. Crane, "Collective Identity, Symbolic Mobilization, and Student Protest in Nanjing, China, 1988–1989," *Comparative Politics* 26, no. 4 (July 1994): 409.
[19] Sullivan, "The 1988–89 Nanjing Anti-African Protests," 454.
[20] Sullivan, "The 1988–89 Nanjing Anti-African Protests," 456; Lufrano, "The 1988 Nanjing Incident," 90.

war dead (including prominent war criminals) at the Yasukuni Shrine in Tokyo,[21] the protests in Nanjing at the end of 1988 were simultaneously antiforeign and antigovernment. Racist anger about African men dating Chinese women overlapped with suspicion that local officials were giving special treatment to foreigners or even protecting an alleged murderer. Nationalistic students criticized the government for appearing weak and incompetent.

Discontent and feelings of impotence were widespread among Chinese university students in 1988 and 1989. The racism at the center of the Nanjing protests, as well as the ethnic tension that characterized fighting between Tibetan and Han students in Lanzhou, showed that, depending on the trigger, frustration could turn into illiberal, menacing violence. During the anti-African marches in Nanjing, local officials banned foreign journalists from the city, sensing the ugliness of the moment and trying to cover it up. But because the targets of the protest were foreign, Nanjing bureaucrats were able to deflect students' legitimate complaints about their substandard living conditions. In the aftermath of the Nanjing clash, for example, the Hehai University president ignored Chinese students' demands and kept the focus on African visitors, issuing even tougher restrictions on foreign students' interactions with Chinese women.[22] Several months later, Communist Party leaders would find it far more difficult to deal with nationalistic protests that directly targeted the government.

★ ★ ★

China's diversity could be seen in violent friction between Han, Tibetans, and foreigners in 1988 and 1989. It was also visible when Uyghur student Örkesh Dölet became one of the main leaders of the movement to reform China's corrupt, repressive government. The high hopes of the 1980s extended to ethnic minorities. According to Nury Turkel, who was in Urumqi at the time, the 1980s were a time of "cultural revival" for Uyghurs. "People were relatively happy and enjoying their daily lives," he remembered.[23]

---

[21] Jessica Weiss Chen, *Powerful Patriots: Nationalist Protest in China's Foreign Relations* (New York: Oxford University Press, 2014), 82.
[22] Sullivan, "The 1988–89 Nanjing Anti-African Protests," 455–56.
[23] Kaiser Kuo, Nury Turkel, and Örkesh Dölet, "A Student Leader 30 Years after Tiananmen: Wu'er Kaixi Reflects on the Movement," *Sinica Podcast*, June 13, 2019, supchina.com/podcast/a-student-leader-30-years-after-tiananmen-wuer-kaixi-reflects-on-the-movement.

Uyghur merchants responded energetically to new economic opportunities, setting up businesses in cities throughout China and cornering the underground foreign currency exchange market. Örkesh remembered how Uyghur mobility and success during the 1980s triggered a racist response among some urban Han:

"Uyghur people, you are kind of cool, you dance, you sing, you make good shish kebab, why don't you just stay in your remote corner, why do you all of a sudden spread to all the cities?" That kind of triggered the discrimination mentality or sensation of the one billion Chinese people.

Örkesh explained, "If you haven't seen a group of people and all of a sudden they are everywhere and you just don't get used to it, the discrimination emerged immediately."[24]

As a student at Beijing Normal University in 1989, Örkesh defied convention. In 1990, a friend described Örkesh's behavior before the student movement erupted in April 1989: "Each night he had only one thing on his mind. He wanted to find a party. If he couldn't find a party, he started his own."[25] Speaking thirty years later, Örkesh reckoned that his upbringing in a Uyghur household instilled in him a spirit of righteous rebelliousness, a willingness to speak up when others were silent. The lesson he learned was, "You have to stand up when someone else is being bullied ... Things like this, you don't find in Chinese, in Han Chinese education."[26] Örkesh said that this is why, on the night of April 17, he made the fateful decision to give a speech to a large gathering of students at Beijing Normal University. When he showed up, the crowd was cursing and waiting for someone to do something. Örkesh called out "make way," and a path to the front of the crowd opened up, where he made a point of saying his Chinese name – Wuerkaixi – his university affiliation, and dormitory number, ensuring that listeners would remember him as a brave rebel.[27] He explained, "In our culture, the way I was brought up ... I just feel in this moment I need to do that, I have to do that, it's an instinctual thing." His speech on April 17 spurred Örkesh to prominence as a leader of the student movement. And although the movement did not emphasize ethnic issues, its collective spirit contributed to a more harmonious atmosphere in Beijing. Örkesh recalled that over the fifty days of protests, he did not feel any discrimination because of his Uyghur background.[28]

---

[24] Kuo, Nury, and Örkesh, "A Student Leader."
[25] Joseph F. Kahn, "Better Fed than Red," *Esquire* 114, no. 3 (September 1990): 190.
[26] Kuo, Nury, and Örkesh, "A Student Leader."
[27] Lim, *People's Republic of Amnesia*, 64.
[28] Kuo, Nury, and Örkesh, "A Student Leader."

During that same period, many Uyghurs and other Muslims through-out China did feel disrespected by the publication of a book called *Sexual Customs* that insulted Islam. Anger at the book sparked large protests in May 1989 that were pointedly separate from student marches but that influenced events nationwide. Protests by Muslims encouraged university students to return to the streets while also reinforcing top leaders' sense that turmoil was coming at them from multiple directions.

Sexual Customs, authored by the pseudonymous Ke Le and Sang Ya, was published by Shanghai Culture Press and Shanxi Hope Books and Periodicals in March 1989. According to anthropologist Dru Gladney, the book "compared minarets to phalli, tombs to vulva, and the pilgrimage to Mecca as an excuse for orgies and sodomy, with camels, no less."[29] On May 6, 1989, censors in Beijing halted sales of the book and ordered the destruction of all existing copies, on the grounds that the book violated China's religious policy. That same day, more than ten thousand Muslims marched in Lanzhou carrying banners written in Arabic and Chinese. One read, "Support the Communist Party." Another demanded, "Execute China's Rushdie," linking *Sexual Customs* to the controversial content of Salman Rushdie's *Satanic Verses*, which had been published in 1988.[30]

Calls to kill the authors of *Sexual Customs* were a clue that banning the book would not be enough to stop protests against it. On May 12, an officially approved march in Beijing that included Uyghur, Hui, Kirghiz, and Khazak representatives demanded the arrest of the book's authors and the closure of Shanghai Culture Press – demands that the state quickly met. Protesters also marched against the book that same day in Hohhot, Lanzhou, and Xining, as illustrated in Figure 18.2. In Lanzhou, people burned more than one hundred copies of the book. They also stormed the provincial government complex, breaking glass and fighting with police. Police arrested thirty-six people, noting that thirty-five of them were Hui and one was Han. In Xining, more than four thousand people marched to the Qinghai provincial leadership compound and staged a sit-in, demanding dialogue with government officials. A delegation of protesters was eventually allowed into the building, where they presented their demands: confiscate all copies of *Sexual*

[29] Dru C. Gladney, "Constructing a Contemporary Uighur National Identity: Transnationalism, Islamicization, and State Representation," *Cahiers d'études sur la Méditerranée orientale et le monde turco-iranien* 13, no. 1 (1992): 165–84.
[30] Ye Lang, "穆斯林们怎么看? 中国的拉什迪事件: 性风俗" (How do Muslims See it? China's Rushdie incident: *Sexual Customs*), August 29, 2008, blog post reposted at douban.com/group/topic/37378495.

Figure 18.2 Protesting against *Sexual Customs* in Beijing on May 12, 1989. Demonstrations against the book also occurred in Hohhot, Lanzhou, Xi'an, Yinchuan, and Urumqi. Catherine Henriette/AFP via Getty Images.

Customs, shut down the publishing house, and execute the book's authors and editors.[31]

Aware of the controversy surrounding the book but hearing no news of government action against its authors or publisher, on May 15 around twenty thousand Muslims marched in Xi'an. Local officials approved the protest. According to Joseph W. Esherick, university students in Xi'an had not taken to the streets in large numbers since May 4, but "no sooner had the Muslims been allowed to demonstrate than the students prepared a massive march of their own … It took the Muslims to break the ban on street theatre in Xi'an."[32]

As it became clear that a quiet ban on *Sexual Customs* was doing nothing to appease anyone, on May 16, authorities in Beijing finally

[31] "五月十二日各地穆斯林学生和群众为抗议性风俗而上街游行的情况" (Muslim students and citizens marching on the streets in various locations on May 12 to protest *Sexual Customs*), *QZ* [89] 144 (May 12, 1989), web.archive.org/web/20140908181054/blog .boxun.com/hero/201304/xsj14/43_1.shtml.
[32] Joseph W. Esherick, "Xi'an Spring," in *The Pro-democracy Protests in China: Reports from the Provinces*, ed. Jonathan Unger (Armonk, NY: Sharpe, 1991), 91.

announced that the book had been banned, 95,240 copies had been destroyed, the publishing house had been shut down, and the authors and editors of the book were being severely punished according to the law. An official from the Shanghai News and Publishing Bureau traveled to Beijing to formally apologize to the Chinese Muslim Association.[33]

This announcement failed to dissuade Muslims from protesting in Urumqi and Yinchuan on May 18. In Yinchuan, capital of the Ningxia Hui Autonomous Region, 4,500 Hui people marched and presented a petition to regional leaders, who "met with these masses."[34] In Urumqi, protesters did not meet with politicians. Instead, they encountered PAP troops who had been ordered by Xinjiang chairman Tömür Dawama to forcibly disperse Muslim demonstrators. Protests in the Xinjiang capital began on the morning of May 18, when around thirty thousand people, many of them university students, marched in support of the hunger strike in Beijing. According to a report by PAP officials, the students were joined by "some Muslim masses, who used *Sexual Customs*, which Party Center had already dealt with long ago, as an excuse to demonstrate about religious issues."[35]

Protests dispersed without incident on May 18, but the next day even larger crowds turned out. When students left Urumqi's main square around 5:30 p.m., several thousand "Muslim masses" marched in and listened to what an official report labeled as "inflammatory speeches." Just before 7 p.m., several hundred protesters besieged the Xinjiang People's Congress and Party headquarters, breaking 7,300 panes of glass and damaging forty-nine vehicles. A fire truck cleared a path through the crowds for more than 650 PAP troops, who used tear gas and nonlethal weapons in three waves of "counterattacks" to disperse people, arresting at least fifty-one.[36] According to Dru Gladney, several Uyghurs who had been arrested for their role in the May 19 protests remained in prison several years later. This seemed unfair to Uyghurs. While Hui in other parts of China had enjoyed government approval and support when they protested against *Sexual Customs*, Uyghurs seemed to have been singled out for harsh treatment.[37]

[33] *RMRB*, May 16, 1989, 2.

[34] "陕西等十二省区五月十八日游行情况" (Demonstrations in Shaanxi and eleven other provinces and autonomous regions on May 18), *QZ* [89] 163 (May 18, 1989), web .archive.org/web/20140908202520/blog.boxun.com/hero/201304/xsj14/62_1.shtml.

[35] Zhongguo renmin wuzhuang jingcha budui silingbu, ed., 处置突发事件战例选编 (制乱平暴专辑) (Selected battle reports on handling sudden incidents (special issue on controlling chaos and suppressing riots)) (n.p., 1990), 89. Reprinted by SCCP, 2009.

[36] Zhongguo renmin wuzhuang jingcha budui silingbu, 处置突发事件战例选编 (Selected battle reports on handling sudden incidents), 90–92.

[37] Gladney, "Constructing a Contemporary Uighur National Identity," 167.

The Muslim reaction to *Sexual Customs*, along with the Lhasa massacre and anti-African protests in Nanjing, have become sidebars in the overall history of 1988 and 1989, marginal stories overwhelmed by the world's focus on the student movement and massacre in Beijing. This is unfortunate. For Muslims in China, insults to their religion were central, not marginal. For Tibetans, the Lhasa massacre was as traumatizing as the Beijing massacre was for residents in China's capital. And the racism directed toward African students in Nanjing, as well as toward China's ethnic minorities, reflected the underlying reality of China during the 1980s. Student protest leaders and top Communist Party officials alike wanted a strong China led by educated, urban Han men who would stand up to foreigners' arrogance and protect the motherland's territorial integrity. But for all the flaws in the Han-centric, male-dominated, city-based democracy movement, ethnic minorities who watched and participated in the events of spring 1989 recognized the possibility of real change. A more transparent, less repressive government, even one dominated by nationalistic Han, would have been a welcome change. Describing the mood of Uyghurs protesting on the streets of Urumqi in May 1989, Nury Turkel said, "If this is successful, we will have a better life."[38]

[38] Kuo, Nury, and Örkesh, "A Student Leader."

19   Outside In

According to political scientist James Tong, the protests of 1989 were the "first nationwide defiant social movement in contemporary China."[1] Provinces and municipalities that led the way, where protests started earlier in April and occurred frequently thereafter, included Shanghai, Tianjin, Jiangsu, Hunan, Sichuan, Shaanxi, Liaoning, Anhui, Zhejiang, and Guangdong. There were fewer protests in Tibet, Ningxia, Xinjiang, Guangxi, and Jiangxi, and they did not erupt until May 16. Tong's spatial analysis of the protests shows that every province and autonomous region in China experienced demonstrations. Tong finds that protests were larger and more frequent in provincial capitals, in cities with more university students, in areas of greater commercialization, and in places that had more direct communication and transportation links to Beijing.

Sociologist Jonathan Unger's edited collection of firsthand accounts of protests in the provinces shows the extent to which people outside Beijing took "cues from events in the capital."[2] News of marches, slogans, autonomous organizations, dialogue between students and officials, and hunger strikes in Beijing, conveyed by phone, fax, and foreign broadcasts, sparked similar efforts in other cities. Many people throughout China, especially in large cities, paid close attention to and were inspired by events in Beijing. But sometimes events and people outside the capital affected what was happening in Beijing and pushed the movement in unexpected directions. In an "outside-in" dynamic, people from all over China provided energy and ideas that fueled the protest movement. In addition, violence and vandalism in Xi'an and Changsha on April 22 helped Deng Xiaoping and Li Peng make the case that turmoil had already occurred and that a harsh crackdown was necessary to prevent it from spreading further.

---

[1] James Tong, "The 1989 Democracy Movement in China: A Spatial Analysis of City Participation," *Asian Survey* 38, no. 3 (March 1998): 325.
[2] Jonathan Unger, "Introduction," in *The Pro-democracy Protests in China*, 3.

Before April 15, 1989, it was not obvious that Beijing would become
the center of a nationwide protest movement. In 1986, student demonstrations began far away from Beijing and focused on local issues. On
November 5, 1986, more than ten thousand students marched in
Changsha, Hunan. They managed to gain an audience with provincial
governor Xiong Qingquan. Around a dozen student representatives met
with Xiong to discuss two specific demands: first, when Hunan Normal
University hired math professor Wei Liren away from Hunan University,
Wei's original employer retaliated against him by sending workers to
force him out of his apartment, assaulting him in the process. The
students wanted the perpetrators brought to justice. The students'
second complaint was that cafeteria food was disgusting and needed to
be improved. Governor Xiong laughed about the canteen slop but said
he would look into it. Xiong also acted on the first issue, punishing Wei's
attackers.

According to Tang Baiqiao, a student at Hunan Normal who was at
the meeting, "The precedent of our campaign had rippled clear across
China." Tang meant that the Changsha students' victory signaled that
large marches targeting provincial leadership compounds could get
results.[3] The next month, in December 1986, protests at the University
of Science and Technology in Hefei, Anhui, focused on the right of
students to nominate People's Congress candidates. Demonstrations
then spread to Wuhan and Shanghai.[4] Students did protest in Beijing
in 1986, but they were reacting to a trend that had started outside
the capital.

University students throughout China reacted simultaneously to the
death of Hu Yaobang on April 15, 1989. In Xi'an on April 20, thousands
of students stormed the Shaanxi provincial government compound.
A delegation of students met with provincial officials and issued
demands: improve education in Shaanxi and explain why Hu Yaobang
had been purged in 1987. On April 21, the day before Hu's funeral in
Beijing, students in Xi'an left a wreath in front of the provincial government building.[5] According to *Shaanxi Daily*, around 10:30 p.m. one
hundred people of "unclear identity" (a euphemism for nonstudents)
put the wreath on a three-wheeled cart and pushed it through city streets,
throwing rocks at buses and overturning two taxis. The procession

---

[3] Baiqiao Tang, *My Two Chinas: The Memoir of a Chinese Counterrevolutionary* (New York:
Prometheus, 2011), 53–57.
[4] Julia Kwong, "The 1986 Student Demonstrations in China: A Democratic Movement?",
Asian Survey 28, no. 9 (September 1988): 970–85.
[5] Joseph W. Esherick, "Xi'an Spring," in *The Pro-democracy Protests in China*, 82.

headed to the train station, where looters stole cigarettes, fruit, and drinks before police arrived and detained eighteen people.[6]

On April 22, the day of Hu Yaobang's funeral, more than forty thousand people gathered at Xincheng Square in Xi'an. Around 1 p.m., a group of protesters forced their way through a police line and tried to get to the provincial government headquarters. Two hours later, the compound's gatehouse was on fire; shortly thereafter, two large trucks went up in flames. At 7:25 p.m., a smaller group of protesters broke into the provincial procuracy and courthouse, setting buildings and vehicles on fire. Half an hour later, five thousand police forcibly cleared protesters from Xincheng Square, arresting 164 people, including 31 university students.[7] According to student accounts, the police clubbed and beat people who were trying to flee the violence.[8]

The next day, top leaders in Beijing received a bulletin from the Ministry of Public Security detailing the "severe beating, smashing, looting, and burning incident" in Xi'an, which reportedly injured more than 150 security officers.[9] They also read a separate bulletin about events in Changsha on April 22. The Changsha protests mirrored what happened in Xi'an: people stormed the provincial government headquarters, trashing six offices. Later that evening, groups of protesters broke off from a crowd of ten thousand who had gathered in Changsha's May First Square, reportedly trashing and looting stores and smashing up the train station. At 1 a.m. on April 23, more than four hundred security officers arrived. It took them one hour to disperse the crowd, out of which 108 people were arrested. Top leaders in Beijing reading the bulletin learned that twenty-five police were injured in Changsha.[10] The official reports I have seen do not mention civilian injuries in either Changsha or Xi'an. Protesters in Xi'an disputed the government's account of what happened on April 22, saying that eleven or thirteen civilians had died and posting photographs of police "kicking and beating bloodied students."[11]

---

[6] Sichuan ribao bianji bu, 学潮, 动乱, 暴乱 *Xuechao, dongluan, baoluan* (Student movement, turmoil, riot) (Chengdu: Sichuan renmin chubanshe, 1989), 21.

[7] "西安市发生严重打砸抢烧事件" (A severe incident of beating, smashing, looting, and burning occurred in Xi'an), *QZ* [89] 106 (April 23, 1989), web.archive.org/web/20180911183142/blog.boxun.com/hero/201304/xsj14/9_1.shtml.

[8] Esherick, "Xi'an Spring," 85.

[9] "西安市发生严重打砸抢烧事件" (A severe incident of beating, smashing, looting, and burning occurred in Xi'an).

[10] "少数不法分子在长沙制造打砸抢事件" (A small number of lawless elements created a beating, smashing, and looting incident in Changsha), *QZ* [89] 108 (April 23, 1989), web.archive.org/web/20180911190856/blog.boxun.com/hero/201304/xsj14/11_1.shtml.

[11] Esherick, "Xi'an Spring," 85–86.

Li Peng expressed serious concern about rioting in the two provincial capitals, writing in his diary on April 22 that the Central Military Commission had approved sending four thousand troops to Xi'an to assist the police.[12] After ordering the PLA to occupy Lhasa a month earlier, top leaders were once again quick to mobilize troops in case they were needed to suppress civilian unrest in Shaanxi. While the soldiers sent to Xi'an did not shoot protesters there, readying the army to move against demonstrators was a first resort on April 22, not a last one. Deng Xiaoping had authorized military force in Lhasa in March and moved troops to Xi'an in April. Ordering soldiers to kill civilians in Beijing never needed to happen, but the path toward the massacre of June 3 and 4 seems less surprising in light of how quickly Deng turned to the army as a solution in March and April 1989.

Commenting on the riots in Changsha, Li Peng noted that "lawless people" had stirred up "pandemonium" by overturning vehicles and injuring police. "A riot this severe has been unheard of since the Cultural Revolution," Li appended to his diary entry dated April 23. "Rioting accompanying the student movement has a lot of momentum that is spreading nationwide."[13] On April 25, Li Peng went to Deng Xiaoping's residence and reported to Deng about the situation. According to Li, Deng "confirmed that this is turmoil aimed at negating the Communist Party's leadership and the socialist system."[14] Before Li Peng talked to Deng Xiaoping about his sense that unrest was spreading throughout China, Deng was already inclined to treat protesters harshly. The meeting on April 25 confirmed Deng's preference for a tough response. The third sentence of the April 26 editorial in *People's Daily*, which was largely adapted from Deng's comments at his home on April 25, prominently mentioned the severe "beating, smashing, looting, and burning incidents in Xi'an and Changsha" as an example of how the "abnormal situation" following Hu Yaobang's death had spiraled out of control.[15]

Students in Xi'an criticized the official version of the April 22 events, arguing that police had violently suppressed a largely peaceful march. One of the main aims of their protests afterward was to push provincial leaders to investigate the matter and provide a more truthful account. Similarly, after April 26, students throughout China demanded that the *People's Daily* article calling the movement turmoil be retracted. The one-sided official versions of events in Changsha and Xi'an contributed to the

[12] *LP*, 73.   [13] *LP*, 75.   [14] *LP*, 84.   [15] *RMRB*, April 26, 1989, 1.

harsh tone of the April 26 editorial, heightening conflict between protesters and Party leaders.

Another way in which the provinces affected the capital is the leadership role played by outsiders. Of the twenty-one student leaders on the Ministry of Public Security's arrest order issued on June 13, 1989, only Örkesh Dölet, Wang Chaohua, and Wang Dan were born in Beijing.[16] Most of the others grew up elsewhere and moved to Beijing for college: Chai Ling grew up in Shandong, Feng Congde in Sichuan, Xiong Yan in Hunan. The students who were wanted for arrest were an elite group of nineteen men and two women (the gender imbalance among student leaders on the arrest order mirrored male-dominated hierarchies in Chinese institutions during the 1980s, including the top leadership of the Communist Party). They had been the top academic performers in their hometowns and tested into China's best universities. Their backgrounds reflect the diversity of the country's culture and geography. Chai Ling described Xiong Yan as a "law student from a peasant family in Hunan ... His passion, his direct temperament and fearless personality, and his resounding Hunan accent endeared him to us all."[17] Wang Zhengyun, another student who ended up on the most-wanted list, was a member of the Kucong ethnicity from Yunnan Province who was attending the Central Institute of Nationalities in Beijing.

Student leaders' diverse experiences growing up outside Beijing gave them an awareness of the nationwide scope of China's problems. But even though Beijing-based student organizations were mostly led by non-Beijingers, they held themselves apart from the influx of university students from the provinces who poured into the capital to offer support. Li Lu, from Nanjing University, was the only student from a university outside Beijing who was on the arrest order. Li grew up in Tangshan in Hebei Province and had been involved in student protests in Nanjing in 1987 and again in April 1989. Discouraged by the April 26 editorial's repressive tone, Li thought that "it had become impossible to carry on the movement in Nanjing," so he decided to travel to Beijing as a "last try."[18] Li had what Chai Ling called "important contacts in Beijing" and by mid-May had become "one of the core leaders at Tiananmen Square." Chai recalled meeting Li around May 1 on the Peking University campus, where "he'd come to offer ideas and suggestions."[19] But Li repeatedly encountered suspicion because he was an outsider who

---

[16] *RMRB*, June 14, 1989, 2. The arrest order erroneously stated that Wang Dan was from Jilin Province; Wang was born in Beijing.
[17] Chai Ling, *Heart*, 105.   [18] Li Lu, *Moving the Mountain*, 115–16.
[19] Chai Ling, *Heart*, 147.

carried no identification. He had left his ID behind because he thought it would get him in trouble if he were arrested on the train from Nanjing to Beijing.[20]

Li Lu was one of the hundreds of thousands of university students who boarded a train to Beijing during the protests of 1989, but his ascension in the leadership ranks was a rare exception. When outsiders tried to offer help to the Beijing Students' Autonomous Federation or the Hunger Strike Committee, or to discuss links between Beijing and protest movements in the provinces, they could not get through. Tang Baiqiao had been elected chair of the Changsha Students' Autonomous Federation on May 4, 1989, after he gave a rousing speech in front of thousands in the city's main square, accusing his university's vice president of "kidnapping" him for four hours that morning to keep him away from the protests. On May 11, the group decided to send Tang to Beijing to lend support and to learn from the capital's students. Tang arrived in Beijing on May 14.[21] He enjoyed the capital's street marches but was frustrated by the lack of interaction between Beijing students and those from the provinces.

Tang had a friend in Beijing, but he had arrived too late to connect with him. Tang never met his contact because "he'd sequestered himself in Tiananmen Square, along with about three thousand other high-level student leaders participating in the hunger strike ... I thought this move ridiculous, a brand-new form of elitism." Tang was mad. "Hurray for you, Beijing! You've replaced governmental insularity with your own," Tang wrote. "By secluding yourself, you cannot unite the nation that stands behind you."[22] Although Tang never got to talk to Beijing student leaders, he did meet with leaders from the provinces who shared his disappointment at the lack of solidarity between capital and hinterland. Tang left Beijing on the night of May 19 and refocused his energy on the local movement in Changsha after his return.

Even though new arrivals from the provinces largely failed in their attempts to work together with Beijing student leaders in May 1989, their presence added to top Communist Party officials' fears of instability. Earlier on May 19, the day of Tang Baiqiao's departure, approximately 304,000 university students had arrived in Beijing on fifty-one separate trains.[23] The Ministry of Public Security reported these numbers to top central leaders in an internal bulletin. Three days later,

[20] Li Lu, *Moving the Mountain*, 116–17.   [21] Tang, *My Two Chinas*, 86–91.
[22] Tang, *My Two Chinas*, 97.
[23] "五月十九日外地动态" (Developments in other parts of the country on May 19), *QZ* [89] 167 (May 19, 1989), http://web.archive.org/web/20140908200008/blog.boxun .com/hero/201304/xsj14/65_1.shtml.

on May 22, leaders reading the security bulletin learned that more than four hundred students in Taiyuan tried to force their way onto a Beijing-bound train. When railway workers would not let them board, thirty students lay down on the tracks. Local officials eventually won one battle, convincing the protesters to stop blocking the train. But they lost the other battle: more than four hundred students got on the train and headed to the capital. That same day, in Inner Mongolia, more than a thousand protesters in Baotou forced their way on to a train to Beijing; at least six hundred people in Hohhot did the same.[24]

Learning about thousands of young people pushing their way onto trains without buying tickets must have reminded top officials of 1966 and 1967, when youths rode the rails for free, visiting Beijing for massive Red Guard rallies and spreading the Cultural Revolution throughout China in what was called the "Great Exchange of Revolutionary Experiences" (大串联).[25] Disruptions to China's rail traffic, as well as the impact of hundreds of thousands of visitors to Beijing, deepened Deng Xiaoping and Li Peng's sense that the protest movement was a chaotic contagion. Li Peng remembered Deng saying at the May 17 meeting, when Deng decided to implement martial law, "We have to stop outsiders from coming to Beijing and we cannot allow turmoil to spread to the rest of the country."[26]

The next day, mechanic Lu Decheng, photographer Yu Dongyue, and teacher Yu Zhijian arrived in Beijing on a train from Hunan. Their agenda in Liuyang that spring had been to denounce authoritarianism and promote democracy; they hoped to add their voices to the protests in the capital. Yu Dongyue and Yu Zhijian wrote a proclamation calling for a general strike and attempted to deliver it to student leaders in Tiananmen Square by passing it to guards who were keeping outsiders out. They wanted their manifesto to be broadcast on loudspeakers, but nothing happened. On May 23, 1989, the three decided to make a decisive statement that nobody could ignore. They bought eggshells from a crepe vendor, filled the empty shells with paint, turpentine, and egg whites, and walked to Chairman Mao's portrait on the north side of Tiananmen Square. There, they posted slogans under Mao's portrait at the Gate of Heavenly Peace ("Five thousand years of dictatorship are

---

[24] "五月二十二日外地动态" (Developments in other parts of the country on May 22), *QZ* [89] 180 (May 22, 1989), web.archive.org/web/20140908211922/blog.boxun.com/hero/201304/xsj14/78_1.shtml.
[25] Roderick MacFarquhar and Michael Schoenhals, *Mao's Last Revolution* (Cambridge, MA: Harvard University Press, 2006), 110–13.
[26] *LP*, 174.

now over" and "The personality cult ends today") and threw the paint-filled egg bombs at Mao's huge face.[27]

According to Chai Ling, "This unimaginable act of sacrilege sent shock waves through the Square. This was an act the government could have used to accuse the movement of anti-Communist, counterrevolutionary turmoil. The three men were immediately apprehended, and to my regret, a zealous student leader handed them over to the police."[28] Lu Decheng, Yu Dongyue, and Yu Zhijian had finally caught student leaders' attention, but not in the way they had hoped. Members of the student groups' own security organization detained the three egg throwers, worried that they might have been agents sent by the government to provoke a crackdown.

Yu Zhijian explained that they had targeted the most prominent symbol of the Communist dictatorship "to motivate the student leadership to question the legitimacy of the Communist regime itself, and therefore its very authority to impose a state of martial law." The students were not impressed. Guo Haifang, a graduate student from Peking University, delivered the three men to a police station. Guo told police that he was secretary-general of the Beijing Students' Autonomous Federation and refused to leave until police gave him a document certifying that they had detained the egg throwers.[29] Lu Decheng eventually received a sixteen-year sentence, Yu Dongyue was sentenced to twenty years' imprisonment, and Yu Zhijian got a life sentence. Guo Haifang and other student leaders seemed to be on the same page as Deng Xiaoping when it came to the way they viewed disruptive outsiders coming to Beijing and trying to radicalize the protest movement.

By the end of May, more students were leaving Beijing than were entering the capital; on May 28, 1,080 students arrived and 10,700 left.[30] This was in part because of official efforts to stop protesters from boarding trains to the capital and also because the movement seemed to be quieting down in Beijing. Not wanting to lose momentum, a group of students in Nanjing decided to make a grand gesture that did not require mass transportation: a "long march" north from Nanjing to Beijing, spreading the message of the democracy movement to villages and towns along the way. Eight hundred students started walking north on the morning of June 1, sent off by more than twenty thousand

[27] Chong, *Egg*, 208, 214–15, 238–39.   [28] Chai Ling, *Heart*, 159.
[29] Chong, *Egg*, 47–49.
[30] "五月二十七日各地动态许多高校学生准备二十八日组织'全球华人大游行'" (Developments elsewhere on May 27, many university students are preparing a "great global march of Chinese people" on May 28), *QZ* [89] 194 (May 28, 1989), web.archive.org/web/20140908192339/blog.boxun.com/hero/201304/xsj14/92_1.shtml.

onlookers as they marched from Drum Tower Square toward the Nanjing Yangzi River Bridge.[31] Local officials and police officers tried to stop student marchers and reportedly even told vendors in towns along the route to not sell the students food or drink.[32] By 8:40 p.m. on June 2, 1989, the marchers had reached Chuzhou in Anhui Province, more than thirty-four miles from their starting point. Jiangsu provincial officials met them there and persuaded around 180 of the students to return to Nanjing, but more than 700 students were determined to keep marching north.[33] The next night, news of the Beijing massacre meant that the march would not be as long as its organizers had hoped.

Protests in Changsha and Xi'an on April 22, plus hundreds of thousands of people forcing their way onto trains to the capital in May, along with Nanjing students' attempted march north on June 1, shaped top leaders' perception and handling of the protests in 1989. Events outside Beijing affected decision making in the capital. But even though most student leaders in Beijing were born and raised elsewhere, they did not pay much attention to events and people from the provinces during April and May 1989 – their concern was changing China as a whole by targeting China's top leadership and occupying Tiananmen Square. A different dynamic was at play in provincial capitals and hinterland towns. People closely followed events in the capital, reacting to news from Beijing and adapting protest strategies to local conditions.

---

[31] "六月一日外地动态" (Developments in other parts of the country on June 1), QZ [89] 205 (June 2, 1989), web.archive.org/web/20190726013102/blog.boxun.com/hero/201304/xsj14/111_1.shtml.
[32] Lufrano, "Nanjing Spring," 33.
[33] "六月二日外地动态" (Developments in other parts of the country on June 2), QZ [89] 207 (June 3, 1989), web.archive.org/web/20130414093239/blog.boxun.com/hero/201304/xsj14/113_1.shtml.

20　Inside Out

Protesters in the provinces wanted a more transparent government that was accountable to citizens and that protected local interests. They were angry about corruption. They hated the police brutality that had occurred in such places as Changsha and Xi'an. They wanted newspapers to print the truth instead of calling patriots rioters. And they wanted to show support for protesters in Beijing. Many simply wanted to vent their anger and frustration. Where better to vent than at the largest symbol of local power in each city or town?

Inside and outside Beijing, protesters occupied large public squares and targeted Communist Party and government leadership compounds. In Beijing, students yelled slogans and pushed guards at Xinhua Gate, the entrance to Zhongnanhai, but never managed to break in. In addition to Changsha and Xi'an, where demonstrators vandalized offices belonging to the Party-state on April 22, many other cities throughout China experienced attacks on leadership headquarters. Sometimes protesters surged past guards and rampaged, sometimes they failed to breach police lines, other times they delivered petitions and spoke with government officials.

At 1 a.m. on May 4, 1989, in Guiyang, the capital of Guizhou Province, more than seven hundred marchers arrived at the Party-government headquarters. Somebody reportedly shouted, "Overthrow Governor Wang Zhaowen!" After that, protesters made three futile attempts to push past guards and enter the compound. By 3 a.m., everyone had given up and left.[1] On May 11 in Taiyuan, the capital of Shanxi Province, more than eight thousand demonstrators targeted provincial Party headquarters. After failing to breach police lines, they

---

[1] "五月四日全国十九个城市九万余名高校学生上街游行" (More than ninety thousand university students marched in nineteen cities on May 4), *QZ* [89] 125 (May 4, 1989), web.archive.org/web/20160703175653/blog.boxun.com/hero/201304/xsj14/26_1.shtml.

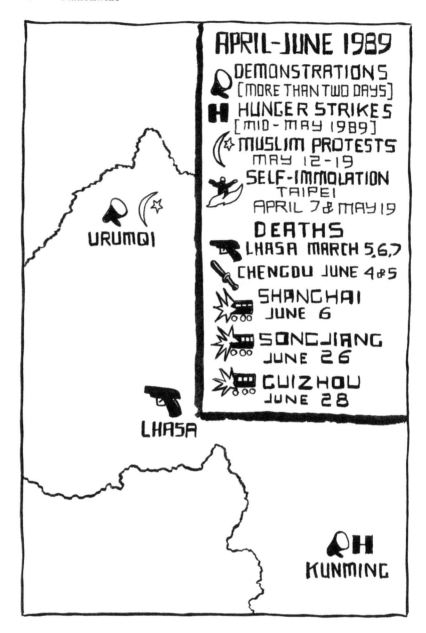

Figure 20.1 Protests and violence beyond Beijing in 1989. Illustrated by Danny Frazier.

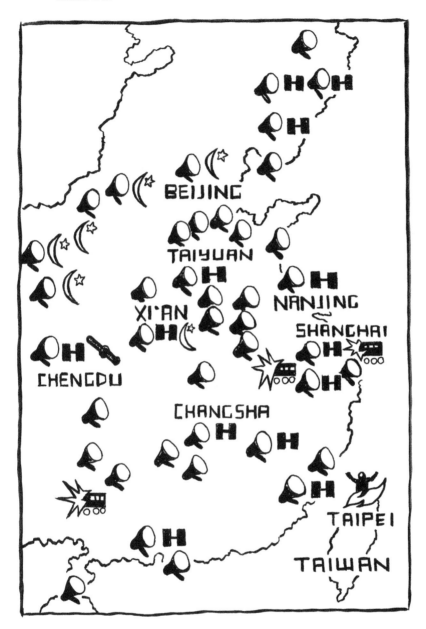

Figure 20.1 (*cont.*)

tore down the Shanxi Provincial Party Committee and Shanxi Provincial Government's name placards.[2]

The high tide of sieges of leadership compounds happened on May 17 and 18, when people moved by the hunger strike in Beijing – and by parallel hunger strikes in the provinces – pressured local officials to tell Party Center to meet the hunger strikers' demands. Face-offs at the gates of provincial Party headquarters happened in Chengdu, Fuzhou, Jinan, Kunming, Nanchang, Taiyuan, and Zhengzhou on May 17. Henan's vice governor emerged to speak with demonstrators in Zhengzhou; Jiangxi's provincial governor Wu Guanzheng came out to ask students to return to their campuses in Nanchang. Only in Kunming did protesters manage to get inside that day – the Yunnan provincial governor ordered guards to open the gates because it was so crowded that people were climbing walls and gathering on nearby roofs. Students entered the courtyard and stayed for a while, until officials eventually persuaded them to leave.[3]

On May 18 protesters targeted Party compounds in multiple provincial capitals including Guiyang, Jilin, Nanchang, Nanjing, Xi'an, and Xining. More than three thousand students made it inside the gates in Nanjing; seven hundred people entered the Party-government courtyard in Jilin. In Xi'an protesters went inside the Shaanxi provincial compound as well, where they marched around and burned an effigy of a top Party leader.[4] When demonstrators forced their way into Party and government offices, local leaders could accuse them of criminal behavior and call in the police. It was more challenging to deal with university students who said they would refuse to eat until the government agreed to dialogue and acknowledged the legitimacy of the student movement.

★ ★ ★

Hunger strikes were a nationwide phenomenon in May 1989. As Table 20.1 shows, protesters staged hunger strikes in at least thirteen cities outside Beijing. They set up encampments in central squares or at

---

[2] "五月十一日各地高校动态" (Developments in universities all over the country on May 11), *QZ* [89] 141 (May 11, 1989), web.archive.org/web/20140908210218/blog.boxun .com/hero/201304/xsj14/40_1.shtml.

[3] "五月十七日各地游行示威情况" (Marches and demonstrations throughout the country on May 17), *QZ* [89] 157 (May 17, 1989), web.archive.org/web/20140908194833/blog .boxun.com/hero/201304/xsj14/56_1.shtml; "云南, 江西一些院校的学生五月十七日上街 游行" (Some university students marched in Yunnan and Jiangxi on May 17), *QZ* [89] 161 (May 18, 1989), web.archive.org/web/20140908174624/blog.boxun.com/hero/ 201304/xsj14/59_1.shtml.

[4] "陕西等十二省区五月十八日游行情况" (Demonstrations in Shaanxi and eleven other provinces and autonomous regions on May 18).

Table 20.1. *Hunger strikes in the provinces, May–June 1989*

City	Number of hunger strikers reported	Approximate dates	Sources
Xi'an	1,300+	May 18	QZ
Hangzhou	700+	May 19	QZ
Taiyuan	500+	May 16–20	QZ; 山西日报 (Shanxi Daily)
Changchun	200+	May 18–20	QZ; Unger, *Pro-democracy Protests in China*, 61.
Changsha	200+	June 1	QZ
Jilin	150	May 18	QZ
Kunming	120	May 19	QZ
Shanghai	100	May 17	QZ
Changsha	60+	May 17–21	湖南日报 (Hunan Daily); Tang, *My Two Chinas*, 92; QZ
Nanjing	59	May 17–19	Lufrano, "Nanjing Spring," 27; QZ
Nanchang	25	May 18	QZ
Shenyang	21	May 18	Unger, *Pro-democracy Protests in China*, 70
Chengdu	?	May 15	Lim, *Amnesia*, 183
Guangzhou	?	?	He, *Tiananmen Exiles*, 71, 73
Xiamen	?	May 17–19	Unger, *Pro-democracy Protests in China*, 158

the gates of leadership compounds. Describing the impetus of the hunger strike in Changsha, Tang Baiqiao wrote that nonviolent action allowed protesters to claim the moral high ground. "By practicing self-deprivation, you show your opponent the strength of your convictions," Tang wrote. "You are saying you'd rather harm yourself than anyone else when effecting change." The Changsha Students' Autonomous Federation decided to start its own hunger strike in a gesture of solidarity with the hunger strikers in Beijing.[5]

A photograph of calm-looking students sitting cross-legged underneath a banner reading "Hunger strike" appeared on the front page of *Hunan Daily* on May 19. A large poster reading "Long live the students" lay on the ground beside them. The newspaper's friendly portrayal of the hunger strike in Changsha reflected a fleeting moment of press freedom and honest reporting about the widespread sympathy people in Chinese cities felt toward students' self-sacrifice. Local leaders felt pressure to appear sympathetic. Officials from the Hunan Party Committee and provincial government met with *Hunan Daily* editors on May 18, 1989,

---

[5] Tang, *My Two Chinas*, 91.

to state that they cared deeply about the hunger strikers' health and had organized medical teams to treat them. The provincial leaders said that they appreciated students' demands to strengthen democracy and the rule of law and would work to address them, but that the only way to do so would be in a stable environment: "The Party Committee and provincial government hopes that the hunger-striking students will look after their health, end the hunger strike, and return to school as soon as possible."[6]

Local news coverage in Taiyuan also played up leaders' concern about protesters who refused to eat. When more than eighty students from Shanxi Finance Academy began a hunger strike on the morning of May 16 in front of the main gate of the provincial leadership compound, deputy governor Wu Dacai and other officials emerged and tried to persuade the students to return to campus. Around 6 p.m. that day, Governor Wang Senhao, not quite understanding the point of a hunger strike, ordered his staff to provide food and water to the students. The students did not touch the supplies. At 11 p.m., Wang himself came to speak to the students, urging them to take care of their health and to go back to school.[7] Two days later, Shanxi Party secretary Li Ligong said that provincial leaders were "very sad" that the hunger strikers had refused to eat and drink the food and beverages that provincial leaders had sent to them.[8]

The collective hunger strikes in provincial capitals mostly concluded with fearful declarations of "victory" after the imposition of martial law in Beijing on May 19, 1989. In Taiyuan, students announced the end of their hunger strike at 12:30 a.m. on May 20. An hour later they had all left the encampment at the gates of the Shanxi provincial leadership compound. News of martial law in Beijing marked the beginning of a new, uncertain phase in the protest movement in the provinces. It ended hunger strikes and also cut short dialogue between local leaders and student representatives.

★ ★ ★

After *People's Daily* reported on the April 29, 1989, dialogue meeting in Beijing, protesters in the provinces demanded dialogue with local leaders, who often said yes. But unlike the sense of victory Tang Baiqiao felt in 1986 after his impromptu meeting with Hunan's top

---

[6] 湖南日报 (Hunan Daily), May 19, 1989, 1.
[7] 山西日报 (Shanxi Daily), May 17, 1989, 3.
[8] 山西日报 (Shanxi Daily), May 19, 1989, 1.

leader, students in 1989 were not satisfied with the results of meetings with provincial leaders. They wanted to set the terms of the meetings. They wanted to speak with the top leader of the province, not random underlings who talked down to them. They wanted to be listened to.

Dialogue in the provinces often focused on procedure: which leaders would attend, what an equal dialogue should look like, and when the next meeting would occur. Students also frequently demanded that local officials properly define the nature of the protests and label protesters as patriots trying to help China, not as criminals sowing chaos. These topics mirrored discussions in Beijing. Local issues, however, also arose during provincial dialogue meetings.

In Taiyuan on May 8, 1989, Li Zhenhua, secretary-general of the Shanxi provincial government, led a delegation of six officials in dialogue with twenty-five student representatives from eight universities.[9] Li's status as secretary-general (秘书长) meant that he was a mid-level functionary lower in rank than a deputy governor, but he spoke authoritatively about whatever issues the students raised. A student from the Taiyuan Institute of Technology opened with a request that workers, farmers, intellectuals, and people from other sectors of society also get regular opportunities for dialogue with government leaders – a rare example of a student's asking for a specific, longer-term systemic change that went beyond the student movement itself. Li Zhenhua was quick to agree, saying, "from now on we will start dialogue at multiple levels and through multiple channels." Li also quickly accepted another student's demand for dialogue "at least twice a year."

Li was apologetic about the topic that dominated the meeting: students' anger that even though Shanxi was one of the poorest provinces in China, provincial leaders had recently built themselves a luxurious office building. If the economic situation in Shanxi were better, it would be acceptable to celebrate opening a fancy building by lighting firecrackers, the student from the Taiyuan Institute for Technology said. But it was hypocritical for the provincial Party committee to do so while talking about "being thrifty" and "sharing adversity" with the people of Shanxi. Later during the meeting, a student from Shanxi University demanded that the provincial leadership openly apologize about the cost of the construction project; another student said that a "monument of disgrace" should be erected in front of the building so that visitors would always remember leaders' profligacy.

---

[9] In this and the following three paragraphs, all details about and quotes from the May 8 dialogue in Taiyuan are from 山西日报 (Shanxi Daily), May 9, 1989, 1, 3.

Li Zhenhua explained the need for a new office building and detailed its costs. He admitted that planners had gotten carried away – they compared themselves with other provinces and wanted a facility on par with the best ones nationwide. This was wrong, he admitted. "We feel deeply that the Party committee building is out of line with Shanxi's economic situation and with the people's standard of living," Li said, and reported that Shanxi leaders had submitted two self-criticisms to Party Center about the project. As for how to best convey these regrets to the people of Shanxi, Li said he would check with higher-ranking provincial leaders and report back.

Other students had plenty more to say. They asked, why is Shanxi experiencing electricity shortages while sending electricity to Beijing, Tianjin, and Tangshan? What are you doing to combat brain drain from our province? What is the provincial government doing about the illegal import of luxury cars? The Taiyuan municipal government said the demonstrations on May 4 were illegal – how is the government going to punish students for this, and may I ask what the government thinks of all of the citizens who supported the illegal march by giving students fruit, bread, and soda? Is the student movement promoting democracy? Please give a positive answer. I heard that a deputy governor was robbed of two hundred thousand yuan and that the brother-in-law of someone affiliated with my school was sentenced to fifteen years for the robbery. What is the income of a provincial leader? Are they taking bribes? Did these things really happen? If yes, how is it being dealt with? If not, then it should be openly refuted.

We know about all of these questions thanks to *Shanxi Daily*'s detailed report about the dialogue. The newspaper article about the May 8 dialogue in Taiyuan records a remarkable exchange of views between students complaining about serious local problems and leaders who offered explanations and promises that the conversation would continue. But around 11 p.m. on the evening of May 8, as soon as the local rebroadcast of the dialogue had finished airing, more than one thousand students marched to the provincial government compound to vent their anger. They chanted, "The dialogue was all empty words, we want a new dialogue, speak the truth!" and "Root out corruption and revitalize Shanxi!"[10] The protesters stayed until 6 a.m. the next morning. They got the do-over they asked for on May 15: thirty-three student representatives from nineteen universities met with higher-ranking officials, including Governor Wang Senhao and deputy Party secretary Wang

---

[10] 山西日报 (Shanxi Daily), May 10, 1989, 1.

Maolin. The two Wangs provided additional details about the new office building's construction costs and confirmed that a top official's residence had been robbed, but the result of the May 15 dialogue was the same as that of May 9: promises of future meetings, but no concrete action.[11]

A final dialogue meeting in Shanxi, this time presided over by Party secretary Li Ligong, the top-ranking official in the province, took place at the Taiyuan Institute of Technology on May 18. The students' main concern was about how provincial leaders characterized the protest movement. Li Ligong said positive things about the students' patriotic motives.[12] The next day, after Li Peng announced the imposition of martial law in Beijing, the doors of local leaders closed nationwide. On May 19, 1989, the Shanxi provincial Party committee and provincial government jointly issued a notice listing six acceptable ways for the masses to contact local authorities with complaints, suggestions, or information about illegal activities. The notice helpfully provided the phone numbers and addresses of the Office of Letters and Visits and five other bureaucratic agencies.[13] What seemed on its face to be a generous gesture of government transparency ("we have given you six different ways to talk to us") was in fact a return to the status quo: citizens would no longer be able to put local leaders on the spot in face-to-face meetings. If they wanted to say something to the Party, they would have to get in line to speak to a powerless bureaucrat who would fill out a form and pass it along to the next functionary.

The window for dialogue in Shanxi was fleeting, but it had been open longer and allowed for more frequent and in-depth interactions between students and officials than in many other parts of China. During a three-hour dialogue meeting on May 18 between Hubei provincial Party secretary Guan Guangfu and students in Wuhan, students asked Guan for his views about the nature of the student movement and what *Hubei Daily* called "some problems specific to Hubei." Guan gave vague answers about working together to solve problems and improve the local economy. He spoke much more clearly when he gave the students a list of rules: do not block traffic on the Yangzi River Bridge, do not storm Party and government offices, do not establish ties with middle school students or factory workers.[14]

Students in Wuhan must not have appreciated Guan's tone, but at least they got a three-hour prescheduled meeting. In Hunan, Governor Chen Bangzhu and Xiong Qingquan, who had been promoted to Party

[11] 山西日报 (Shanxi Daily), May 16, 1989, 1.
[12] 山西日报 (Shanxi Daily), May 19, 1989, 1.
[13] 山西日报 (Shanxi Daily), May 24, 1989, 1.
[14] 湖北日报 (Hubei Daily), May 19, 1989, 1.

secretary since his meeting with Tang Baiqiao in 1986, showed up at
4:45 a.m. on May 18 to speak with students gathered at the leadership
compound. *Hunan Daily* called Chen and Xiong's appearance a "frank
and honest dialogue," but that claim rang false for the exhausted students, who asked the officials to schedule an "official dialogue" that
would be broadcast live. Xiong said he could not give a definite answer
about broadcasting because he was unsure about the technical details; he
and the other officials left at 6 a.m.[15]

Xiong Qingquan once enjoyed a good reputation among Hunanese
students, according to Tang Baiqiao, because they had heard he had
once served as Hu Yaobang's secretary and was unhappy about how Hu
had been purged. But Xiong "cast us aside at the critical juncture in
1989," Tang recalled in an interview.[16] That turning point came on May
19 and 20. The announcement that martial law would be imposed in
Beijing cut short planning for future dialogue between Hunan's leaders
and student activists. In the early hours of May 20, after watching Li
Peng and Yang Shangkun's speeches, members of the Hunan Party
Standing Committee gathered for a "study session." They drafted a
telegram to Party Center pledging to firmly endorse the measures to curb
turmoil.[17] A month after his early morning dialogue with protesters,
Xiong Qingquan would be issuing orders to arrest the leaders of
Hunan's student and workers' autonomous federations. On the run and
trying to escape China, Tang Baiqiao was arrested in Guangdong on
July 13, 1989. He received a three-year sentence for "instigating
counterrevolutionary propaganda."[18]

As in Hunan, dialogue barely got off the ground in Shaanxi. Students
in Xi'an delivered three petition letters to provincial leaders on May 4.
On May 10, a student called the governor's office to ask when they might
expect a response. The next day, officials from the Shaanxi Office of
Letters and Visits said that dialogue would proceed through multiple
channels and that details about the timing and participants would be
provided later.[19] *Shaanxi Daily* then reported that a "dialogue" had
occurred on May 15 between Party secretary Zhang Boxing, Governor
Hou Zongbin, and provincial Youth League officials and cadres from the
officially approved student association. Protesters and leaders of newly

[15] 湖南日报 (Hunan Daily), May 19, 1989, 1.
[16] Ya Yi, "我心中永远关注中国 – 访唐柏桥" (I will care about China forever: An interview
with Tang Baiqiao), *Beijing zhi chun*, January 24, 2003, beijingspring.com/bj2/1997/290/
2003124155134.htm.
[17] 湖南日报 (Hunan Daily), May 22, 1989, 1, 3.   [18] Tang, *My Two Chinas*, 138, 171.
[19] 陕西日报 (Shaanxi Daily), May 12, 1989, 1.

formed autonomous federations were not invited.[20] Zhang and Hou had engaged in dialogue, but not with anyone who had asked for it.

Suddenly, on the afternoon of May 19, Zhang and Hou sent a bus to Xi'an's central square. They had decided to summon more than thirty protesters and to accept their petitions. Liu Ziyang, a student from Shaanxi Normal University, told the provincial leaders, "We are here today to deliver petitions, not for dialogue. We would need to be notified about a dialogue in advance so that we can prepare. We were just now called here from the square." Other students echoed Liu Ziyang's complaint that the hasty summons from the province's top leaders was not the kind of dialogue they were asking for.

Two students left after delivering their petition, but others seemed to realize that this might be their only chance to confront Zhang Boxing and Hou Zongbin in person. Unhappy with the official characterization of the events of April 22, students asked for a full investigation and wanted to know why press coverage had mentioned how many police had been injured that night but ignored student casualties.[21] Hou Zongbing responded on behalf of the leaders. Hou said that it had never been the government's intention to accuse students of having had anything to do with the turmoil of April 22. "On the contrary," Hou said, "we have affirmed students' role in maintaining order" that night. The government had always made a clear distinction between rioters and the students who were properly mourning Hu Yaobang, Hou claimed. He ended by asking students to stop their hunger strike.[22] At around 2 a.m. on May 20, 1989, the hunger-striking students who remained at Xincheng Square decided to end the strike and return to campus. It is likely that the martial law declaration in Beijing, not Hou's request, sparked this decision.

[20] 陕西日报 (Shaanxi Daily), May 16, 1989, 1.
[21] 陕西日报 (Shaanxi Daily), May 20, 1989, 1.
[22] 陕西日报 (Shaanxi Daily), May 20, 1989, 3.

21 Rage

Just as the protest movement was not confined to Beijing, neither were deaths and injuries limited to China's capital. After the Beijing massacre there were local killings by security forces that were smaller in scale but no less traumatic for those who were affected. Like hunger strikes and dialogue meetings, violence in the provinces followed an "inside-out" dynamic. In the early hours of June 4, reports of shooting in Beijing sparked enraged uprisings throughout China in which citizens marched, occupied public squares, blockaded roads and rail lines, tried to organize general strikes among workers, organized new political parties, and even carried out murderous terrorist bombings. Although local leaders in at least one city followed Deng Xiaoping's example and allowed deadly force, most provincial, city, and county officials found ways to restore order without widespread killing.

Clashes between angry citizens and security forces were especially violent in Chengdu, the capital of Sichuan. Louisa Lim calls Chengdu residents' impulse to fight on June 4 "an act of sheer solidarity and outright bravery; protesters were taking to the streets in the full knowledge that troops had opened fire on unarmed civilians in Beijing." Protesters wielding rocks, bottles, and other improvised weapons faced off against PAP soldiers and police officers who used batons, tear gas, and – according to some reports – bayonets and guns. Lim received a handwritten report from someone who saw the violence in Chengdu, naming "six people who had been wounded by gunshots."[1]

According to another eyewitness in Chengdu, "Most of the action consisted of isolating groups of demonstrators and stabbing them and beating them to the ground ... Even after they had beaten demonstrators down, they would continue attacking them with truncheons and knives until they were motionless. There was a pattern to it: with males, the

---

[1] Lim, *People's Republic of Amnesia*, 186, 188.

Figure 21.1 Face-off in Chengdu, June 4, 1989. AFP via Getty Images.

preferred area of attack was the head, with females it was the abdomen."[2]
In addition to pitched street battles on June 4, violence in Chengdu
included police beatings of detainees on June 5. Western visitors staying
at Chengdu's Jinjiang Hotel described seeing summary executions of
prisoners. They saw security officers using clubs or iron rods to repeatedly bash in the heads of detainees whose hands were wired behind their
backs. Between twenty-five and one hundred "lifeless bodies" were then
thrown into the backs of trucks and driven away.[3] We do not know how
many people died during the killings of June 4 and 5 in Chengdu.
Anthropologist Karl Hutterer, who left the city on June 7, wrote that
"there was a consensus that from 300 to 400 people had been killed and
upward of 1,000 wounded. A doctor from one hospital reported a
personal count of 27 deaths in that medical facility."[4]
    Based on Public Security situation reports from June 4 and 5, it
appears that authorities in Chengdu thought that because top leaders in

[2] Amnesty International, *The Massacre of June 1989 and Its Aftermath*, March 31, 1990,
ASA 17/009/1990, amnesty.org/download/Documents/200000/asa170091990en.pdf.
[3] Lim, *People's Republic of Amnesia*, 194–95; Amnesty International, *The Massacre of June
1989 and Its Aftermath*.
[4] Karl Hutterer, "Chengdu Had Its Own Tiananmen Massacre," *New York Times*, June 23,
1989, A28.

Beijing had used lethal violence to "clear the square," they needed to rapidly take control of Chengdu's Tianfu Square in the same way, a decision that escalated violence and culminated in summary executions of prisoners.[5] Most other local bosses of China's large cities exercised restraint compared with Deng Xiaoping and Chengdu Party secretary Wu Xihai. For example, after learning about the Beijing massacre, protesters paralyzed Chongqing by blocking roads and train tracks. Authorities in Chongqing used persuasion and police investigations rather than violence to clear the streets and crack down on organized dissent. Rumors circulated that Party secretary Xiao Yang "had scaled down the seriousness of the situation by characterizing it as 'purposeless commotion' (乱动) rather than as 'political turmoil' (动乱)."[6]

Xu Wanping, a twenty-eight-year-old who worked at a factory in Chongqing, had been active in the city's democracy movement in May 1989. He reacted to the Beijing massacre by establishing the China Action Party on June 5, 1989. The court case against Xu claimed that he had designed a flag and constitution for his new party, and had written essays stating that the China Action Party's goal was to wipe out the Communist Party by stealing guns, robbing banks, and setting up a military base area. Dai Yong, a twenty-two-year-old coworker of Xu's, joined the new party, as did Tong Bi'an and Zhang Junfeng. Chongqing authorities detained the men in July; Xu served eight years in prison, Dai was sentenced to two years, and the other men were sent to reeducation through labor.[7]

Police action shut down Xu Wanping's resistance and also quashed activist organizing in other parts of China. Angry people nationwide reacted to the Beijing massacre by calling on workers to strike, building on efforts in April and May to form independent unions and forge links between students and workers. Starting on June 7, two brothers named Chen Gang and Chen Ding in Xiangtan, Hunan, tried to shut down the Xiangtan Electrical Machinery Factory where Chen Gang worked. They organized more than one thousand workers to block access to the factory. According to court documents, on June 9 security officials from the

---

[5] Two reports about Chengdu security forces forcibly clearing Tianfu Square use "forcibly expelling" (强制带离) and "clear the square" (清场) – language that seems to be modeled on the clearing of Tiananmen Square. See *QZ* [89] 210 (May 5, 1989) and *QZ* [89] 213 (June 5, 1989), web.archive.org/web/20130414093751/blog.boxun.com/hero/201304/xsj14/116_1.shtml, web.archive.org/web/20200212181454/blog.boxun.com/hero/201304/xsj14/119_1.shtml.

[6] Anita Chan and Jonathan Unger, "Voices from the Protest Movement in Chongqing: Class Accents and Class Tensions," in *The Pro-democracy Protests in China*, 122–23.

[7] Support Network for the Persecuted in China (Australia), ed., "六四"抗暴者法庭档案 (Court files of civil disobedience against government violence on June Fourth, 1989) (Deerpark, NY: Guoshi chubanshe, 2019), 123–25.

factory, including chief Fang Fuqiu, injured Chen Ding's arm while trying to force the factory's gates open. Chen Ding's injury shifted angry workers' energy toward seeking revenge. A large crowd raced to the factory's security office to look for Fang. When they failed to find him they entered Fang's home, questioned his wife, and burned some of his belongings. Hunanese legal officials threw the book at Chen Gang, who they saw as the main instigator of unrest – he received a death sentence while three other worker leaders named Peng Shi, Liu Zhihua, and Liu Jian were sentenced to life imprisonment.[8] When workers at the Xiangtan factory heard that Chen Gang was scheduled to be executed on April 22, 1990, they did go on strike.[9] The next month, Chen Gang's sentence was commuted to a death penalty with a two-year reprieve (effectively a life sentence). Chen and Peng were released from prison in 2004, Liu Zhihua was released in 2009.

In Anhui Province, students protested alongside workers at the Hefei Steel Company on June 7, 1989, but the people who police identified as ringleaders received minor slaps on the wrist compared with Chen Gang and his colleagues in Xiangtan. Students in Hefei blocked the entrances to the city's main ironworks, forcing it to shut down for almost ten hours. A female worker named Zhang Xuezhi accused the steel company's security guards of stealing money that had been donated to protesters. Zhang then reportedly cut her hand by breaking a window and yelled, "Blood has been spilled." This led to wider protests against security officials after people heard that a worker had been hurt. As in Xiangtan, angry crowds in Hefei targeted the home of a police officer. They pulled officer Li Xuchang, known as Big Cannon Li, out of his residence in the middle of the night, vandalized his home, and brought him to Hefei Polytechnic University to parade him in front of students.[10] After the unrest on June 7, five young workers at Hefei Steel, including a woman named Huang Dezhen, were arrested and released after receiving "education" or serving one-year labor reform sentences.[11] If Huang and her coworkers had been in Hunan it is likely that they would have

[8] Support Network for the Persecuted in China (Australia), "六四" 抗暴者法庭档案 (Court files of civil disobedience against government violence on June Fourth, 1989), 17–21; Dui Hua Foundation, "Last-Known June Fourth 'Hooligan' Released from Prison," May 18, 2009, duihua.org/last-known-june-fourth-hooligan-released-from-prison.

[9] Human Rights Watch, *Anthems of Defeat: Crackdown in Hunan Province, 1989–92* (Washington, DC: Human Rights Watch, 1992), 52.

[10] 安徽日报 (Anhui Daily), August 12, 1989, cited in Dui Hua Foundation, "Outside Beijing: Official June Fourth Accounts (Part II)," May 20, 2014, duihuaresearch.org/2014/05/outside-beijing-official-june-fourth.html.

[11] Dui Hua, "Outside Beijing."

suffered much harsher punishments. Provincial leaders had latitude in choosing hard or soft approaches toward those who lashed out in anger after learning of the Beijing massacre.

In Shanghai, leaders made a point of appearing to take a soft approach toward residents' widespread outrage after June 4. Top Shanghai authorities also organized workers to restore the city to normalcy. Shanghai leaders' official statement responding to the crackdown in Beijing was far more moderate than the harsh words issued by other provincial leaders, according to Australian diplomat Shelley Warner: "going sufficiently far in its condemnation of the 'rebellion' in Beijing to be acceptable to the central leadership, without being excessive and thus totally implausible to the people of Shanghai." Nonetheless, Shanghai students and members of the city's autonomous workers' union shut down the city in protest. They blocked 234 intersections with buses that drivers had offered to the students in solidarity. The vehicles, parked sideways and with deflated tires, created what Warner called "an obstacle course that impeded an advance into the city centre at many points." Students also displayed posters about the Beijing massacre and organized blockades of train tracks. Trains on the Shanghai–Ningbo and Shanghai–Hangzhou lines were unable to run for fifty hours and 281 trains were unable to run as scheduled.[12]

On the evening of June 6, train number 161 from Beijing plowed into protesters who were blocking the tracks at Shanghai's Guangxin Road crossing, as depicted in Figure 20.1. According to Shanghai mayor Zhu Rongji, the train killed six people and injured six others (Taiwan's *China Times* reported eight dead and more than thirty wounded).[13] News of the atrocity spread quickly; a crowd of thirty thousand people gathered at the scene. Some people set the train on fire and battled with police. Firefighters managed to extinguish the flames and police arrested seventy-four people, all of whom were, in Mayor Zhu's words, "the dregs of society." Zhu said that the riot sparked by the train crash was a "bad thing and also a good thing. It taught people that if we do not stop bad people from wreaking havoc, we won't be able to return to normal life."[14] On June 15, Shanghai's highest court delivered a death sentence verdict and immediately executed three men who had taken part in burning train cars nine days earlier: Bian Hanwu, who was unemployed; Xu Guoming,

---

[12] Quotations in this paragraph are from Shelley Warner, "Shanghai's Response to the Deluge," in *The Pro-democracy Protests in China*, 217, 219; statistics are from *RMRB*, September 24, 1989, 4.

[13] 中國時報 (China Times) (Taipei), June 8, 1989, 3.

[14] *Zhu Rongji Shanghai jianghua shilu* bianji zu, ed., 朱鎔基上海講話實錄 (Zhu Rongji's Shanghai speeches) (Hong Kong: Sanlian, 2013), 279.

a temporary worker at the Shanghai Beer Brewery; and Yan Xuerong, a worker at a radio factory.[15]

In addition to broadcasting show trials, Zhu Rongji used television to try to convince Shanghai residents to return to work and stop disrupting traffic, promising that a deadly crackdown was not even under consideration. In what Shelley Warner described as a "finely tuned political speech,"[16] Zhu told Shanghai residents on June 8 that he had chosen not to authorize violent force because overexcited students behaving irrationally had been joined by the "dregs of society," making it difficult to distinguish between good and bad people. "In this situation," Zhu said, "it is very likely that good people would be mistakenly hurt if we use harsh measures." He pledged that city officials "have never considered using the army and have never planned to implement military control or martial law."

Instead, Shanghai's leaders mobilized factory workers to clear barricades and restore traffic – 6,500 workers removed obstacles on June 5, 36,000 on June 6, and 20,000 on June 7.[17] The city government paid generous wages to members of the clearing teams, who were mostly made up of politically reliable Party members and factory administrators rather than rank-and-file workers. Several thousand students marched in the city on June 9; two days later, more than one hundred students protested the arrests of members of Shanghai's autonomous workers' union, which had been declared illegal. Over the following week, Shanghai police rounded up the leaders of other student and worker organizations. Shanghai's unrest had ended.[18] Zhu Rongji's methods – calming a tense standoff by ruling out a harsh crackdown, prohibiting military involvement, and straightforwardly telling residents what he was doing in nightly televised speeches – showed that a softer approach could save lives. By declaring martial law in Beijing, Deng Xiaoping and Li Peng had unwisely exacerbated tensions that led to the unnecessary deaths of hundreds of civilians.

Other cities experienced a similar pattern of marches, traffic shutdowns, and arrests of activists in early and mid-June 1989 before protests died down and people grimly returned to daily routines. A small number of individuals, however, refused to quietly submit to the post-massacre

---

[15] 聯合報 (United Daily News) (Taipei), June 16, 1989, 1; Chen Hansheng, "為了從未紀念的紀念" (Commemorating the never commemorated), June 4, 2014, web.archive.org/web/20180207123115/http://www.chengmingmag.com/t346/select/346sel21.html.
[16] Warner, "Shanghai's Response," 227.
[17] *Zhu Rongji Shanghai jianghua shilu* bianji zu, 朱鎔基上海講話實錄 (Zhu Rongji's Shanghai speeches), 283–84.
[18] Warner, "Shanghai's Response," 228–29.

order. They vented their rage by resorting to terrorism. On June 26, 1989, at Songjiang on the outskirts of Shanghai, an explosion rocked passenger train number 364, which was traveling from Hangzhou to Shanghai (see Figure 20.1). Twenty-four people died in the blast and fifty-one were injured. Security officials determined that this was a "human-caused explosion" that occurred when dynamite ignited in the washroom of car number seven.[19] Zhu Rongji visited victims in the hospital and Minister of Railways Li Senmao rushed to Shanghai to lead the investigation.[20]

Two days later, in what might have been a copycat attack after *People's Daily* reported on the bombing of train number 364, another blast derailed a train traveling through Guizhou Province, killing five people and injuring twelve. The second deadly explosion received no media coverage, but the State Council issued a notice to "take strict precautions against enemies blowing things up" and to be aware that many incidents of people trying to derail trains by putting obstacles on tracks or dismantling railway infrastructure had occurred since June 4. Who caused the train explosions and how officials and survivors dealt with the aftermath of the tragedies are some of the many things about 1989 that will remain mysteries until it is possible to openly research the topic in China. But at the time, top officials in Beijing warned that the explosions were a result of "counterrevolutionaries refusing to admit defeat" and that the nation's transport infrastructure was a major target of "enemy sabotage" in the aftermath of the crackdown of June 3 and 4.[21]

[19] Guowuyuan, 关于加强铁路治安保卫工作: 严防敌人爆炸, 破坏铁路设施的紧急通知 (Urgent notice about strengthening railway security protection work: Take strict precautions against enemies blowing things up), web.archive.org/web/20130416064624/blog.boxun.com/hero/201302/xsj14/45_1.shtml.

[20] *RMRB*, June 28, 1989, 3.

[21] Guowuyuan, 关于加强铁路治安保卫工作 (Urgent notice about strengthening railway security protection work); see also Beijing shi gongan ju, 关于加强铁路运输安全防止发生爆炸, 颠覆列车等恶性事故的意见 (Opinion on strengthening rail transport safety and preventing such severe accidents as explosions and trains overturning), July 7, 1989, circulated by the Beijing Municipal Government as *Jingzhengfa* [1989] 55 (July 24, 1989), web.archive.org/web/20200214214700/http://www.beijing.gov.cn/zhengce/zfwj/zfwj/szfwj/201905/t20190523_71503.html.

22 Rural Actions and Reactions

The first deadly train explosion of late June 1989 occurred on Shanghai's rural-urban periphery; the second took place in the rural mountains of Guizhou's Qiandongnan Miao and Dong Autonomous Prefecture. About 75 percent of China's population lived in rural areas in 1989. Even though every province in China experienced protests and crackdowns in 1989, most of the action occurred in cities, especially provincial capitals and other hubs of higher education. Beyond terrorist bombings that killed train passengers outside urban centers, what happened in the countryside in 1989? How did rural people get involved in the protests, how did the events of spring 1989 affect them, and what did they think about the demonstrations and Beijing massacre?

In 1989, many university students came from rural backgrounds. Their families back home in villages felt bewildered and worried that their children – an elite group of high achievers who had the rare privilege of going to university – were putting themselves in danger and threatening their futures by becoming political activists. University student Shen Weirong returned to his rural home during the middle of the protests. "In villages like ours, the student movement did not mean a lot. My mother and my grandma did not care much about politics. They were only concerned about my well-being." Ding Huizhen, Shen's mother, explained, "I didn't agree with the student movement opposing Deng Xiaoping. It was only after Deng came to power that my son could go to college based on his own merits." Shen added, "Freedom and democracy were too far removed for them. They had no concept of such things. They'd say, 'What kind of freedom do you want? You are in college. You can say and do anything you like. What more freedom do you want?' I could not communicate with them."[1]

The urban-rural divide between young protesters in cities and older rural people was evident in students' elitist conception of democracy.

---

[1] Sue Williams, *China: A Century of Revolution, Part Three: Born under the Red Flag*, DVD (New York: Ambrica, 1997), 1:30:23–1:31:33.

It was difficult to find student protesters calling for a democratic election system based on one person, one vote, which would have given rural people a voice commensurate with their majority status in China. University students' specific demands focused not on elections but on greater freedom of speech, transparency and accountability, and protection from dictatorial persecution. People in the countryside needed these rights at least as much as city-dwellers did, but student protesters did not prioritize farmers' concerns.

The gap between urban and rural people was on display for the world to see on April 29, 1989, when student leaders followed by a group of foreign journalists visited government offices in Beijing to demand genuine dialogue instead of stilted exchanges. At the gate of one leadership compound, a group of rural petitioners was trying to get the central government to address their grievances. When the villagers saw journalists holding cameras, they knelt on the ground, cried dramatically, and held up their petition documents in the air. But most cameras stayed focused on the students, not on the rural people. Wang Dan walked away awkwardly.[2] Even though the same authoritarian system was failing petitioners from the countryside as much as it was bothering elite urban student protesters, the two worlds remained separate.

One month after Wang Dan missed an opportunity for villagers and urbanites to connect about their grievances, a few rural voices offered support to students in Beijing. An unverifiable story circulated about a horseman from Inner Mongolia who rode to Beijing to give five thousand yuan from his village to the students.[3] More concrete evidence of at least some rural support came in an open letter purportedly written by an anonymous "farmer from Sichuan" that circulated on the Peking University campus in late May 1989. The author claimed that farmers were increasingly unhappy about corruption and inflation, with some saying that officials "only care about collecting grain and fees, they don't care whether the farmers live or die." This is why farmers, who had long been repressed by corrupt officials but had no way to publicize their ills, supported the patriotic young students and were upset that the government had declared martial law.[4]

Aside from possibly noticing this open letter – one among many manifestos circulating in the capital in May 1989 – Beijing students rarely

---

[2] *Gate of Heavenly Peace*, VCD, Disc 2, 4:00–4:31.
[3] Black and Munro, *Black Hands*, 260.
[4] Yiwei laizi Sichuan de nongmin, "农民的呼声政府听到没有?" (Has the government heard the farmers' voice?), 民主運動原始資料 (Original materials from the democracy movement, May–June 1989), Universities Service Centre, Chinese University of Hong Kong, JQ-3.2 69316.

listened to or involved rural people. But teachers and students at schools in the countryside did pay close attention to the protest movement. Some tried to mobilize villagers. One schoolteacher in rural south central China set up a propaganda station to broadcast Voice of America reports about what was happening in Beijing. He talked to every villager he could to share news about the protest movement. At first, the conversations were awkward: people reacted as Ding Huizhen did, wanting the privileged students to go back to class. The teacher said that some people's attitudes changed after the hunger strike began. Villagers worried about students' health, sympathized with them, and thought that the central government should compromise. But after June 4, the villagers stopped talking publicly. News of the massacre and arrests of activists convinced them to stay quiet to protect themselves.[5]

Reactions to the massacre were similarly muted in rural Guangdong and rural Fujian. In Chen Village near Hong Kong, rural people who had benefited from the economic reforms of the 1980s "feared that any rocking of the boat might endanger their present lifestyles, and therefore there was little sympathy for the protests." Older men who saw television footage of the massacre broadcast by Hong Kong stations "argued that the demonstrators had gone too far, and that they deserved what they got."[6] Access to media beyond the reach of the Communist Party's propaganda apparatus did not necessarily lead to views that clashed with the Party's post-June 4 version of events. For some people in rural areas far from Beijing, the crackdown might have been something to notice or even comment on, but did it not seem earthshaking. On June 6, 1989, an English teacher from Australia named Rod Curnow visited a village in the mountains above Fuzhou in Fujian Province. The villagers had heard about bloodshed in Beijing "but were indifferent. They thought Deng was a fine leader."[7]

In the aftermath of the massacre, villagers refrained from saying critical things about Deng Xiaoping, especially in front of a foreign visitor. Other people were so angry at the dictator that they traveled to his rural birthplace with plans to desecrate the Deng family's ancestral graves. Lei Fengyun convinced a group of friends at Chongqing's Southwest Normal University to travel to Guang'an County, where Deng's family compound was located. In an interview in 2017, Lei explained his

---

[5] Author conversation 10 (teacher at a rural school). To protect the anonymity of people I spoke with about June Fourth, I am deliberately vague in citing my conversations with them and in providing details about their identities.
[6] Chan, Madsen, and Unger, *Chen Village*, 327.
[7] Mary S. Erbaugh and Richard Kurt Kraus, "The 1989 Democracy Movement in Fujian and Its Aftermath," in *The Pro-democracy Protests in China*, 156.

thinking: "In our Sichuan, if someone has done evil things that cause widespread indignation, people often dig up their ancestral graves to teach them a lesson."[8] Lei was so vocal in his organizational work in the two days after the Beijing massacre that someone leaked his plans to security officials. By June 7, 1989, top police authorities in Beijing received reports that two hundred students were threatening to attack the Deng compound and dig up the graves; in response, Sichuan's provincial security chiefs had deployed guards to control the area.[9] Lei and his friends took a train to Guang'an County, where they recited a "Grave Digging Declaration" in the train station waiting room and then tried to buy shovels, but they never made it to the Deng family cemetery.[10] The grave diggers learned that "there were no vehicles within a ten-kilometer area and police were already in combat readiness," Lei said. "We could not get a car and all the hotels refused to put us up." A police officer told Lei that a full military battalion had been transferred to Guang'an to set up three security cordons. Unable to breach the blockade and get close to Deng's birthplace, Lei and his team gave up and returned to Chongqing.[11] He was arrested on June 19, 1989, and was eventually sentenced to twelve years in prison for counterrevolutionary propaganda and incitement.

In Youyang County in the far southeast corner of Sichuan, hundreds of miles from the Deng ancestral graves, more than thirty students were arrested in the aftermath of the massacre. According to a student named Zhang, many students returned to their rural homes during summer 1989. The people they encountered wanted to know what had happened in Beijing. On a boat on the Yangzi and Wujiang rivers, Zhang and other students soon tired of telling the same story over and over to individual passengers who were curious to learn about the student movement and its violent end. To better reach a bigger audience, Zhang got up on the boat's stage and used a loudspeaker to denounce the massacre. Zhang recalled, "There was a visitors' logbook on the ship, in which the students wrote satirical sayings about Deng Xiaoping, Li Peng, and others that we had heard in Beijing." The speeches and written remarks became evidence of the students' "crimes" after they arrived in Youyang.[12]

[8] Zhou Fengsuo interview with Lei Fengyun, *China Digital Times*, January 31, 2017, bit.ly/chinadigitaltimesleifengyun.
[9] *QZ* [89] 218 (June 7, 1989), web.archive.org/web/20200218234158/blog.boxun.com/hero/201304/xsj14/124_1.shtml.
[10] Liao Yiwu, *Bullets and Opium*, 204.   [11] Zhou Fengsuo interview with Lei Fengyun.
[12] Youyang Tujia and Miao Autonomous County is now part of Chongqing Municipality, which became a separate administrative region in 1997. You Weijie, "大地之子陈永廷" (Chen Yongting, son of the earth), *Human Rights in China*, April 10, 2014, hrichina.org/chs/ren-quan-lun-tan/da-di-zhi-zi-chen-yong-ting.

Zhang's boat ride and Lei Fengyun's failed trip to Deng Xiaoping's hometown were attention-getting reactions to the Beijing massacre. Other people in villages had quieter responses that were equally risky. They actively helped or turned a blind eye toward activists who were trying to escape the crackdown. Students and workers had largely ignored rural people in April and May 1989, but after June 4 getting along with villagers, or even pretending to be a farmer, became a way to stay out of prison. Worker leader Han Dongfang rode his bicycle out of Beijing after the massacre and slept in farm fields in Hebei Province for several nights. One day, he spoke to a watermelon farmer about "democracy, the need for a genuinely elected government – things I had learnt just in the last month – and I realized that he did not have that many complaints about the Communist Party." The two men failed to connect, but they had a friendly conversation, and the farmer made no move to alert the authorities to Han's presence in the countryside. A few days later, Han decided to turn himself in. He rode his bicycle back to Beijing, walked into the Ministry of Public Security, and suffered badly in jail until 1991.[13]

Another BWAF leader received far greater rural support than Han Dongfang did. Zhao Hongliang was smuggled out of Beijing in the back of a stinking garbage truck with other activists. The group ended up in Inner Mongolia, where villagers helped them hide in caves and gave them four thousand yuan when the fugitives had to move on. With help from democracy supporters in Hong Kong, Zhao and two others eventually made their way to Guangzhou, Shenzhen, and finally Hong Kong.[14] Chai Ling and Feng Congde followed a similar route to freedom. Like Zhao Hongliang, they would not have been able to escape China without help from rural people. Chai recalled that when Feng was moving to a new safe house in south China, a "farmwoman in a field asked if they were helping students from Beijing. She pointed to a shed on the side of the road ahead and warned them that security forces were waiting there," allowing Feng and his helper to narrowly avert capture. Chai herself spent several weeks hiding in the home of what she called a "family of simple peasants. They were gentle and kind, free from anger and gossip. They found joy in the small things of life."[15] Chai Ling and Feng Congde eventually made it to Hong Kong; decades later, Chai still had fond memories of the rural people who had helped her.

---

[13] Han Dongfang, "Chinese Labour Struggles," *New Left Review* 34 (July–Aug 2005), newleftreview.org/issues/II34/articles/dongfang-han-chinese-labour-struggles.

[14] Black and Munro, *Black Hands*, 263, 277–78.   [15] Chai Ling, *Heart*, 208, 210.

Zhang Boli, who was number seventeen out of twenty-one on the list of most-wanted student leaders issued by the Ministry of Public Security on June 13, 1989, got lots of help from farmers. He even became one himself. The twenty-nine-year-old was older than many of the other student leaders in 1989. After working as a journalist in his native Heilongjiang Province, Zhang entered a writers' training program at Peking University in fall 1988 and became an activist after Hu Yaobang's death. Following the Beijing massacre, he made his way back to northeast China, where his relatives helped to hide him.

Zhang successfully bluffed his way through a police checkpoint in rural Heilongjiang by driving a horse cart and speaking the local dialect. Zhang and his cousin's husband hunkered down for part of summer 1989 in a crude hut they built at the junction of the Hulan and Songhua rivers outside Harbin. Zhang then spent a week as a short-term laborer hoeing yellow beans, badly blistering his writer's hands, before making it to the home of his well-connected uncle. Zhang's uncle boasted that hiding a fugitive from the post-massacre crackdown was "what real communists would do ... The Communist Party's glorious name was ruined in the hands of this little Deng fellow, damn him!" Zhang's uncle spoke widely of his contribution to real communism, and one day he told Zhang that "at least fifty" rural relatives and friends knew Zhang's whereabouts. None gave Zhang up to the police, but he was nervous. Early the next morning, Zhang recalled, "I changed into my peasant costume" and slipped away. "I assumed a peasant's identity – seldom talking, keeping to myself." He managed to survive while working as a farm laborer in fall 1989.[16] Zhang crossed into the Soviet Union in winter 1989. Authorities declined to grant him asylum or allow him to travel to the West, but they did permit him to quietly return to China, where he survived until 1991, when he finally escaped to Hong Kong and then to the United States.[17]

Villagers were not only harborers of fugitives in 1989. Some became persecuted, stigmatized, and impoverished mourners. The rural family members of people killed in Beijing faced anguish and loneliness. Fang Guizhen and her husband, Lei Guangtai, lived in a village in Huairou County about forty miles away from Tiananmen Square. In June 1989, Lei was working as a driver on an earth-moving project for a high-rise tower in Jianguomen. According to Ding Zilin, around 10 p.m. on June 3, Lei and two other drivers went to see the Goddess of Democracy

[16] Zhang Boli, *Escape from China*, 85, 90, 93.
[17] Verna Yu, "Tiananmen Activist Zhang Boli Keen to Spread Gospel in China," *South China Morning Post*, June 2, 2013, scmp.com/news/china/article/1251647/tiananmen-activist-zhang-boli-keen-spread-gospel-china.

statue. After 11 p.m., the men were smoking cigarettes near Nanchizi. Martial law troops shot Lei. In the chaos of the shooting, someone put Lei on a flatbed tricycle, and he became separated from his coworkers.

Fang Guizhen knew nothing about this when, on June 4, village officials told her that her husband had gotten lost and not returned to work. This sounded strange to Fang. She wondered how a grown man could get lost in Beijing. The next day, she heard the evening news denouncing the "false rumor" that people had been shot and killed at Tiananmen Square. "This made me very worried," Fang said. Over the next few days, she visited eighteen hospitals in Beijing, looking through thick stacks of photographs of corpses and reading through name lists of victims of the massacre. She never found Lei. He has been missing ever since the night of June 3, 1989. From then on, Fang has had to farm more than three acres of land on her own while struggling to raise the couple's two children (one was seven and the other an infant in 1989). Not only did the massacre rob her of a husband and the family's main source of income, it stigmatized her and subjected her to persecution. For a period after Lei went missing, village authorities cut off electricity to her house. And every year in the lead-up to June 4, police officers pay a visit to make sure that she is not planning to "stir up trouble." The officers know that Fang once confronted Beijing mayor Chen Xitong at a "meet-the-mayor" event and demanded justice and compensation for the loss of her husband.[18]

Cheng Renxing and Tian Daoming of Hubei, Chen Yongting and Wu Guofeng of Sichuan, and Li Haocheng of rural Tianjin were all celebrated as being the first people from their villages to test into universities in Beijing. This brought great honor to their hometowns. The prospect of a decent-paying, stable job after graduation also promised economic stability for their families back home. After June 1989, honor turned into shame and financial promise became destitution for the rural families of those who were murdered by PLA troops. Cheng Renxing's family lived in Tongshan County in a large compound with the characters "Daoist Master" written above the gate. After Cheng's father returned from Beijing, where he had met with staff at Renmin University and attended to his son's cremation, he got drunk every day, sitting at his doorstep and crying out for Renxing to come home. Cheng's father had sold piglets,

---

[18] Ding Zilin, "京郊的难属 – 赤贫的农妇" (A victim's family member in the Beijing suburbs: An utterly destitute rural woman), *Tiananmen Mothers*, April 20, 2004, tiananmenmother.org/the%20truth%20and%20victims/Authentic%20records%20of% 20visiting%20the%20victims/authentic_18.htm; see also video testimony from Fang Guizhen at youtube.com/watch?v=pcJfigeumWg&feature=youtu.be.

ducks, sweet potatoes, rice, and vegetables to pay for his son's education. Eventually, he drank himself to death, according to his daughter-in-law Xia Xiya. After other villagers learned that Renxing had been shot and killed in Beijing, they called him a counterrevolutionary and ostracized the family. During an interview in 2013, Cheng's mother Jin Yaxi mostly stayed quiet while her daughter-in-law did the talking. When pressed to speak about Cheng Renxing's death, she shook her head and cried. "She can't take it," Xia Xiya said.[19] Jin Yaxi died in April 2019 at the age of ninety-three.[20]

Cheng Renxing's, Tian Daoming's, and Chen Yongting's families were blindsided by the news that their sons had died. Li Haocheng's mother, Liu Jianlan, got no news at all. Trying to protect Liu from unbearable grief, her other children never told her the news that Li Haocheng had been shot and killed, but she knew that something was wrong when he never came home. Liu guessed that Li had died. She tried to act normally around others but cried herself to sleep in her village home in Wuqing County west of Tianjin. When she finally asked Li's brother if Li had died, he lied and said no. Eventually, she figured it out.[21]

Wu Dingfu's experience as a parent was different. He knew early on that his son Wu Guofeng was involved in the protests. Wu Guofeng sent a long letter home to Sichuan describing the scene in Beijing after Hu Yaobang's memorial service.[22] His father wrote a letter back saying that the young protesters were failing to understand the Communist Party's extreme brutality. Wu Dingfu admonished his son: "Remember this: do not get involved in politics no matter what." Wu Guofeng never got around to writing another letter to his parents. After he was killed in Beijing, township officials called his father to the government compound, gave him the news, and asked if his son was a rioter. "I said that even if he did riot, he should not be shot and killed," Wu Dingfu recalled. "Fine, arrest him and lock him up for ten or twenty years. Then give my son back after twenty years. I did not expect them to be that brutal."

---

[19] You Weijie and Guo Liying, "我的儿子被打死了，我不甘心." (My son was shot to death; I can't take it), *Human Rights in China*, May 21, 2014, hrichina.org/chs/ren-quan-lun-tan/wo-de-er-zi-bei-da-si-liao-wo-bu-gan-xin; video of the interview with Jin and Xia is available at youtu.be/BKjXpZayYQo.
[20] "Cheng Renxing," *Human Rights in China*, 2019, truth30.hrichina.org/cheng_renxing .html.
[21] Video of an interview with the late Liu Jianlan is available at youtu.be/Nw49Z5t84n4.
[22] Material in this and the following paragraph are from an interview with Wu Dingfu and Song Xiuling available at youtu.be/GMka7KyvdBA.

Wu Dingfu did, however, manage to take advantage of Beijing officials' stereotypes about rural people. Wu traveled to Beijing along with an uncle who looked like an "old farmer." The two washed and photographed Wu Guofeng's body, which had bullet wounds in his head, shoulder, and chest, along with a stab wound in his belly. The uncle, dressed like a country bumpkin, smuggled the film out of Beijing in his clothes; nobody searched him because he looked like a peasant and could hardly be considered a threat. A relative in Chengdu developed the film, which provided crucial evidence that PLA soldiers used bayonets to stab civilians.

23 Alternative Paths Nationwide

Looking beyond Beijing presents a world of alternative histories of 1989. Wu Dingfu suggested one: even if the "extremely brutal" Communist Party felt compelled to punish "rioters," why not imprison protesters instead of shooting and stabbing them? Wu Dingfu made his preference clear when he thought about embracing his son, Wu Guofeng the ex-convict, on his imaginary release from prison in 1999 or 2009. By authorizing soldiers to kill, Deng Xiaoping condemned the relatives of the dead to a lifelong nightmare.

The experiences of the hundreds of cities throughout China where Communist Party leaders exercised relative restraint during the protests, blockades, and strikes offer countless alternative paths and show how unnecessary it was for the PLA to open fire in Beijing on June 3 and 4. In Shanghai, Zhu Rongji dealt with a tense situation in which a train smashed into and killed at least eight protesters; Zhu also authorized the execution of three men who set the train on fire. The family members of Bian Hanwu, Xu Guoming, and Yan Xuerong, as well as the victims of the train disaster, are in the same boat as Wu Dingfu. But imagine how many more Chinese parents would be mourning if more city leaders had followed the Beijing, Chengdu, and Lhasa models instead of ruling out military force as Zhu Rongji did.

Chai Ling thought that bloodshed in Beijing would show Chinese people the truth about the nature of Communist Party rule and spark a nationwide uprising. Chai was not alone. Enraged protesters in Shanghai, Wuhan, and other major cities threw themselves into action after the Beijing massacre, trying to shut down traffic, organize massive strikes, and somehow bring about regime change. They failed.

There were two precedents for regime-changing revolution in twentieth-century China. The most recent example was the Communist takeover of the mainland in 1949. The Communists came to power by defeating the Kuomintang in a civil war. Revolution by way of military victory was not replicable or relevant in 1989. One side – the perpetrators of the Beijing massacre – had guns and tanks. The other side had bricks and stones. Those opposed to the army's butchering of civilians had no way to defeat the army in a fight. The events of June 3 and 4 showed that a modern army using lethal weapons could overcome fierce resistance by hundreds of thousands of civilians wielding crude tools.

The more distant historical precedent was the 1911 revolution, when New Army officers and revolutionaries opposed to the Manchu-led Qing monarchy seized power in a succession of southern provinces. A wave of provincial declarations of independence from the Qing resulted in the abdication of the emperor and the establishment of the Republic of China on January 1, 1912. But revolutionaries did not take charge of the new republic. Instead military strongman Yuan Shikai brokered the Qing abdication and became president. Li Lu mused about the possibility of 1911-style provincial declarations of independence in 1989.[1] What if coordination among angry civilians and sympathetic officials had gained enough traction to actually topple Party Center in June and July 1989? Zhu Rongji did not call up provincial leaders in Hubei and Sichuan to discuss seceding from the PRC. Instead, he called on Shanghai factory leaders to clear roadblocks and get the city back to work. Zhu's reward was promotion to the Politburo Standing Committee in 1992, to vice premier of the PRC in 1993, and to premier in 1998.

China under Communist Party rule during the 1980s was fundamentally different from the Qing empire under a Manchu-led dynasty in the first decade of the 1900s. The provincial leaders who declared independence from the Qing dynasty had gained their positions by keeping the Qing afloat during and after the Taiping civil war. They enjoyed relative autonomy, cultivated provincial identities, and – crucially – controlled New Army soldiers who were more loyal to them than to the decaying Qing. During the 1980s, municipal and provincial leaders had all gained their positions through loyalty to the Communist Party rather than to place-based strongmen. Politicians such as Zhu Rongji had enough autonomy to choose a softer approach toward protesters but were not inclined to turn against the Party to which they owed their careers and political futures.

---

[1] Li Lu, *Moving the Mountain*, 195.

Part Five

The Aftermath

24   The Purge as History

"China has cancer," bellowed a sixty-one-year-old professor on the evening of June 3, 1989. The man was listening to the radio with his students in a town far from Beijing. When he heard reports that the People's Liberation Army (PLA) was shooting at civilians in the capital, the professor cried out in despair and then fainted, striking his head. He quickly recovered from his head injury, but three months later, the professor once again passed judgment on what had happened in June. The PLA, he said, had erected a "Great Wall against counterrevolutionary rebellion."[1] What had happened between June and September to make him change his tune? The professor's diametrically opposed statements suggest that the aftermath of the Beijing massacre was as momentous as the crackdown itself.

"During the turmoil of 1989, not even one of the five hundred Party members in our department took part in marches, protests, and other such activities."[2] So claims the official history of the Ministry of Railways' Sixteenth Engineering Bureau's Fourth Engineering Department. "At the time, many units were working on projects in urban Beijing and there was a large probability that workers would get swept up in the political turbulence," the official history states. "But from beginning to end the entire department's staff stayed in line with Party Center – not one person watched or participated, showing quite a high level of political awareness."[3]

---

[1] Author conversation 1 (student at a university in China in 1989). For an account of professors in Beijing who displayed a similarly dramatic shift, from supporting the student movement to denouncing it, see Michael David Kwan, *Broken Portraits: Personal Encounters with Chinese Students* (San Francisco, CA: China Books and Periodicals, 1990), 186.

[2] *Tiedao bu di shiliu gongcheng ju di si gongcheng chu jianshi* bianweihui, ed., 铁道部第十六工程局第四工程处简史 (Concise history of the Ministry of Railways' Sixteenth Engineering Bureau's Fourth Engineering Department) (Beijing: Zhongguo tiedao chubanshe, 2000), 161.

[3] *Tiedao bu di shiliu gongcheng ju di si gongcheng chu jianshi* bianweihui, 铁道部第十六工程局第四工程处简史 (Concise history of the Ministry of Railways' Sixteenth Engineering Bureau's Fourth Engineering Department), 154.

It seems possible that laborers laying track in rural Hebei or building roads in Fujian – two of the Fourth Engineering Department's main projects in 1989 – might have had nothing to do with the protests. But the department was also working on construction projects in and around Beijing. On both May 17 and 18, 1989, millions of workers, officials, and ordinary citizens took part in demonstrations in the capital. Is it really possible that nobody from the Fourth Engineering Department even peeked at the marches or listened to speeches?

Normally, I would assume that the Fourth Engineering Department's official history was false – one of the many lies, omissions, and mischaracterizations about the Tiananmen Square protests perpetrated by censors, editors, and officials since shots rang out in Beijing on the evening of June 3, 1989.[4] I would also assume that more reliable answers might be found in the archives, if and when grassroots documents from 1989 become available to scholars. As it turns out, Stanford University's East Asian Library holds a set of original archival documents about how cadres from the Fourth Engineering Department performed during the 1989 protests.

What do the archival documents say? At first glance, they confirm and elaborate on the official history. Thirty-four "personal summaries" (自我总结) written in September 1989 all state that nobody from the Fourth Engineering Department marched or protested, nor did anyone observe any marches or protests.[5] What's more, employees did not gossip or listen to rumors about what was happening. Everyone worked hard and resolutely supported the crackdown. The compilers of the Fourth Engineering Department's official history may not have been lying. They were faithfully relying on archival documents.

Is it a coincidence that the only work unit-level files about June Fourth that I have seen all claim that "nobody did anything" and originated from a unit that was under direct military control until 1984?[6] Probably not.

---

[4] Michel Bonnin, "The Chinese Communist Party and 4 June 1989: Or How to Get Out of It and Get Away With It," in *The Impact of China's 1989 Tiananmen Massacre*, 33–48.

[5] These individual summaries are backed up by reports by the department's Party committee. See Zhongguo Gongchandang tiedao bu di shiliu gongcheng gongsi si chu jianzhu shigongduan weiyuanhui, 关于制止动乱，平息暴乱的情况写实报告 (Report about curbing the turmoil and quelling the rebellion), October 15, 1989, Stanford University East Asian Library, Collection of Contemporary Chinese Political Archives (hereafter abbreviated as SCPA), Box 17.

[6] The Fourth Engineering Department began as the Sixty-Third Regiment of the People's Liberation Army's Railway Corps in 1964 and was based in North Vietnam during the late 1960s. *Tiedao bu di shiliu gongcheng ju di si gongcheng chu jianshi* bianweihui, 铁道部第十六工程局第四工程处简史 (Concise history of the Ministry of Railways' Sixteenth Engineering Bureau's Fourth Engineering Department), 1.

But it is not surprising that documents produced during the purge that followed the Beijing massacre deny or downplay what people did between April and June 1989. Such documents reveal plenty about the purge (officially called "purging and sorting-out work," 清查清理工作) and little about the protests. This is useful because scholars know a lot about the protests but not much about their aftermath, when all Beijing work units were compelled to investigate people who had been involved in the spring's demonstrations, and when all urban Party members were required to reregister and affirm their loyalty.

Combining the Stanford files with memoirs, oral history interviews, and policy documents held at the Princeton and UCLA libraries allows for a new analysis of the post-June Fourth purge. Previous descriptions of the purge are impressionistic and vary widely, from political scientist Richard Baum's claim that the "campaign reportedly fizzled" because of a "tacit conspiracy of silence among leading cadres" to historian Maurice Meisner's assertion that intellectuals "became arbitrary targets of official criticism and found themselves the victims of Kafka-like inquisitions."[7] Each statement is insightful, but neither one is based on solid evidence. Baum is correct that many officials protected their subordinates, but his misreading of a source leads him to downplay what he calls the "surprisingly small" number of Party members who were punished and purged.[8] Meisner's idea of "Kafka-like inquisitions" is also speculative, but it comes closer to what the purge was like for those who experienced it. The point of the purge was not to formally punish huge numbers of people. The point was to remind the millions who wrote self-criticisms and filled out Party reregistration forms to obey, or else. The alternatives were arbitrary detention, interrogation, demotion, or exile to the hinterland. The fact that most people managed to pass

---

[7] Richard Baum, *Burying Mao: Chinese Politics in the Age of Deng Xiaoping* (Princeton: Princeton University Press, 1994), 316; Maurice J. Meisner, *The Deng Xiaoping Era: An Inquiry into the Fate of Chinese Socialism, 1978–1994* (New York: Hill and Wang, 1996), 475.

[8] Baum, *Burying Mao*, 316. Baum mixes up numbers from a Central Commission for Discipline Inspection report passed by the Fourteenth Party Congress on October 9, 1992. The number 13,254 includes Party members punished for having made political mistakes during the five years preceding 1992, not in the "post-Tiananmen" period. The number 1,179 refers not to those who "were punished for having participated in mass demonstrations and related 'disturbances,'" as Baum writes, but instead to the number of higher-ranking leaders who were included in the total of 13,254. The Central Commission for Discipline Inspection report did not release specific figures related to the post-June Fourth purge. See Zhongyang jiwei bangongting and Zhongyang jiwei yanjiushi, eds., 党的十四大以来中共中央纪律委员会历次全会工作报告汇编 (Collected work reports of the Central Commission for Discipline Inspection since the Fourteenth Party Congress) (Beijing: Zhongguo fangzheng chubanshe, 2005), 6–7.

through the purge unscathed did not diminish the specter of being arbitrarily targeted.

As lawyer Pu Zhiqiang has insightfully observed about his own experience, the Party was more interested in having people debase themselves, even by lying or by simply going through the motions during the purge, than in punishing them for what they had done. "Maybe the Communist Party didn't actually want people to sincerely examine their thinking and submit," Pu wrote. "It just made everyone bow their heads superficially, to make them despise themselves in the face of reality."[9] Pu refused to bow his head and has paid a heavy price. Ever since 1989, the Party has handled the aftermath of June Fourth like an abusive partner who knows that they have done something wrong but still uses the threat of violence to force compliance from the citizens of China. People who protect themselves and others by staying silent or lying about what happened in 1989 can get by. Those who stand up and resist the Party's version of events get smacked down and made examples of.

---

[9] Pu Zhiqiang, "向党交心: 我在六四清查运动中提交的反思" (Baring my heart to the Party: The thought report I turned in during the June Fourth purge movement), April 28, 2004, in 浦志强文集: 删不掉的博客 (Pu Zhiqiang's collected writings: The uncensorable blog), March 4, 2007, puzhiqiang999.blogspot.com/2007/03/blog-post_04.html. For an alternate translation of this excerpt see Philip P. Pan, *Out of Mao's Shadow: The Struggle for the Soul of a New China* (New York: Simon and Schuster, 2009), 276.

25 "Rioters"

On June 13, 1989, the Beijing Public Security Bureau ordered the arrest of twenty-one student leaders: nineteen men and two women. Wang Dan, Örkesh Dölet, and Chai Ling were at the top of the list.[1] While global attention focused on the fates of the students, some of whom managed to flee China, others of whom were quickly arrested, a wider crackdown on the working-class men who opposed martial law was already unfolding. The crimes committed by these "counterrevolutionary rioters" were impulsive acts – split-second angry reactions to the massacre that they had witnessed. But the nonelite men who set fire to or urinated on military vehicles received much harsher punishments than did the student leaders. Wang Dan received a four-year sentence for counterrevolutionary incitement, while Lu Decheng, who had thrown eggs at Mao's portrait, was sentenced to sixteen years in prison.[2]

Wang Dan and Lu Decheng's lives changed dramatically because of their decisions to protest in spring 1989. Wang's incarceration was shorter because of his high profile and the special status held by students at China's elite universities, but Lu Decheng survived his incarceration and was released in 1998, seven years before his sentence was supposed to end.[3] Other working-class men who opposed martial law were less fortunate: their lives ended just two weeks after the massacre. On June 22, 1989, five days after being sentenced to death for riot-related crimes, Ban Huijie, Chen Jian, Lin Zhaorong, Luo Hongjun, Zhang Wenkui, and Zu Jianjun were executed by shooting.[4] Their names do not appear on the Tiananmen Mothers' list of victims, but they also died in June 1989 because of their encounters with martial law troops. Around 1 a.m. on June 5, Lin Zhaorong, a worker in a Beijing hospital, allegedly set fire to a transport truck and stole seven army uniforms. Ban Huijie, who was

---

[1] *RMRB*, June 14, 1989, 2.   [2] *RMRB*, January 27, 1991, 4; *RMRB*, August 12, 1989, 1.
[3] Chong, *Egg*, 225.   [4] *RMRB*, June 23, 1989, 2.

from rural Xinle County in Hebei Province, allegedly hit soldiers with the metal end of his belt on the evening of June 3.[5]

Because executioners' bullets silenced Ban Huijie and Lin Zhaorong's voices in 1989, we can only guess what they were thinking when they lashed out in anger against the army that was violently occupying Beijing. But thanks to the efforts of Liao Yiwu, a poet and dissident now based in Germany who interviewed sixteen men who opposed the massacre and served sentences for counterrevolutionary rioting, we have a better picture of how and why ordinary people responded to the PLA's violent crackdown.

Zhang Maosheng was a twenty-year-old worker in Beijing in 1989.[6] When Liao Yiwu interviewed Zhang in 2006, Zhang remembered that he was not especially moved or impressed by the democracy movement's protests and marches. Zhang lived near Tiananmen Square and watched the action every day after work, but he felt that all of the speeches, singing, leaflets, and hunger striking were "inappropriate" because they had "messed up the heart of the motherland." Zhang transformed from a passive observer to an active resister on the evening of June 3. At Fucheng Road, Zhang saw an anguished mother carrying the dead body of her eight-year-old child, who had been shot and killed by martial law troops. "Fuck their mothers!" Zhang said of the soldiers as he recalled his reaction to seeing the dead boy. "My head hummed and I felt a surge of heat. Are they even human? They're worse than dirty swine. I wished that I had a gun in my hand. If I had run into soldiers, I would have mowed them all down!"

Zhang's rage intensified as he watched Beijing residents rushing wounded civilians to the Peking University hospital. He could not hold back as he watched a standoff between soldiers and Beijingers. He yelled, "Never! Never! Never let these gun-wielding sons of bitches slaughter the innocent! Fellow Chinese, we must do whatever we can to stop them from continuing to murder." Zhang noticed a piece of cloth on the gas tank of a military truck. He opened the gas cap, used one of his matches to set the cloth on fire, and stuffed it into the tank. Within a minute, the entire vehicle was in flames. Zhang turned around and headed home. A few days later he went back to work, and later in June seven police officers arrested him at a job site in Tianjin. In September 1989 Zhang received a suspended death sentence for the crime of counterrevolutionary arson; he was released in 2006.

---

[5] Zhonggong Liaoning shengwei gongchandangyuan zazhi she, 平息反革命暴乱500题 (Five hundred questions about quelling the counterrevolutionary rebellion), 205.

[6] Details and quotes in the next two paragraphs are from ZY, 77–79.

Other "rioters" (暴徒) interviewed by Liao Yiwu tell similar stories. They had little or nothing to do with the protests of April, May, and June 1989, but when they saw or heard about the massacre, they lashed out. Wang Lianhui, a twenty-two-year-old temporary worker in Daxing County outside Beijing, was trying to get home from his girlfriend's place on the night of June 3 when he encountered a large crowd blocking the road.[7] Wang ran into someone he knew and said he was heading home because it was late and he needed to go to work tomorrow. His friend reminded him that the next day was Sunday, a day off work, saying, "Come on, let's go be patriotic together." Wang succumbed to peer pressure and joined the crowd. Li Peng's rationale for clearing Tiananmen Square before Sunday to prevent large protests on a non-workday had backfired: people felt free to resist the military advance because they did not need to work the next day.

According to Wang Lianhui, the focal point of the protest he joined was a disabled APC that had been part of a convoy rushing toward Beijing from the Nanyuan military airport in Daxing. The APC had taken a corner too fast and crashed into a large tree. Protesters gathered around the vehicle and talked about how soldiers had shot unarmed civilians. The more he heard, the angrier Wang got. He jumped on top of the APC and broke its periscope and side-view mirrors. Someone suggested that pouring lots of water on the vehicle might be a good way to damage it further, but nobody had any water. Wang decided to pee on the APC.

"You're joking," Liao Yiwu said when Wang told him the story. "Yes, it was a joke," Wang responded, but this joke became a serious crime, "because my stream of piss almost caused the mass asphyxiation of the soldiers inside the vehicle." Wang had not known it at the time – he thought he was peeing on an empty object – but the APC's crew had stayed hidden inside. Police officers showed up at Wang's workplace on June 12, 1989, and took him away in handcuffs. Wang received a life sentence in December 1989 and was released in February 2005.

Wu Wenjian, who worked at the Yunshan Petrochemical Company and had found student activists' speeches "refreshing," was sentenced to seven years in prison for loudly denouncing the massacre, shouting slogans against Deng Xiaoping and Li Peng, and calling for a mass strike. Wu summed up the motives of "rioters" like himself, Wang Lianhui, and Zhang Maosheng:

[7] Details and quotes in the next three paragraphs are from *ZY*, 165–73.

We are all common Beijingers, with strengths and weaknesses, aroused by our sense of justice, so we stepped up. Throwing a few bricks, bottles, a basket. Or blocking military vehicles, giving speeches, disabling tank treads. But we all had the same goal, which was to stop the army from entering the city and massacring the students.

Wu, who was nineteen in 1989, lamented that the stories of elites had overshadowed the stories of those who had been imprisoned as rioters. "Later," Wu said, "the students who withdrew from Tiananmen Square became the main players of the 'Tiananmen Incident,' thanks to exaggerated attention from the Western media. But the real main players have been relegated to the shadows of history."[8]

---

[8] *ZY*, 60.

26 Don't Call It a *Yundong*

While China's legal system punished thousands of alleged criminals – arsonists, vandals, and ringleaders of illegal organizations – a larger movement known as "double *qing*" (双清) subjected millions more people to interrogations, investigations, meetings, and administrative and Party sanctions. Similar to the fate of the young men who impulsively resisted the massacre, the broader post-massacre purge has remained in the shadows of history.

One week before gunshots rang through Beijing, a purge had already begun, as officials associated with General Secretary Zhao Ziyang were taken away in unmarked cars to clandestine detention centers. Zhao himself was removed from his position and was ritualistically denounced by at least ten elders at the 4th Plenary Session of the 13th Central Committee in late June 1989.[1] Zhao remained under house arrest until his death in 2005. In most places, the purge wrapped up in 1990, although in some work units it dragged on until 1992. In some ways, it has never really ended.

After the declaration of martial law on May 20, 1989, the purge started at the top. Bao Tong, director of the Office of Political Reform and Zhao Ziyang's political secretary, heard that Li Peng had accused him of leaking the decision to impose martial law. Bao showed copies of the PRC and Communist Party constitutions to his family, saying, "These things are probably not enough to protect me."[2] He was right. On May 28, a car took Bao to Zhongnanhai, where Song Ping, minister of the Party's Organization Department, told him that because his home and office were "unsafe," he would need to go somewhere else. Bao was then driven directly to Qincheng Prison, where he became prisoner 8901.[3]

---

[1] The text of the elders' remarks pledging loyalty to Deng Xiaoping and blaming Zhao Ziyang for a series of crimes can be found in Tsoi Wing-Mui, *The Last Secret*.
[2] Lim, *People's Republic of Amnesia*, 154.
[3] Wu Wei, 中國80年代政治改革的台前幕後 (Onstage and backstage: China's political reform in the 1980s) (Hong Kong: Xin shiji chubanshe, 2013), 541–42.

A few days earlier, Bao Tong had visited Wu Wei, his secretary, and told him to study up on the Party constitution and other regulations. "I immediately knew what Bao was getting at," Wu wrote. "Bao and the rest of us could be arrested and locked up at any moment," so they needed to inform themselves about ways to resist illegal detention. On May 28, Wu was driven to a compound in Changping County on the outskirts of Beijing, where he was held and interrogated until the morning of June 4, when he was transferred to a Ministry of Public Security guesthouse adjacent to Qincheng.[4]

Wu Wei demanded to see his interrogators' identification cards and argued that his detention went against Party rules. Similarly, Zhao Ziyang accurately pointed out that his removal as general secretary violated the Party constitution, and he repeatedly questioned the legality of his house arrest. But as Roderick MacFarquhar writes, "legality didn't figure at all in the handling of the Zhao case, only power and stability."[5] The same can be said for the broader post-June Fourth purge, which can be seen as a bridge between the political movements of the Mao Zedong era and the stability-maintenance regime of the 2000s.

At the Third Plenum of December 1978, Party leaders decried special-case groups as a vestige of the Cultural Revolution and pledged to "permanently abolish" extralegal investigations of cadres.[6] In August 1980, Deng Xiaoping said that China would no longer have large-scale political movements known as *yundong* (运动).[7] This explains why internal documents as well as a handful of brief mentions in *People's Daily* all referred to the purge as "work" (工作) rather than as a movement, even though on the surface it shared many characteristics with the special-case groups and political movements of the Cultural Revolution, including work teams, arbitrary detentions, criticism meetings, reflection essays, standardized forms determining the nature of targeted individuals' problems, and attempts to get people to accuse and expose each other.

Central Document Number Three, issued on June 30, 1989, outlined the scope and scale of the purge. All work units in Beijing were ordered to do purge work, as were offices and schools in "large and medium

---

[4] Wu Wei, 中國80年代政治改革的台前幕後 (Onstage and backstage: China's political reform in the 1980s), 552, 555.
[5] Roderick MacFarquhar, "Foreword," in *PS*, xxiv.
[6] 中国共产党第十一届中央委员会第三次全体会议公报 (Communiqué of the Third Plenary Session of the 11th Central Committee of the Chinese Communist Party), December 22, 1978, cpc.people.com.cn/GB/64162/64168/64563/65371/4441902.html.
[7] Deng Xiaoping, "Answers to the Italian Journalist Oriana Fallaci," August 21 and 23, 1980, in *Selected Works of Deng Xiaoping (1975–1982)*, 330.

cities" throughout China "where turmoil occurred." Work teams made up of politically reliable retired cadres were to take charge of the purge in units where leadership was deemed to be "severely impure."[8] While the purge was ubiquitous in Beijing, it also affected faraway cities and counties: Harbin set up purge offices in 165 work units and uncovered 265 "incidents" that involved 8,763 people; a total of 1,064 cadres were investigated in Xianyang, just outside Xi'an in Shaanxi Province; and 4,559 cadres in Guangdong Province were determined to have "committed mistakes," of whom 248 were "handled by the organization," 51 received Party disciplinary sanctions, and 29 lost their Party membership.[9]

Purge policy mandated leniency toward "people who for a short while did not understand the truth and took part in marches, sit-ins, hunger strikes, and protests, especially young students," who should do self-criticisms but who would not be otherwise punished.[10] In a speech on August 21, 1989, new general secretary Jiang Zemin reiterated that the Party should "be a bit forgiving toward the majority of young students, because after all they are young and politically naive. But be strict toward cadres."[11] As for "those who have committed heinous crimes and whose being left alive would be insufficient to calm popular outrage," Central Document Number Three ordered, "they must be resolutely killed; as

---

8 中共中央, 国务院转发中共北京市委, 北京市人民政府 "关于彻底清查, 坚决镇压反革命暴乱分子的工作方案的请示" 的通知 (Party Center and State Council notice circulating the Beijing Party Committee and municipal government's request for instructions about a work plan to thoroughly ferret out and firmly suppress counterrevolutionary rioters), June 30, 1989, in Zhongguo renmin jiefangjun zong zhengzhi bu bangongting, 政治工作手册 (Political work manual) (n.p., 1990), 34, reprinted in SCCP, special series 27, volume 69 (2013).

9 Haerbin shi difang zhi bianzuan weiyuanhui, ed., 哈尔滨市志: 中共地方组织 (Harbin municipal gazetteer: Local Communist Party organization) (Harbin: Heilongjiang renmin chubanshe, 1999), https://web.archive.org/web/20190121203146/http:/218.10.232.41:8080/was40/detail?record=109&channelid=50196&back=-3; Xianyang shi zhengwu menhu wangzhan, "1989 年" (1989), *Zouxiang Xianyang*, October 19, 2010, web.archive.org/web/20190121203250/http://www.xianyang.gov.cn/zjxy/xydsj/7836.htm; Zhonggong Guangdong shengwei zuzhi bu, Zhonggong Guangdong shengwei dangshi yanjiushi, Guangdong sheng dang'anguan, eds., 中国共产党广东省组织史资料 (Materials on the organizational history of the Communist Party in Guangdong Province) (Beijing: Zhonggong dangshi chubanshe, 1994), https://web.archive.org/web/20170629210900/http:/www.gdzz.cn/javaoa/article/zzs_p1/zzs-3.htm.

10 中共中央, 国务院转发中共北京市委, 北京市人民政府 "关于彻底清查, 坚决镇压反革命暴乱分子的工作方案的请示" 的通知 (Party Center and State Council notice circulating the Beijing Party Committee and municipal government's request for instructions about a work plan to thoroughly ferret out and firmly suppress counterrevolutionary rioters), 35.

11 *RMRB*, October 17, 1989, 1.

for those whose circumstances allow for leniency, and who could be killed or not killed, try to not kill them."[12]

There was a huge gray area between executing "rioters" who had fought against the martial law troops on June 3 and requiring "naive" students to write self-criticisms. What happened to people in this gray zone depended on the leaders of the purge in each work unit or school. Following the release of Central Document Number Three, every work unit in Beijing, and many outside the capital, formed a Purging and Sorting-Out Work Leading Small Group (清查清理工作领导小组). These committees ultimately reported to the Central Purge Office (中央清查办), the leaders of which included former minister of railways Ding Guan'gen, another former railway official named Gu Yunfei, and Liu Zepeng from the Party's Organization Department.[13]

Purge leaders issued a flurry of documents in late 1989 and early 1990 explaining steps, targets, and protocols for examining and penalizing people. One key variable was whether marches and protests had occurred before or after May 20, when martial law went into effect. Marching or protesting before May 20 was not a big deal; doing the exact same things during the martial law period was more serious. Another variable to consider was whether the content of slogans, leaflets, and posters opposed the "four cardinal principles" (meaning that they questioned the leadership of the Communist Party and the socialist system). Other distinctions also mattered: donating personal funds or goods to the hunger strikers was fine, but using public monies or giving "huge sums" demanded punishment. Signing a petition or showing up at a march could be forgiven, but collecting signatures or ordering subordinates to join protests had to be punished.[14] And if memorial services for people killed during the crackdown were held by "close relatives grieving in accordance with old customs," they were merely subject to

---

[12] 中共中央, 国务院转发中共北京市委, 北京市人民政府 "关于彻底清查, 坚决镇压反革命暴乱分子的工作方案的请示" 的通知 (Party Center and State Council Notice circulating the Beijing Party Committee and municipal government's request for instructions about a work plan to thoroughly ferret out and firmly suppress counterrevolutionary rioters), 36.

[13] Wu Wei, 中國80年代政治改革的台前幕後 (Onstage and backstage: China's political reform in the 1980s), 560, 563, 565. Song Ping, head of the Organization Department, "supervised the purge," according to James Miles, *The Legacy of Tiananmen: China in Disarray* (Ann Arbor: University of Michigan Press), 28.

[14] 中央纪委, 中央组织部转发北京市清查领导小组 "关于对在动乱和反革命暴乱期间参加非法游行等问题的若干处理意见" 的通知 (Central Commission for Discipline Inspection and Central Organization Department notice circulating the Beijing Municipal Purge Leading Small Group's "Several opinions on handling illegal marches and other problems during the period of turmoil and counterrevolutionary rebellion"), September 5, 1989, in 政治工作手册 (Political work manual), 63–66.

criticism, but if funerals promoted "counterrevolutionary propaganda," the organizers could be criminally charged.[15]

One of the biggest distinctions of all in dealing with the aftermath of the protests was whether people were Party members. On July 20, 1989, the Central Commission for Discipline Inspection mandated that Party members who had taken part in or organized "turmoil and counter-revolutionary rebellion activities" should be stripped of their Party membership; lesser offenses could be punished by various forms of Party discipline.[16] Scrutiny of Party members increased beginning in late August 1989, when two new central documents ordered that as part of the broader purge, all cadres at the county level and above throughout China needed to be inspected. More significantly, cadres in central and provincial organs, as well as in cities where "turmoil" had taken place, had to reregister with the Party to maintain their membership.[17] Because a "counterrevolutionary rebellion" had occurred in Beijing[18] (as opposed to more widespread but less severe "turmoil" throughout China), this test of loyalty extended to every Party member in the capital except for village officials in outlying rural areas.[19]

The reregistration of Party members was the final stage of the purge. It involved extra paperwork and meetings and was supposed to proceed in three steps. The first was to educate Party members on the standard they had to meet to maintain their membership. In short, everyone needed to

---

[15] 最高人民法院，最高人民检察院对各地处理政治动乱和反革命暴乱案件中提出的一些政策法律问题的意见（节录）(Opinion of the Supreme People's Court and Supreme People's Procuratorate on policy and legal questions in handling political turmoil and counterrevolutionary rebellion throughout China (extracts)), November 11, 1989, in 政治工作手册 (Political work manual), 69.

[16] 中央纪委关于印发"中央纪律检查委员会关于共产党员和党的组织参加动乱反革命暴乱活动党纪处分的若干规定"的通知 (Central Commission for Discipline inspection notice on printing and distributing "Several rules from the Central Commission for Discipline Inspection about Party discipline punishment for Party members and Party organizations participating in turmoil and counterrevolutionary rebellion activities"), July 20, 1989, in 政治工作手册 (Political work manual), 52–56.

[17] 中共中央关于加强党的建设的通知 (Party Center notice on strengthening Party construction), August 28, 1989, in 政治工作手册 (Political work manual), 158–59.

[18] 中共中央转发 "中央组织部关于在部分单位进行党员重新登记工作的意见" 的通知 (Party Center notice circulating "Opinion of the Central Organization Department on carrying out reregistration of Party members in some work units"), September 7, 1989, in Zhongyang zuzhi bu ganbu shenchaju, 干审工作政策文件选编 (Selected policy documents on cadre inspection work) (n.p., 1993), 1442, reprinted in SCCP, series 5, vol. 100 (2005).

[19] 中共中央组织部关于转发中共北京市委组织部 "关于党员重新登记工作的安排意见" 的通知 (Central Organization Department notice circulating the Beijing Municipal Organization Department's "Opinion on arranging reregistration of Party members"), November 21, 1989, in 干审工作政策文件选编 (Selected policy documents on cadre inspection work), 1453.

follow Party Center in lockstep and endorse the crackdown. Second was a written "personal summary" including self-criticism and a recounting of their thoughts and actions during spring 1989. The final step was a Party branch meeting featuring a "fair and just democratic discussion," followed by a decision on whether to reregister the member. If someone's application was denied, an official from the higher levels of the bureaucracy had to chat with the person to determine whether the expulsion was justified. The higher-up could unilaterally overturn the Party branch's decision.[20]

Purge policy was so convoluted, open to interpretation, and full of potential loopholes that officials had wide latitude in deciding whether to protect, punish, or ignore people. This should come as no surprise. During the political movements of the Mao years, local officials tended to tweak, overrule, or ignore vague and contradictory central directives.[21] By calling the post-massacre purge work instead of a movement, however, officials faced a slightly different problem. At a minimum, work needed to be completed, but it could be perfunctory and slapdash: just another routine task on the local Party branch agenda.

Central leaders knew about the problem with work, but they had few answers. In a speech to leading Beijing municipal cadres on August 25, 1989, Beijing Party secretary and Politburo member Li Ximing said, "Currently, the biggest danger facing purge work is going through the motions, minimizing big things, disguising small things, and quitting halfway." Li's only solution to this problem was to "do a thorough job with purge work."[22] More than a month later, a *People's Daily* editorial about protecting stability and unity exhorted readers to "take purge work seriously, absolutely do not just go through the motions" (绝不能走过场).[23]

---

[20] 中共中央组织部关于转发中共北京市委组织部 "关于党员重新登记工作的安排意见" 的通知 (Central Organization Department notice circulating the Beijing Municipal Organization Department's "Opinion on arranging reregistration of Party members"), 1453–55.

[21] For examples, see Brown, "Moving Targets: Changing Class Labels in Rural Hebei and Henan, 1960–1979"; and Chan, Madsen, and Unger, *Chen Village*.

[22] *RMRB*, August 26, 1989, 1.   [23] *RMRB*, October 10, 1989, 1.

27   Going through the Motions

"We knew what we had to say and we just tried to get it over with," remembered a former Peking University graduate student who experienced the purge during fall 1989. Following weekly study sessions at which someone recited speeches by central leaders and *People's Daily* editorials, the student and her peers wrote self-criticisms. "Nobody took it seriously," she said. "We said we weren't involved, but in order to make it sound okay we said we had followed others and went to the square a few times because we were lacking in revolutionary consciousness."[1] Two phrases from this student's testimony accurately describe how participants in the purge went through the motions: knowing what they "had to say" and making it "sound okay." In various schools and workplaces, different people had to say distinct things in order to sound okay: university students could not deny that they had marched and gone to the square, so they minimized what they had done. Other strategies included rambling about irrelevant matters, shifting blame, and outright lying.

I do not know the extent to which cadres at the Fourth Engineering Department lied about what they had done during the democracy movement, but the department's purge was clearly an exercise in going through the motions. An eleven-page report from October 6, 1989, outlines how the department's Party branch was steadfast from start to finish, lists all the important speeches that cadres studied to get in sync with Party Center, and admits to no significant mistakes or problems. "Some comrades had confused understanding," the report writer noted, but did not explain any specific confusion. In a discussion meeting, some workers admitted that they had heard on Voice of America that "Tiananmen Square was awash in blood." Of course, later study sessions convinced them that this was untrue.[2]

---

[1] Author conversation 2 (graduate student at a university in Beijing in 1989).
[2] Zhongguo gongchandang tiedao bu di shiliu gongcheng ju di si chu di yi gongchengduan weiyuanhui, 关于在制止动乱，平息反革命暴乱期间的情况报告 (Report about the

The October 6 report tantalizingly mentioned "major local disturbances" near a track-laying project north of Tangshan but claimed that cadres prevented workers from getting involved. Department leaders also noted that on May 23, 1989, some Shandongese workers began two months of family leave from a project in Fujian. To ensure that the workers did not "encounter problems," they were sent home via Tangshan instead of through Beijing. "In closing," the report bragged, "we not only made sure that there was no chaotic thought, but we also increased our vigor ... handing over profits of 1,309,500 yuan, which represents 65.14 percent of the annual quota."[3] Fourth Engineering Department cadres knew what they had to say, and they made it sound okay.

Nine days later, however, another report about the department's performance during the "curbing of the turmoil and quelling of the rebellion" was due. Leaders seemed to have run out of things to say, so they listed the names of five investigation committees they had formed. They also noted that they had discovered "five comrades using hotplates and thirteen comrades using rice cookers in violation of the rules." The illicit appliances were confiscated and offenders had to write self-criticisms. Without a hint of irony, the report writer closes with bromides that he himself had ignored for twelve pages and that many of his colleagues brazenly disregarded when writing their own personal summaries: "use your own brain to think about problems, do not parrot others' words or drift with the current."[4]

Many cadres from the Fourth Engineering Department failed to use their own brains in September 1989 when they filled out a one-page "Cadre Performance Investigation Form" about what they had done during the "turmoil" and "rebellion."[5] Even more of them parroted others' words. The cadres began by filling in basic information in five boxes: name, position, date of birth, the date they began work, and the

---

situation during the period of curbing turmoil and quelling counterrevolutionary rebellion), October 6, 1989, 4, 7, SCPA, Box 17.

[3] Zhongguo Gongchandang tiedao bu di shiliu gongcheng ju di si chu di yi gongchengduan weiyuanhui, 关于在制止动乱，平息反革命暴乱期间的情况报告 (Report about the situation during the period of curbing turmoil and quelling counterrevolutionary rebellion), 9, 7, 11.

[4] Zhongguo Gongchandang tiedao bu di shiliu gongcheng gongsi si chu jianzhu shigongduan weiyuanhui, 关于制止动乱，平息暴乱的情况写实报告 (Report about curbing the turmoil and quelling the rebellion), 3–4, 12, SCPA, Box 17.

[5] Unless otherwise noted, all details and quoted material from the forms are from Tiedao bu di shiliu gongcheng ju sichu di yi gongcheng duan, 制止动乱，平息反革命暴乱期间干部表现考察登记表 (Cadre performance investigation forms for the period of curbing turmoil and quelling rebellion), September 1989, SCPA, Box 17.

date they entered the Party. They then wrote their personal summary in a large box that filled the top half of the page. A note at the bottom indicated, "if there is not enough space for the personal summary, you may append an additional page."[6]

The personal summary of Zhang Yinglong, the thirty-five-year-old political instructor of the second team, is identical to that of twenty-nine-year-old team leader Song Yueshi. The bland contents (I wasn't even in Beijing and did nothing wrong; Party Center was correct) are an exact character-for-character match, and the handwriting is the same. In the Party branch appraisal box on Zhang's form, Song's stamped name appears in red ink approving of Zhang's statement. In the same box on Song's form, Zhang signed off on his colleague's summary. But the language in each appraisal box is identical and written by the same hand, praising the cadre's firm standpoint in not spreading rumors, not protesting, and not donating money. This blatant double plagiarism passed muster with whoever wrote "on investigation, we agree with the individual's summary and the Party branch's opinion" at the bottom of each form.

The person who wrote summaries on behalf of Song and Zhang also filled out forms for Fu Junming and Li Youlin – same handwriting, same contents – but thoughtfully changed one detail: while Song and Zhang were laying track north of Tangshan, Fu and Li were working on a road project in Fujian. Zhang Yinglong's name stamp and the exact same boilerplate approval closed out the forms for Fu and Li. Investigation over.

At least Song, Zhang, Fu, and Li thought that it would be wise to have someone else evaluate their summaries. Four other cadres from the Fourth Engineering Department blithely signed off on their own reports. Yu Zhigen, a Party secretary and director of the workplace union, wrote that "Comrade Yu Zhigen" performed admirably during the "turmoil." Or maybe he had someone else write the summary and the appraisal on his form; at any rate, his name is the one that approves its contents. Five other forms have a different problem entirely: nobody signed off on them at all – the appraisal box and the box indicating the higher-ups' opinion are empty. This is true of fifty-one-year-old vice department head Cui Shijun, the oldest and highest-ranking cadre featured in the files held at

---

[6] Only two out of the thirty-four form fillers added extra pages. They were both in unique and relatively precarious positions. One was not a Party member, the other was a recent graduate of the Shijiazhuang Railway Institute who had joined the work unit in July 1989 and had to explain how he had ignored his classmates' effort to "empty out the school" in protest after the massacre in Beijing.

Stanford. Cui, who had been named a labor model in April 1989 by the Sixteenth Engineering Bureau,[7] mentioned that he "persuaded" his own children studying at universities not to take part in any "activities." But he saw no need to show his form to anyone else. This looks like an example of what Beijing Party secretary Li Ximing had called "quitting halfway" a month earlier. No matter. Cui's purge work was done.

While some cadres at the Fourth Engineering Department nonchalantly breezed through the investigation, others thought harder about what to write. Not all of the forms were plagiarized or incomplete. In fact, the personal summaries that were not barefaced copies contain diverse contents and a variety of stylistic approaches. A thirty-four-year-old accountant named Zhou Weiguo lambasted the role of the "dregs of society" (a phrase used by Deng Xiaoping in speeches) in inciting rebellion, mentioned Mikhail Gorbachev's visit to China, and asked why Party Center had not used force even earlier to stop the protests. Quoting or paraphrasing Deng Xiaoping was a safe move adopted by others, including two cadres who wrote that events had been determined by the "broad international environment and the smaller domestic environment."[8]

In addition to Deng Xiaoping and Gorbachev, other names that appear in the summaries include deposed leader Zhao Ziyang, who one cadre accused of "supporting turmoil and splitting the Party," as well as Zhao's replacement Jiang Zemin. Huang Zhengchang wanted to say that he "firmly endorsed the leading group at Party Center led by Comrade Jiang Zeming [江泽明, sic]." By September 1989, Huang had probably heard Jiang's name mentioned at meetings, but he may not have seen it in print, so he wrote it incorrectly. Huang was not alone in not knowing much about the new general secretary. When Jiang appeared at a food market in Beijing to meet and greet ordinary people in January 1990, "it took a few minutes before any of the busy shoppers even recognized him."[9]

It was safe to criticize Zhao Ziyang and to praise Jiang Zemin, but some cadres took the riskier step of lauding the students' goals in starting

---

[7] *Tiedao bu di shiliu gongcheng ju di si gongcheng chu jianshi* bianweihui, 铁道部第十六工程局第四工程处简史 (Concise history of the Ministry of Railways' Sixteenth Engineering Bureau's Fourth Engineering Department), 303.

[8] Details in this paragraph come from summaries held in a separate folder, Tiedao bu di shiliu gongcheng ju sichu di yi gongcheng duan, 制止动乱，平息暴乱的自我总结 (Personal summaries about curbing turmoil and quelling rebellion), September 1989, SCPA, Box 17.

[9] Bruce Gilley, *Tiger on the Brink: Jiang Zemin and China's New Elite* (Berkeley: University of California Press, 1998), 169.

the protests and even in launching a hunger strike. Political instructor Liu Xiyang wrote that he originally thought that the students' marches, petitions, and hunger strike were part of a "democratic" and "righteous" movement aimed at strengthening the rule of law and rooting out corruption. Team leader Cao Xinming agreed, admitting that he once thought that the students were full of "patriotic zeal." Similarly, Chen Tie thought that the students' methods were correct. Liu, Cao, and Chen worked together on the same team and followed a set formula in their summaries: after the publication of the April 26, 1989, *People's Daily* editorial labeling the student movement as "turmoil," they came to realize that their thinking was wrong. The only hole in their logic was that the hunger strike, which all three men had once endorsed, did not begin until May 13, 1989, more than two weeks after the "turmoil" editorial appeared in print. This chronological gaffe did not trouble the Party branch representative who approved the summaries. Why not? Because Liu Xiyang signed off on all three of them, including his own.

This mistake slipped through, but another cadre's characterization of the student movement did not. In a longer draft essay, an official with the surname of Wang wrote, "I thought the students' slogans opposing corruption and official profiteering were correct. Sometimes I felt a bit sympathetic." Someone else with notably different handwriting then crossed out those sentences and replaced them with "because I did not understand that a small number of people were using such slogans as 'oppose corruption' and 'oppose official profiteering' to camouflage their turmoil, I developed sympathetic feelings. I did not recognize that this was a plot carried out by only a few people."[10] Wang had been too sincere in voicing his original feelings. The revision may have been the editor's well-meaning attempt to protect a boss. The editor understood that the purge was never intended as an honest exercise in truth telling.

---

[10] Tiedao bu di shiliu gongcheng ju sichu di yi gongcheng duan, 制止动乱, 平息暴乱的自我总结 (Personal summaries about curbing turmoil and quelling rebellion).

28 Falsehoods and Defiance

Since the Anti-Rightist Movement of 1957, if not earlier, the Chinese Communist Party has cultivated a culture of lying. After seeing tens of thousands of people ostracized and exiled for openly expressing critical opinions about Party policy, many people adopted prevarication as a survival strategy. This culture of lying was alive and well in the second half of 1989. It undermined Li Ximing's admonitions against "minimizing big things" and "disguising small things" during purge work. Clearly the purge was not the time for the Party to change one of its basic operating principles. In most schools and offices, people got away with cover-ups and falsehoods.

One graduate student at Peking University who defended her thesis in summer 1989 remembered that she and her classmates successfully negotiated the purge by writing a single sentence: "I did not take part in the turmoil." The students did not want to admit to anything at all, but their professor convinced them to write the phrase, saying, "this is the way political movements go, you're young, just write it down and leave." According to the official definition of "turmoil," they had just lied, because all of them had marched and protested in Tiananmen Square. But because none of them believed that their actions qualified as "turmoil," the student said, "In the end we felt like we had not lied."[1]

Something similar happened at a university in north China outside Beijing, where in one department students had to write statements about whether they had marched or given donations supporting the protests. They then had to provide testimony from a classmate confirming their answers. Everyone wrote the same thing: nobody from the department had marched or donated. The witness statements all agreed. A student

---

[1] Author conversation 3 (another graduate student at a university in Beijing in 1989). This student's experience of the purge was more perfunctory than what an undergraduate at Peking University described as a rigorous "reeducation course" in Link, *Evening Chats in Beijing*, 303. Graduate students who had already finished their theses might have been treated differently than undergraduates, and it is likely that each department handled its own purge differently.

who had marched and then covered up his participation remembered that after his department's reports were sent up the ladder, someone asked, "if nobody marched, then where did the eight thousand marchers come from?" The question was met with shrugs and everyone moved on.[2]

The students got away with their denials, but others who had been more active during the democracy movement faced bigger challenges. Another student at Peking University remembered that during May and June 1989, her roommate had spent hours at the university's broadcasting station reading reports produced by autonomous student associations. She could have been labeled as an "inciter of counterrevolutionary propaganda," one of the main purge targets listed in Central Document Number Three. During the purge, the roommate made it clear that she would not mention anything about the broadcasts; she hoped that her friends would also maintain silence. Everyone stayed quiet.[3] In this case, omission was as effective as lying.

Omission was more difficult, but not impossible, for those who found themselves on special lists of "main purge targets" (重点清查对象) drawn up by purge leaders in each school or work unit.[4] One such target, an undergraduate student at a university in Beijing, had served on a prominent student organization and had worked with a protest leader who fled China after the massacre. In fall 1989 she was summoned for twice-weekly interrogation sessions at the campus security director's office. "My schooling was totally disrupted," she said. "I didn't learn anything that term. The purge took priority." She fended off questions, she said, by pretending to be "naive and stupid, an innocent girl." As long as there was no written record or proof of what she had done, her answer to every question was "I don't know." If her questioners asked her about a specific person, she would feign ignorance, saying, "I saw so many faces every day." It worked. "This was a very successful strategy," she said, noting that she was allowed to graduate with a "demerit" in her dossier (档案). She did not take full credit, however, for her successful evasions. She sensed that university security officials had no interest in finding incriminating evidence or in seriously punishing students.[5] She was protecting herself, but she was also being protected.

---

[2] Author conversation 4 (student at a university in China in 1989).
[3] Author conversation 2.
[4] Author conversation 5 (instructor at a university in Beijing in 1989).
[5] Author conversation 6 (student at a university in Beijing in 1989).

As Perry Link perceptively noted at the time, this "impulse of mutual protection" was "especially strong" in the aftermath of the massacre.[6] While the survival strategy of lying persisted in 1989, another vestige of the political movements of the Mao years – informing on others – was remarkably rare during the purge. Instead of raising their hands to report the misdeeds of their colleagues, most people stayed quiet. Others bravely spoke up to protect their friends. Sometimes this required trickery, but it often worked. Ms. Liu, a woman who was a second-year undergraduate at Tsinghua University, had taken part in the hunger strike at Tiananmen Square. This became an issue during the purge, but someone said that she was only going to the square and forgoing food because she needed to lose weight.[7] She breezed through the investigation.

Jiang Zemin himself said that students were to be treated gently during the purge, so it is no surprise that a joke equating hunger striking with dieting counted as an acceptable explanation at Tsinghua. Similar strategies also worked, however, in more sensitive offices. According to political scientist Bruce Gilley, Jiang Zemin "made no attempt to conciliate with the media" and poured "vitriol" on the press in the aftermath of June Fourth.[8] Nonetheless, Zhang Wanshu, a leader at the Xinhua News Agency in Beijing, managed to deflect attention from a colleague in his department. At Xinhua, where an outside work team led by Duan Junyi of the Central Advisory Commission (CAC) managed the purge, finger-pointing and informing on others were more common than they were on university campuses. Someone from a different office tattled on Zhang's younger colleague, saying that he had shouted reactionary slogans at two different marches in May 1989. When a cadre from the Xinhua purge office asked Zhang about the accusation, Zhang replied, "Because he is an athlete and is tall, everyone pushed him to the front to shout slogans. But he only yelled about opposing corruption and that type of thing." This explanation "blocked the inquiry," Zhang remembered.[9]

Zhang Wanshu had to think creatively and invent excuses to protect the people under his supervision. In other workplaces, supervisors issued blanket denials that stopped investigations into what people had done during spring 1989. Li Kan, the top leader at the Zhonghua Book

---

[6] Link, *Evening Chats in Beijing*, 189.
[7] Shao Gang, 我的青春, 我的64: 六四真相访谈录 (My youth, my June Fourth: Interviews about the true June Fourth) (Hong Kong: Meijia chuban, 2014), 75.
[8] Gilley, *Tiger on the Brink*, 153.
[9] Zhang Wanshu, 歷史的大爆炸 (Historical explosion), 414.

Company in Beijing, had an unblemished revolutionary record dating back to before the founding of the People's Republic. In 1989, Li opposed the protests as they were unfolding, saying that not all mass movements are inherently correct and telling his subordinates to avoid Tiananmen Square. Even though many employees ignored Li's advice and took part in protests, after the crackdown Li issued a sweeping declaration that there were no "turmoil elements" to be found at the book company. Because Li had a clean record and had spoken out against the protests from the beginning, nobody questioned him. His subordinates wrote perfunctory summaries of what they had supposedly done; none of them were punished.[10]

★ ★ ★

Even though Li Kan had not supported the student movement, his protection of his subordinates was an act of defiance. By covering up what employees had done and allowing them to write dishonest and superficial self-criticisms, Li was contravening purge policy, as were the many others who protected themselves through lies and omissions. But by covering up the extent of their involvement in the protests and by writing token self-criticisms – rather than owning up to what they had done or refusing to take part in the purge – people were tacitly submitting to the post-massacre order. A student who had frequently marched to Tiananmen Square in 1989 put it to me this way: "There is no way to talk or debate if one side uses violence. It's like if I disagree with a point in your book, but instead of talking about it, I take out a knife and attack you."[11]

Recognizing that it was pointless to try to meaningfully engage with a murderous opponent – and that the price of doing so could be a prison sentence, expulsion from school, or getting fired – many people went through the distasteful motions of the purge. But others refused to do so. Knowing full well that their only weapon was the moral high ground in a debate against a violent adversary, some people used the purge as a platform to openly denounce the massacre. Older truth tellers who were already retired or near retirement operated in the spirit of Zhao Ziyang's final public statement at Tiananmen Square ("We are old, it doesn't matter" what happens to us), figuring that they had little to lose.[12] Others, like Pu Zhiqiang, had been so prominent during the student

---

[10] Author conversation 7 (employee at a work unit in Beijing in 1989).
[11] Author conversation 8 (student at a university in Beijing in 1989).
[12] Lu Chaoqi cites Zhao's statement to explain why he agreed to step in as top editor at *People's Daily* in June 1989 after other colleagues went on sick leave. He was about to

movement that there was no way they could conceal what they had done, and in any case their personalities made it difficult for them to lie.

In 1989, Pu Zhiqiang was a graduate student at the China University of Political Science and Law. During the student movement, he was part of the first group of hunger strikers from his university. On May 19, 1989, he gave an interview to ABC television in which he denounced the April 26 editorial, and on June 3, 1989, he spoke at Tiananmen Square, equating decades of Communist rule with slavery. Pu figured he would be on his university's list of purge targets. He was right.

As an undergraduate in Nankai University's history department, Pu had studied the political movements of the Mao era.[13] He wondered about the extent to which the purge would resemble earlier political movements and was pleasantly surprised when school leaders treated students gently and students protected each other. Nonetheless, Pu himself was unwilling to say that his actions during the student movement had been mistaken, and he was even less willing to praise Party Center's decision to forcefully suppress the demonstrations. Nothing he wrote was acceptable to university authorities. By late 1990, Pu was on the verge of graduating and school officials determined that they could no longer ignore him. Write one more reflection essay explaining what you did, they told him. Pu titled his piece "Baring My Heart to the Party," in honor of "rightists" who had been asked to do the same thing in the late 1950s.[14]

Pu's essay, which he wrote on October 27 and 28, 1990, is unrepentant and sarcastic. He admitted that he had given an interview to a foreign television station, criticized central leaders in public speeches, and transferred one thousand yuan from the square to another protest leader at Xinhua Gate. Pu did not say what he was supposed to say. He wrote what he really thought:

Thinking back on it now, I still don't believe that there was an organization leading the student movement, let alone a plot to turn it into turmoil and a counterrevolutionary rebellion! Otherwise, there is no way to explain why such

retire and did not care if his reputation was ruined. Lu Chaoqi, 六四內部日記 (Inside journal of June Fourth), 149.

[13] Liu Zehua, the Nankai professor who had encouraged Pu to analyze whether Cultural Revolution-style denunciations might recur in China, was himself a victim of the purge after June Fourth. Liu was removed from his position as department chair because he had written a petition in support of the students.

[14] On the movement to "bare" or "Open Your Heart to the Party" in Henan Province in 1958, see Cao Shuji, "An Overt Conspiracy: Creating Rightists in Rural Henan, 1957–1958," in *Maoism at the Grassroots*, 77–101.

intense disorder appeared within the student movement, or why students and Beijing residents scattered like birds after tanks showed up.

In addition to opposing the Communist Party's characterization of the student movement, Pu also mocked the purge itself, spilling out details that his readers surely did not want or need to know about. After explaining how he had come to deliver one thousand yuan to someone he did not know, he argued that he had not committed financial malfeasance. "I can only testify, based on my own character and conscience – if my character and conscience are still recognizable to any extent at all," Pu rambled, "that I never spent one cent that I was not supposed to spend, except for buying a pair of athletic shorts." He then explained in parentheses, "around noon on May 18, I pooped my pants because I was inattentive to my intestinal inflammation. Someone accompanied me to buy shorts."

Pu concluded his thought report by quoting Liang Qichao, Lu Xun, and Sun Yat-sen to bolster his argument that China belonged to its people, not to political leaders. "I believe that tomorrow will be a better day!" he wrote in closing. "This is the conscience of a young person toward this country and this nation!"[15] On December 30, 1990, Pu was called in to the graduate studies office, where a teacher named Liu Tingji handed him a form and told him to sign it. Pu was a couple of weeks away from his twenty-sixth birthday. Under "Graduate Student Registration for Graduation," the form read, "Because of this student's problems in the turmoil and rebellion, he is hereby punished with a severe administrative warning." Next to his signature, Pu wrote, "I've finally been purged."[16] The punishment may have seemed like a slap on the wrist, but in the context of the early 1990s, it meant something far more serious: unlike every other graduating student, Pu would not be assigned a job at a work unit.[17] He was on his own.

Figuring out his own path instead of receiving a comfortable job assignment ended up suiting Pu, but his decision to openly defy the Party during the purge dramatically reshaped his future. Older professionals who had behaved as defiantly as Pu did not experience major life changes. The prominent seventy-four-year-old translator Yang Xianyi had donated money and bottles of water to demonstrating students and had also signed several petitions asking the government to continue with

[15] Pu Zhiqiang, "向党交心: 我在六四清查运动中提交的反思" (Baring my heart to the Party: The thought report I turned in during the June Fourth purge movement).
[16] Pu Zhiqiang tweeted the story of Liu Tingji and the graduation form on July 20, 2009, twitter.com/puzhiqiang/status/2741387142.
[17] Author conversation 5.

political reforms and to allow increased freedom of the press. More serious was his interview with the BBC on June 4, 1989. Yang recalled that a journalist called from London "and asked me what I thought of the massacre. I was still in a towering rage and through the phone I denounced the people responsible for the crime, calling them fascists."[18]

A few days later, Yang heard from a friend that the police were planning to arrest him. He sought refuge at the friend's house and then traveled by train to Changchun to hide at his daughter's home. After three days, he returned to Beijing and wrote a note to the Party secretary of *Chinese Literature* magazine, saying that he had spoken to foreign journalists without permission, which was "a breach of party discipline ... I asked for disciplinary punishment. I did not say that I was sorry or regretted what I had done."[19] In the months that followed, Vice Minister of Culture (and famous actor) Ying Ruocheng visited Yang on three separate occasions.[20] Yang recalled that each time, Ying vaguely said that he "hoped that I would change my mind." Yang would not. When the men crossed paths in the future, Yang wrote, "he did not try to brainwash me again."[21]

Yang's routine continued as usual until early 1990, when Party re-registration began at *Chinese Literature*. Yang wrote a note asking to quit the Party. "Since I felt that I could not admit that I had done anything wrong, and I still condemned those in power who were responsible for the tragic incident," he explained, "I decided I could not take part in this reregistration process." The Party secretary said exactly what he was supposed to say according to central reregistration rules: Yang's problems were serious, but he could be pardoned if he honestly repented.[22] A dozen people from Yang's Party branch gathered to discuss and vote on his case. Half of those present criticized Yang's outspokenness in the aftermath of the massacre. When the time came to vote, everyone raised their hands to expel him from the Party. According to purge policy, people who proactively asked to quit the Party were not allowed to do so. They had to be formally expelled – asking to quit was grounds for expulsion.[23] Yang accepted his Party branch's decision and faced no further consequences for his defiance.

[18] Yang Xianyi, *White Tiger: An Autobiography of Yang Xianyi* (Hong Kong: Chinese University Press, 2002), 291.
[19] Yang, *White Tiger*, 295.
[20] Yang's autobiography does not name Ying Ruocheng, but Ying is identified in Lei Yin, 楊憲益傳 (Biography of Yang Xianyi) (Hong Kong: Mingbao chubanshe, 2007), 388.
[21] Yang, *White Tiger*, 296.   [22] Yang, *White Tiger*, 297.
[23] According to Article 20 of the Central Commission for Discipline Inspection's initial guidelines for punishing Party members, "Even if someone asks to quit the Party, if they have committed mistakes that are punishable by expulsion ... they should be expelled." See 中央纪委关于印发 "中央纪律委员会关于共产党员和党的组织参加动乱反革命暴乱

If Yang had wanted to, he probably could have maintained his opinion about the massacre and kept his Party membership. That was what happened to poet Shao Yanxiang, who turned fifty-four just six days after the massacre. In 2009, Shao was going through some old files and found the China Writers Association Purge Work Leading Small Group's judgment on his Party reregistration, dated February 23, 1991. Shao's memories about the process, as well as the text of original documents from the purge, are available online.[24] In Shao's personal summary, written in June 1990, he noted that he had been in the United States for a conference between April 25 and May 18, 1989. After he returned, he participated in a march on May 25, following the imposition of martial law. This was a violation of Party discipline, Shao wrote, and he was "willing to accept punishment" for this transgression.

Shao was unwilling to say anything positive, however, about what happened next. "Perhaps using modern weapons to solve problems was not the best choice," he wrote. As a Party member, Shao admitted, he had no option but to obey the official assessment of what had happened in May and June 1989. "But whenever I think back on the way that Beijing's political turbulence was resolved," Shao held,

I remember my revolutionary mentors always pointing out that rulers should not use force rashly against their own people. In the 1950s, Mao Zedong admonished us that it was absolutely forbidden to open fire on the masses. For this reason, please allow me to maintain my personal opinion about this matter.

Shao's Party branch had no problem with his defiance. On July 28, 1990, fifteen colleagues unanimously approved his reregistration, saying that Shao "maintained his Communist beliefs, endorsed the Party's basic line ... and conducted a self-criticism about his mistakes during the turmoil." The person in charge of the Purge Work Leading Small Group at the China Writers Association, however, noticed Shao's "personal opinion" and not only wanted to deny his reregistration but also criticized his Party branch for negligence. When the purge boss asked how Shao had gotten away with this act of defiance, a Party branch leader

---

活动党纪处分的若干规定" 的通知 (Central Commission for Discipline Inspection notice on printing and distributing "Several rules from the Central Commission for Discipline Inspection about Party discipline punishment for Party members and Party organizations participating in turmoil and counterrevolutionary rebellion activities"), 55. See also Miles, *The Legacy of Tiananmen*, 28.

[24] The details and quotes below are from Shao Yanxiang, "'六四'后我所经历的'党员重新登记'" (My experience during the "reregistration of Party members" after "June Fourth"), March 28, 2009. The original posting is no longer accessible online, but it has been reposted at bit.ly/blog51cashaoyanxiang.

said that because Shao had quoted Chairman Mao's sacred words, there was no way to refute him. This made the purge boss even angrier, and he asked the Central Organization Department for permission to expel Shao from the Party. Central authorities responded that Party members have the right to hold their own personal opinions. His work unit's purge office ultimately issued Shao an "internal Party warning," which his Party branch finally discussed and voted on in September 1991. Nine people voted in favor, five were opposed, five abstained, and one person was silent.

The purge boss at the China Writers Association was plausibly following the Central Organization Department's reregistration guidelines issued in February 1990 about how to handle Party members who had "failed to correct their mistakes." Being forced by the purge to say a few words in support of the four cardinal principles did not count as an honest change of opinion, according to the policy.[25] By this measure, Shao's open denunciation of the crackdown should have gotten him kicked out of the Party. But the purge office in his work unit had apparently not received the memo reporting that in late May and early June 1990, former economic czar Chen Yun, one of the "eight elders" and director of the CAC, had essentially prohibited any further expulsions for political reasons.[26] Faced with the prospect of stripping four members of the CAC of their Party membership (Du Runsheng, Li Chang, Li Rui, and Yu Guangyuan, who took a stand similar to that of Shao Yanxiang), Chen ordered that people who had made mistakes during the "turbulence" of 1989 could stay in the Party. Li Rui remembered that Chen Yun said, "We can't do this kind of thing anymore. If we do [kick them out], we'll have to rehabilitate them later."[27] Everyone still needed to wrap up the reregistration drive, but Chen's unwillingness to purge his immediate colleagues – or to revisit their cases in the future – overrode all previous policy guidelines. Purge work ended with a whimper.

★ ★ ★

[25] 中央组织部关于印发 "党员登记工作座谈会纪要" 的通知 (Central Organization Department notice distributing the summary minutes of a conference on Party member registration work), February 2, 1990, in 干审工作政策文件选编 (Selected policy documents on cadre inspection work), 1460–61.

[26] Chen's official biographers discuss this episode in surprising detail and portray his reasoning in a positive light ("doing it this way benefits stability and unity"). See Jin Chongji and Chen Qun, 陈云传 (Biography of Chen Yun) (Beijing: Zhongyang wenxian chubanshe, 2005), 2:1806–1808. See also Yang Jisheng, 中国改革年代的政治斗争 (Political conflict in China's reform era), 15.

[27] Li Rui, "李锐对改革开放的个人回顾" (Li Rui's personal recollections of reform and opening up), Wang Jianxun, comp., *Yanhuang chunqiu*, no. 11 (2008): 18.

If the purge was intended to weed out people who were opposed to the Party's handling of the protests or to provide a true reckoning of what people had said and done during the democracy movement, it had clearly failed. But to stop the analysis there ignores two important points. First is Pu Zhiqiang's suspicion that the purge was about making people bow down to the post-massacre reality, not about sincere expressions of loyalty. Viewed in this light, the purge served its purpose. Most people turned in lame and dishonest reflection essays. They knew the potential costs of defiance. Second, focusing on the perfunctory nature of the purge ignores significant counterexamples. Some work units were labeled "severe disaster zones" (重灾区) because their collective behavior during spring 1989 was considered unacceptably opposed to Party Center.[28] In these places, which included the Office of Political Reform, *People's Daily*, and Xinhua News Agency, the purge was not a routine administrative task. It looked more like a Mao-era political movement, complete with accusations, betrayals, and shrill criticism speeches. These were all intended to confirm purge leaders' predetermined verdict that each workplace was involved in a plot linking Zhao Ziyang to the students in the square.

When Bao Tong's secretary Wu Wei was released from detention in August 1989 and allowed to return to the Office of Political Reform, he was eager to see his old colleagues. He quickly sensed that something was wrong. His coworkers came out to greet him, but he no longer felt the "harmony and closeness" he had been used to. Most of his colleagues quickly returned to their own offices; those who stayed behind to chat told him that an outside work team had already begun conducting the purge. Someone asked Wu about his experience being locked up. Wu responded, "I said everything that I was supposed to say. I didn't say one word of what I shouldn't tell." Later that afternoon, the purge work team leader called Wu in for a talk. The purge boss said, "I heard that you didn't say anything you weren't supposed to say at Qincheng. What things weren't you supposed to say?" Wu was shocked that one of his coworkers had tattled on him so quickly. "I realized that the office had changed," Wu wrote. "I needed to watch what I said."[29]

Compelling people to inform on their colleagues was an important strategy for purge work teams in "disaster zones." This was in line with Central Document Number Three, which read, "Mobilize the masses to expose and accuse ... keep the identity of accusers secret and protect

---

[28] Author conversation 5.
[29] Wu Wei, 中國80年代政治改革的台前幕後 (Onstage and backstage: China's political reform in the 1980s), 559.

accusers from retaliation that they might encounter."[30] In late October 1989, *People's Daily* editor Lu Chaoqi had been removed from his position while he was being investigated. Gao Di, the new leader at the newspaper, told Lu that in addition to examining his own mistakes, he would have to report on others. Lu knew that Gao was trying to incriminate Bao Yujun, who was under suspicion for having worked alongside Bao Tong earlier in the 1980s. Bao Yujun had handled administrative tasks at *People's Daily* during the student movement and was not involved in producing controversial content. In fact, at first he had been appointed to the paper's purge leadership. But then a former university classmate tattled on Bao Yujun, saying that his relationship with Bao Tong was "unusual." This accusation got Bao Yujun kicked off the purge committee. He became a target himself.[31]

In addition to behind-the-back accusations, people also criticized purge targets face-to-face in heated criticism meetings. Gao Wenqian, who worked at the Central Documents Research Office, had led a group of officials during a protest march and also put his name on an open letter to Party Center affirming the patriotism of the student movement. During the purge, instead of downplaying or minimizing Gao's involvement, his coworkers exaggerated it, saying that he had stabbed the Party in the back.[32] Similar scenes occurred at Xinhua in February 1990, when cadres who had stayed quiet during the student movement took turns standing up to criticize purge targets. One critic accused former Xinhua vice director Guo Chaoren of having said, "let's protect Zhao Ziyang." Another enthusiastic accuser was Xu Guangchun, who was director of Xinhua's Beijing branch. He gave a long speech essentially accusing his colleagues of treason, equating their unwillingness to distribute martial law notices with generals failing to follow military orders. Regrouping with his friends after Xu's vitriolic speech, Guo Chaoren laughed it off, remembering that his colleagues had once said of Xu Guangchun, "He

---

[30] 中共中央, 国务院转发中共北京市委, 北京市人民政府 "关于彻底清查, 坚决镇压反革命暴乱分子的工作方案的请示" 的通知 (Party Center and State Council notice circulating the Beijing Party Committee and municipal government's request for instructions about a work plan to thoroughly ferret out and firmly suppress counterrevolutionary rioters), 40.

[31] Lu Chaoqi, 六四内部日记 (Inside journal of June Fourth), 211.

[32] "高文謙: 我所見證的六四 (上)" (Gao Wenqian: What I witnessed on June Fourth (part 1)), *Dajiyuan*, June 1, 2004, epochtimes.com/b5/4/6/2/n556323.htm. Gao recalled that going through the purge convinced him that he could not continue as a "political tool" writing official history. "I determined to never again lie or go against my convictions," he explained in 晚年周恩來 (Zhou Enlai's later years) (Carle Place, NY: Mirror Books, 2003), 608, which he wrote after leaving China.

sure can generalize and exaggerate. It's the whole Cultural Revolution package."[33]

In the face of intense criticism, targets could either fight back or try to throw someone else under the bus. Both phenomena occurred. In August 1989, *People's Daily*'s internal newsletter published a self-criticism by Li Pu, who had served as a vice director at Xinhua before retiring. Li flagellated himself for his "severe mistake" of having taken part in an "illegal march" on May 18, 1989. Zhang Wanshu of Xinhua was furious that *People's Daily* leaders were using a pensioner as a punching bag to deflect attention from their own behavior – which had been undeniably sympathetic to the students and opposed to martial law.[34]

People's Daily editors found that passing the buck only offered a temporary reprieve. They ended up having to actively refute increasingly ludicrous charges. The purge at *People's Daily* not only focused on the newspaper's transgressions during 1989 but also argued that the paper had been opposed to Party Center ever since 1976. This accusation appeared in the transcript of a discussion between Hu Qiaomu of the CAC and the newspaper's new post-purge leaders. A former director at the newspaper fought back. He compiled a list of all the times that Party Center had officially praised *People's Daily* since the 1970s and asked, "Who gave you the right to negate Party Center's judgments about *People's Daily*'s work?" Hu Qiaomu backed down, saying that he had not had a chance to approve the transcript before it was circulated.[35] This moral victory failed to blunt the purge at *People's Daily*. At least eight editors were removed from their positions at the paper.[36]

★ ★ ★

The contentious arguments and sweeping demotions at *People's Daily* make it difficult to characterize the purge as a campaign that "fizzled." Even though such "disaster zones" were not representative of the purge, they served as examples of what might happen to people who appeared to

---

[33] Zhang Wanshu, 歷史的大爆炸 (Historical explosion), 420–22. Zhang does not name Xu Guangchun but I can, thanks to a quick internet search. I insist on identifying Xu by name because he is a public figure who went on to become a prominent provincial leader.

[34] Zhang Wanshu, 歷史的大爆炸 (Historical explosion), 414–15. See also Frank Tan, "The *People's Daily*: Politics and Popular Will – Journalistic Defiance in China during the Spring of 1989," *Pacific Affairs* 63, no. 2 (July 1990): 151–69.

[35] Lu Chaoqi, 六四內部日記 (Inside journal of June Fourth), 213–14.

[36] Tan, "The *People's Daily*," 169.

be out of sync with Party Center. More broadly, the massacre and its aftermath set people on radically different life trajectories. People who had planned on pursuing careers inside China fled the country (or stayed abroad). Elite university students who would have received good job assignments instead got demerits in their files that prevented them from getting hired in Beijing. For some people this was a permanent stain, for others it was a temporary inconvenience – prominent intellectual Wang Hui was "sent down" to Shaanxi in 1990 to "temper himself" for a year; another university graduate had to endure a miserable experience in the countryside enforcing the one-child policy before being allowed to take her job at the Ministry of Finance.[37]

These punishments may not seem like the end of the world. Wang Hui and the woman at the Ministry of Finance have done fine for themselves. Even people who lost their jobs or became unemployable in regular state work units because of the purge found ways to thrive afterward. Liu Suli, a lecturer at the China University of Political Science and Law, led an organization at Tiananmen Square in 1989 and was imprisoned until 1991. Liu was kicked out of the Party and fired from his job. But he went on to establish the independent All Sages Bookstore, which became a hub of intellectual life in Beijing. And look at Pu Zhiqiang, who became a highly successful lawyer.

Liu and Pu's success, however, was incredibly fragile. They show that the post-June Fourth purge is ongoing. Liu Suli's release from prison was conditional on his not giving interviews about 1989. He broke his pledge days before the twentieth anniversary of the crackdown, when he told a *New York Times* reporter that he was constantly watched by security agents and had this to say about China's direction since 1989: "You can raise pigs to be very strong and very fat. But a pig is still a pig. And a pig has no rights."[38] The next year, Liu was restricted from traveling and was assaulted by a security agent.[39]

As Pu Zhiqiang's 1990 essay "baring his heart" to the Party might lead us to expect, he has remained defiant. He pledged to pay his respects to the victims of the massacre by visiting Tiananmen Square every year on June 3, a streak that was broken in 2006, when police detained him. They

---

[37] Ma Wenchuan, "汪晖: 渐行渐远的思想者" (Wang Hui: The drifting thinker), *Jingji guancha bao*, August 6, 2007, 42, epaper.eeo.com.cn/shtml/jjgcb/20070806/27775 .shtml; author conversation 3.

[38] Michael Wines, "After Tiananmen and Prison, a Comfortable but Uneasy Life in the New China," *New York Times*, June 4, 2009, nytimes.com/2009/06/04/world/asia/ 04protester.html.

[39] Andrew Jacobs, "China Bars Travel for 2 Rights Advocates," *New York Times*, November 9, 2010, nytimes.com/2010/11/10/world/asia/10china.html.

prevented him from reaching the square, but he decided that his time with the cops counted as an adequate memorial.[40] In May 2014, Pu was detained after attending a meeting to commemorate June Fourth. He remained in custody until December 2015, when he was found guilty and given a suspended sentence for "inciting ethnic hatred" and "picking quarrels."

During the purge after June Fourth, a few people remained defiant. Many others went through the motions. But there is a third group of people whose performance during the massacre and purge deserves special mention. Their fate helps to explain how the purge continues to this day, and why it is unlikely to end any time soon. This third group consists of those who enthusiastically defended the crackdown and purge. Xu Guangchun, the rampaging critic at Xinhua in 1990, was awarded with promotion after promotion. In 2004, he became first Party secretary of Henan Province.[41] This trend was replicated in many other levels of Chinese society, including the PLA. As Wu Renhua has shown, martial law officers have received commendations for meritorious service, as well as steady promotion through the ranks, based on their performance in 1989.[42] In one Beijing cultural office in 1989, a leading cadre was conspicuously absent from group marches and protests. His coworkers teased him and asked him why he was not taking part. The man blamed his wife, saying that she had locked him in at home. He was implying that he had to stay inside to protect family harmony. During the purge, however, the cadre said that he had really avoided Tiananmen Square because he was steadfastly defending Party Center. After another leader who had supported the students was demoted, the supposedly steadfast comrade took his job, and he eventually rose up to become a department director.[43]

This third group of purge defenders includes officials at much higher levels than lowly department directors. Ever since July 1989, every general secretary of the Chinese Communist Party – beginning with Jiang Zemin, continuing with Hu Jintao, and extending to Xi Jinping – owes his position to the violent crackdown and the purge that followed. Without the massacre and purge, there would be no chairmanship for

---

[40] Pu Zhiqiang, "'June Fourth' Seventeen Years Later: How I Kept a Promise," trans. Perry Link, *New York Review of Books*, August 10, 2006, nybooks.com/articles/2006/08/10/june-fourth-seventeen-years-later-how-i-kept-a-pro/.

[41] Zhang Wanshu, 歷史的大爆炸 (Historical explosion), 424, provided the thread that led me to Xu. See also 徐光春简历 (Xu Guangchun's CV), *Xinhua*, https://web.archive.org/web/20160304112221/http:/news.xinhuanet.com/ziliao/2002-03/05/content_300373.htm.

[42] *LSJ*, 72–82.   [43] Author conversation 9 (employee at a Beijing office in 1989).

these men and no power for their underlings. This is why the purge continues today. As historian Glenn Tiffert writes, "In the Party's eyes, Tiananmen also stood for the proposition that a decisive leader could galvanize the CCP to determine its own fate against formidable odds by sheer force of will."[44] Xi Jinping has been inspired by June Fourth to consolidate his own power as a dictator rivaling Deng. The post-massacre repression is likely to continue as long as Xi remains in power.

---

[44] Glenn Tiffert, "30 Years after Tiananmen: Memory in the Era of Xi Jinping," *Journal of Democracy* 30, no. 2 (April 2019): 40.

29   Aftermath
Alternative Paths

On May 28, 1989, Chai Ling told journalist Philip Cunningham, "Only when the square is awash with blood will the people of China open their eyes. That's when they will really unite."[1] After the massacre did occur, Chai fled Beijing and recorded a statement about the bloodshed. She concluded by saying, "Compatriots, all citizens with a conscience, all Chinese, awaken! The final victory will be yours! The day is fast approaching when the Central Committee that pretends to speak for the Party – Yang Shangkun, Li Peng, Wang Zhen, and Bo Yibo – will be annihilated!"[2]

Chai Ling was not the only student leader who hoped that the massacre would lead to a wider popular uprising that would overthrow the government. Li Lu recalled his thoughts when he learned that soldiers were violently advancing toward the square on the evening of June 3: "Would the workers strike? Would some leaders publicly oppose the Government? Would some cities and provinces declare their independence? What should the Democracy Movement do next?"[3]

On the run and in hiding in the days after the massacre, Li Lu hatched a plan to occupy a central radio or television station. "I felt that even one hour of broadcast time would be enough to persuade the Chinese people to rise up peacefully," Li wrote in his memoir. "If we used this opportunity well opposition within the army and the Government would follow, and the Government would fall."[4] Li never got his hour. Armed soldiers guarded the gates of media outlets in Beijing; there was no way in. Li's plan B failed when police confiscated a private radio transmitter he had his eyes on. Plan C – to steal a bus, pick up foreign correspondents one by one, and hold a press conference – never got off the ground.

---

[1] Transcript of Chai Ling interview, May 28, 1989, *The Gate of Heavenly Peace*, tsquare.tv/chinese/archives/chailin89528.html.
[2] Han Minzhu, *Cries for Democracy*, 366.   [3] Li Lu, *Moving the Mountain*, 195.
[4] Li Lu, *Moving the Mountain*, 206–7.

Even though Li's media takeover fell flat, word of the Beijing massacre did spread throughout China. The uprising that Li Lu and Chai Ling hoped for in the immediate aftermath of the massacre never happened. Why not? Even in the absence of regime change, what if the official celebration of the martial law troops as heroes and condemnation of the protesters as rioters had somehow turned into a reevaluation of the democracy movement and massacre, instead of shifting toward erasure and amnesia?

Sociologists Yang Su and Ting Jiang argue that there was no revolution in the immediate aftermath of the Beijing massacre because of the government's "counterframing" in the media. Su and Jiang hold that because top leaders' pronouncements about needing to quell a counter-revolutionary rebellion in June were consistent with their call to oppose chaos ever since the *People's Daily* editorial of April 26, 1989, people who had not witnessed the Beijing massacre "believed them ... this explains the absence of moral outrage among the Chinese people in the wake of the massacre."[5] Su and Jiang are correct that Deng Xiaoping and Li Peng never wavered from their initial condemnation of chaos. But the sociologists' argument about how people received and understood the government's counterframing is unconvincing. Understanding the truth undergirding the government's messaging – that brutal violence had killed a peaceful protest movement – was not the same as believing its content.

There was plenty of moral outrage in and beyond Beijing in June 1989. Some people, such as Pu Zhiqiang, Yang Xianyi, and Shao Yanxiang, bravely proclaimed their sense of outrage. Others, like the anguished professor who fell backwards and hit his head on the night of June 3, felt immediate anger but eventually fell silent or even parroted the official line about opposing chaos and quelling the counterrevolutionary rebellion. They knew that resistance was too risky because they knew about the massacre and purge, not because they had been convinced by propaganda. The army's use of deadly force, followed by arrests of "rioters" and widespread purges, confessions, and reregistration of Party members, sowed fear and resignation that subdued and demoralized many who had sympathized with the protests. Mowing down civilians with machine guns – not counterframing – kept the Communist Party in power.

---

[5] Yang Su and Ting Jiang, "Government Counterframing and the Revolutionary No-Show in 1989," in *China's Transition from Communism: New Perspectives*, ed. Guoguang Wu and Helen Lansdowne (New York: Routledge, 2016), 89.

There is another alternative path that many hoped for in the aftermath of the massacre: an official reevaluation of the protests and crackdown, along with the rehabilitation of victims. Participants in the protests and witnesses of the massacre felt that they were on the right side of history and that Deng Xiaoping, Li Peng, and the PLA officers and men who issued – and acted on – orders to shoot civilians were perpetrators of a grave injustice that, sooner or later, would be redressed. Every year in the lead-up to the anniversary of June 4 there are petitions and calls for the Communist Party to redress the massacre and rehabilitate its victims. The Chinese word *pingfan* (平反) refers to this process of redress, rehabilitation, and reversing verdicts.

Ever since the 1930s, the Communist Party has followed a pattern of reevaluating the recent past and redressing injustices in the aftermath of periods of state violence and persecution.[6] High officials and ordinary protesters alike had historical precedents in mind following the Beijing massacre. Their freshest memories were of the late 1970s. In 1978, Hu Yaobang personally intervened on behalf of such senior officials as Peng Zhen, who had been purged during the 1960s.[7] High-level rehabilitation was most urgently relevant for Zhao Ziyang, who while under house arrest in 1990 and 1991 kept himself busy writing a series of letters protesting his detention to Deng Xiaoping, Jiang Zemin, Li Peng, and the entire Politburo Standing Committee. Zhao recalled that "All these letters of mine fell like stones dropped into the sea, disappearing without a trace."[8] In February 1997, Deng Xiaoping died. Zhao Ziyang, still under house arrest, wrote a letter calling for a Party-led reevaluation of June Fourth following the model of post-Cultural Revolution *pingfan*. Zhao must have known that a reassessment was unlikely as long as Deng Xiaoping was alive. But after Deng died, no *pingfan* followed. Instead, Zhao was denied permission to attend a colleague's funeral, visitors were barred from his house, and guards searched his wife's purse after her shopping trips.[9]

Ordinary people who had been arrested or otherwise punished for their involvement in the Tiananmen protests of 1989 might have also remembered precedents from the late 1970s. In November 1978, more than

---

[6] Daniel Leese and Puck Engman, "Introduction: Politics and Law in the People's Republic of China," in *Victims, Perpetrators, and the Role of Law in Maoist China: A Case-Study Approach*, ed. Leese and Engman (Berlin: De Gruyter, 2018), 13–17.
[7] Peng Zhen eventually turned on Hu and played a central role in removing Hu from his position as general secretary. Chung, "The Ousting of General Secretary Hu Yaobang: The Roles Played by Peng Zhen and Other Party Elders."
[8] *PS*, 58–59.   [9] *PS*, 78–81.

three hundred people who had been imprisoned as counterrevolutionaries for their role in the Tiananmen protests of April 1976 were officially
exonerated. What *People's Daily* had once characterized as a counterrevolutionary plot masterminded by Deng Xiaoping was now declared a
proper movement by the revolutionary masses to memorialize Zhou
Enlai and denounce the Gang of Four.[10]

Imagine a scenario in which the top leaders of the Communist Party
relabeled the events of April, May, and June 1989 as a patriotic movement meant to improve China. Imagine *People's Daily* articles announcing the rehabilitation of Zhao Ziyang; the early release from prison of
Wang Dan, Han Dongfang, and Lu Decheng; along with the return from
abroad of such exiles as Chai Ling, Feng Congde, Li Lu, Örkesh Dölet,
and Shen Tong. If this type of official reevaluation of June Fourth had
occurred in the early 1990s, while Deng was still alive, or in the late
1990s after his death, might Zhao Ziyang have been able to lead a
government pushing for the type of political reforms that he had pursued
in 1988? Zhao remained committed to one-party rule while working for
reform within the system during the 1980s. His memoir does suggest,
however, that the longer he was subjected to house arrest, the more
supportive of democracy he became. But Zhao stayed out of sight and
under house arrest until his death in 2005. He remained radioactive in
Chinese politics. Why? All of the shrill criticisms of Zhao lodged by the
elders in July 1989 and documented in *The Last Secret* boil down to a
single problem: Zhao had defied Deng by saying that there was no major
turmoil in China and by quitting when Deng proposed implementing
martial law.

Deng's centrality explains why there has been no official reevaluation
of the protests and massacre of 1989. One important factor is missing
from the imaginary June Fourth scenario that was present in the real-life
pingfan of 1978: bad guys on whom to pin the blame. In 1978 the Gang
of Four was a clear enemy, an easy target to vilify. The arrest of Jiang
Qing, Wang Hongwen, Yao Wenyuan, and Zhang Chunqiao in
1976 paved the way for a reversal of verdicts. There was no similar
scapegoat after 1989 because the perpetrator stayed in power. Deng
Xiaoping has always been the main obstacle standing in the way of an
official reevaluation of the massacre, even to this day. Reevaluating the
massacre would be tantamount to repudiating Deng Xiaoping.

Because Deng Xiaoping himself called the protests turmoil, declared
martial law, and issued orders to violently clear the square, he could not

---

[10] *RMRB*, November 19, 1978, 1.

plausibly blame the massacre on an underling.[11] It is even more difficult to imagine Deng openly acknowledging that he was wrong to order the military to attack civilians, even if he might have regretted the bloodshed in private moments with his family.[12] In May 1989, Deng showed impatience when Zhao Ziyang argued for a retraction of the April 26 editorial. Deng remained convinced that "turmoil" was the correct way to characterize the protests. Likewise, Deng had no interest in listening to those who objected to martial law in late May, pushing aside Xu Qinxian and ignoring the retired generals who wrote a letter begging the people's army not to fire on the people.[13] By 1990, public celebrations of the martial law troops' performance ended. Media coverage shifted into downplaying and gradually erasing the army's role in dealing with what came to be benignly called a "political disturbance."[14] Deng chose enforced amnesia rather than *pingfan*.

As for the post-Deng leadership, because Jiang Zemin owed his position as general secretary to the purge of Zhao Ziyang, he had nothing to gain by pushing to reevaluate June Fourth. Hu Jintao's ascension was less obviously linked to the Beijing massacre. Hu, however, had been Party secretary in Tibet when martial law was declared in Lhasa in March 1989. His role in forcibly ending the protests in Lhasa might have contributed to his future rise to power – and likely shaped his unwillingness to *pingfan* the events and victims of 1989. If Deng Xiaoping wanted to make sure that there would be no reevaluation of June Fourth in the decades after he died, boosting the career of a young provincial-level leader who had endorsed a violent crackdown in March 1989 might have been a clever choice.

If an official reevaluation of the Tiananmen protests and Beijing massacre had occurred in late 1997, as Zhao Ziyang had hoped, it could have offered a different path forward for China by putting the protest movement's demands for transparency and freedom of the press back on the

---

[11] Former Beijing mayor Chen Xitong did complain that he was unfairly associated with the massacre, but he went to prison in a corruption scandal, not as a war criminal. Yao Jianfu, 陳希同親述 (Conversations with Chen Xitong).

[12] Yu Hongshan claims that Deng expressed regret about the massacre but wanted to wait twenty years before revisiting the incident. Yu's book also claims that at various times Jiang Zemin, Wen Jiabao, and Li Ruihuan pushed for *pingfan*, but were rebuffed by Hu Jintao. Yu does not provide evidence for these claims. Yu predicted that an official reevaluation would come in 2013. Yu Hongshan, 平反六四之謎 (The mystery of reevaluating June Fourth) (Hong Kong: Beiyunhe chubanshe, 2012).

[13] Bao Pu interviewed by Louisa Lim, "Tiananmen's Final Secret," *Little Red Podcast*.

[14] The term "political disturbance" (政治风波) first appeared in *People's Daily* on July 4, 1989, to refer to the entire period between Hu Yaobang's death and the violent crackdown of June 3 and 4, 1989.

table. If a *pingfan* had been handled on the Communist Party's own terms, possibly by recharacterizing the movement and offering compensation to victims but not punishing soldiers and officers who carried out orders, there is no reason to believe that such a humane gesture would destabilize China. The expensive but limited transitional justice after the Cultural Revolution, which included lots of compensation but did not pursue many perpetrators of violence, even offered a model for how the Communist Party could stay in power after reevaluating a historical trauma.

Official acknowledgment that the victims of the massacre were patriotic citizens rather than thugs would have offered a measure of solace to victims' family members. And a reversal of verdicts would have cut short the suffering of "rioters" languishing in jail. These would have been meaningful changes. But calling on the Communist Party to *pingfan* the events of 1989 implies that the Party is a legitimate arbiter of Chinese history, a proper judge of right and wrong. Not surprisingly, Zhao Ziyang had no problem with this. But others find it distasteful. By calling for "truth, compensation, and accountability" – not for *pingfan* – the Tiananmen Mothers have positioned themselves as critics of the regime that killed their children, rather than as supplicants.[15] They expose the main problem with addressing the massacre on the Party's terms: whose voice counts, that of the victim or that of the perpetrator?

---

[15] Tiananmen muqin, 哭六四大屠杀中罹难的亲人和同胞们 – 致中国国家领导人公开信 (An open letter to China's leaders from the relatives who mourn those who were murdered in the June Fourth massacre), March 7, 2019, www.tiananmenmother.org/ TiananmenMother/30%20years/m20190306001.htm.

30 The Future of June Fourth

June Fourth can become an all-consuming obsession for people affected by it. At times the obsession seems out of proportion to the event itself. The death toll of the Beijing massacre pales in comparison to famines, natural disasters, pandemics, and even traffic accident deaths. But June Fourth captures public interest, as evidenced by commemorations and media coverage outside China each year, far beyond the scale of the massacre itself. Perry Link explains why. First, because millions of people witnessed the killings (or at least evidence of them) in person, and millions more saw news coverage of the massacre, the event "probably has had the highest bystander-to-victim ratio of any disaster in history."[1] Second, Link argues, the killings in Beijing "had to do with the fate of a nation. They were an important turning point for a society of more than a billion people."[2]

Obsession is therefore warranted. Sometimes it can be useful; sometimes it can be paralyzing. Wu Renhua embodies this phenomenon. After leading his students to the square in April 1989, experiencing the highs and lows of May, and evacuating from the square in the early hours of June 4, Wu fled China and ended up in southern California before moving to Taiwan. Even though Wu has no institutional affiliation, he has become the world's leading researcher in June Fourth studies, pouring his obsession into three books that he published himself. Whenever I have questions about what happened in the spring of 1989, I get in touch with Wu, who possesses encyclopedic knowledge about June Fourth.

I first met Wu in person in Liberty Square in Taipei on June 4, 2019. He was speaking at a thirtieth-anniversary vigil. Wu was swamped with admiring questioners, many of whom were mainland Chinese students studying in Taiwan, but I said a quick hello. When I emailed him a few

---

[1] Link, "June Fourth: Memory and Ethics."
[2] Perry Link, "Foreword," in *Tiananmen Exiles: Voices of the Struggle for Democracy in China*, xii.

weeks later with a list of questions related to what the military had done in Beijing on June 3 and 4, he never wrote back. When I finally tracked him down on Facebook, he explained that he was too traumatized to write another word about June Fourth, even by email. But he did not mind talking, so we met in a coffee shop.

Wu explained that he had been suffering from writer's block ever since he published *The Full Record of the Tiananmen Movement* in 2014. He said that every time he tried to write, he got depressed and upset, so he was instead putting his energy toward compiling a list of victims. As we parted ways, I confided to Wu that I had also struggled with writing about the massacre, even though I had not lived through it myself. Some days I thought about the victims, listened to their stories, and could not bring myself to write a word. Wu told me to persevere and said that the importance of the topic merited pushing through the challenges. In his view, June Fourth was more consequential to China's fate than May Fourth was. He predicted that someday June Fourth studies would surpass research on the May Fourth Movement and foresaw a future in which June Fourth research centers would be established in major universities worldwide.

Is Wu overly optimistic? At first, the research of historian Rowena Xiaoqing He suggests that Wu is being too hopeful. Rowena He's conversations with exiled former leaders Shen Tong, Wang Dan, and Yi Danxuan show survivors' inner conflict: "They were all struggling between sacrificing for an unfinished cause and living an ordinary life."[3] Not only does the activists' cause seem unfinished, but they appear to be losing badly. The officially enforced amnesia about June Fourth within China, combined with "patriotic education" over the past three decades, means that many young Chinese people have never heard of June Fourth. If they have heard about it, they know that it is not safe to speak about it. As Louisa Lim has discovered, it is not uncommon for parents to lie to their children about what they did or what happened in 1989.[4] This reality is depressing. As Rowena He writes, "the victims are no longer considered victims and the perpetrators no longer perpetrators. Rather, the latter have become the winners against the backdrop of a 'rising China.'"[5]

Wang Dan, who spent 1989–93 and 1995–98 in prison, refuses to be depressed by losing. He sees patriotic youth who know nothing about June Fourth or who criticize him as anti-China as victims who deserve sympathy. Wang also thinks that the perpetrators' status as winners and

---

[3] He, *Tiananmen Exiles*, 84.   [4] Lim, *People's Republic of Amnesia*, 95–96.
[5] He, *Tiananmen Exiles*, 28.

his position as a loser is a temporary but necessary step in a longer-term process. "I view the democracy cause as a process of accumulating failed experiences," Wang told Rowena He. Wang explained:

For me, the democracy cause, or say the opposition movement, is doomed to failure again and again. It is not possible to succeed. It is the fate of the opposition to lose. If you are part of an opposition movement, you always lose because once you succeed, you will no longer be in the opposition – you will have already taken over power. So before you come to power, as long as you are still the opposition, failure is just a matter of course (理所当然). We need to learn from the experience of failure so we will be able to succeed one day.[6]

Wang's road to success seems exceedingly difficult. There is no organized opposition or democracy movement inside China – repression and surveillance by agents of the Ministry of Public Security's Bureau to Guard Domestic Security and the Ministry of State Security make activism highly risky.[7] Exiled democracy activists like Wang Dan are too distant to influence events inside China and have been constantly riven by infighting.

But then I think of the opposition victories that I have witnessed in my lifetime. I was living in Mexico during the presidential election in which the opposition Partido Acción Nacional (PAN) defeated the Partido Revolucionario Institucional (PRI), ending the PRI's seven-decade dictatorship. And as Wu Renhua and I drank tea in Taipei, we touched on how Xi Jinping's handling of protests in Hong Kong was affecting Taiwan President Tsai Ing-wen's reelection prospects. Tsai's Democratic Progressive Party (DPP) is another opposition force that experienced failure after failure before it overcame the dictatorship of the Kuomintang (KMT). Mexico and Taiwan's political trajectories are different from China's, but looking at the fates of the PRI and KMT makes Wang Dan's long view seem less unreasonable and Wu Renhua's optimism appear less misguided.

Another reason for optimism about the future growth of June Fourth studies is how personally offended people become when they discover that someone is lying about or covering up the truth, especially about something as consequential as what happened in 1989. During historian Paul G. Pickowicz's decades of researching Chinese film, he often found himself in the middle of "bitter political struggles that pit people who are determined to conceal against people who want to reveal." He encountered many revealers in China "who work openly or behind the scenes to

---

[6] He, *Tiananmen Exiles*, 138.
[7] Xu Youyu and Hua Ze, *In the Shadow of the Rising Dragon: Stories of Repression in the New China* (New York: Palgrave Macmillan, 2013).

tear down barriers and eliminate taboos."[8] When it comes to June Fourth, the concealers are in charge. They have political power, technological advantages, and brute force. But the revealers remain irrepressible.

My experience teaching about June Fourth in Canada to university students, many of whom were born and raised in China, shows that the more exposure people get to forbidden topics, the more interested they get in listening to revelations and in becoming revealers themselves.[9] Students in my introductory lecture class spend three hours learning about and discussing June Fourth. Since I started teaching the class in 2009, students from China have become more skeptical and critical. Earlier in my career, reactions were more extreme, ranging from indignant nationalistic defense of the army's use of force to tearful shock that the Chinese Communist Party could have done something so bad. More recently, students from China are less indignant and less shocked. They know that the Party is capable of repression. They have more difficulty understanding the students in Tiananmen Square and the people in the streets of Beijing. Many students wonder about the "personal interests" and ulterior motives of student protesters and ask whether a foreign plot manipulated and tricked people into protesting. It seems unfathomable to young people who came of age during the 2000s that millions of people, all of whom had pressing personal interests and diverse motives, would put their individual goals aside at great risk to themselves – spontaneously, without prodding from foreign agents. But that is indeed what happened in 1989.

Three hours in an introductory undergraduate class is not enough to overcome the power of the concealers to hide and twist the history of June Fourth. It does, however, spark thinking and questioning that often leads to longer-term learning. Some Chinese students ask their parents what they were doing in 1989 and learn for the first time that their mothers and fathers were shouting slogans in the streets. During group office hours in spring 2020, one student from China told me, "my dad said that I shouldn't be brainwashed by your class." Her classmate then said, "my mom said the same thing." Their parents' warnings were counterproductive. The students were hungry to learn more.

When I reflect on the four times I have taught a full-term, thirteen-week undergraduate seminar about June Fourth, I begin to understand

---

[8] Paul G. Pickowicz, *China on Film: A Century of Exploration, Confrontation, and Controversy* (Lanham, MD: Rowman and Littlefield), 1.

[9] Jeremy Brown, "High Stakes: Teaching Tiananmen to Chinese Students in Canada," *PRC History Review* 4, no. 2 (August 2019): 29–31.

where Wu Renhua is coming from when he talks about the bright future of June Fourth studies. Deep immersion in primary sources from and scholarship about 1989 can quickly undermine decades of censorship and amnesia. Of course, students who enroll in my June Fourth seminar have already chosen to defy the concealers. They have become such experts in the topic that they have made seventy-two original Wikipedia contributions.[10] Not every student in the course has become an obsessive anti-concealment activist, but some have. When censorship about the coronavirus outbreak in Wuhan became widespread in January and February 2020, the first reaction of a group of Chinese-born students who had taken the June Fourth seminar was to archive social media posts about what was happening in Wuhan before the censors could remove them. My students in Canada were not alone: thousands of people inside China have defied the authorities by documenting the history of the outbreak in China.[11] Some have been detained and charged with the crime of "picking quarrels."[12]

Preserving, discussing, and writing about the past in ways that question or challenge the concealers' control of recent Chinese history remains dangerous. The stakes remain high for the Beijing massacre's perpetrators and their enablers and beneficiaries. Knowing the risks, revealers continue to reveal. The irrepressibility of revealers inside and outside China suggests that amnesia about June Fourth is fragile and temporary. There are as many alternative paths for China today as there were in 1989.

---

[10] SFU Tiananmen Square Project, en.wikipedia.org/wiki/Wikipedia:School_and_university_projects/SFU_Tiananmen_Square_Project; Jeremy Brown and Benedicte Melanie Olsen, "Teaching Tiananmen: Using Wikipedia in the Undergraduate Classroom to Write about Recent History," *Perspectives on History: The Newsmagazine of the American Historical Association*, April 2012: 18–19.

[11] Christoph Koettl, Muyi Xiao, Nilo Tabrizy and Dmitriy Khavin, "China Is Censoring Coronavirus Stories. These Citizens Are Fighting Back," *New York Times*, February 20, 2020, nytimes.com/video/world/asia/100000006970549/coronavirus-chinese-citizens.html.

[12] "China: Free Covid-19 Activists, 'Citizen Journalists': Arbitrary Detentions, 'Disappearances,' for Sharing Coronavirus Information," *Human Rights Watch*, April 27, 2020, hrw.org/news/2020/04/27/china-free-covid-19-activists-citizen-journalists.

Further Reading

Part One: China's 1980s

Timothy Cheek. *Living with Reform: China since 1989.* London and New York: Zed Books, 2006.

Denise Chong. *Egg on Mao: The Story of an Ordinary Man Who Defaced an Icon and Unmasked a Dictatorship.* Toronto: Random House of Canada, 2009.

Fang Lizhi. *The Most Wanted Man in China: My Journey from Scientist to Enemy of the State,* trans. Perry Link. New York: Henry Holt, 2016.

Joseph Fewsmith. *Dilemmas of Reform in China: Political Conflict and Economic Debate.* Armonk, NY: Sharpe, 1994.

Julian Gewirtz. *Unlikely Partners: Chinese Reformers, Western Economists, and the Making of Global China.* Cambridge, MA: Harvard University Press, 2017.

Perry Link. *Evening Chats in Beijing: Probing China's Predicament.* New York: Norton, 1992.

Yang Jisheng. 中国改革年代的政治斗争 (Political conflict in China's reform era) Hong Kong: Excellent Culture Press, 2004.

Part Two: The Tiananmen Protests

Craig J. Calhoun. *Neither Gods nor Emperors: Students and the Struggle for Democracy in China.* Berkeley: University of California Press, 1994.

Han Minzhu, ed. *Cries for Democracy: Writings and Speeches from the 1989 Chinese Democracy Movement.* Princeton: Princeton University Press, 1990.

Michel Oksenberg, Lawrence R. Sullivan, and Marc Lambert, eds. *Beijing Spring, 1989: Confrontation and Conflict: The Basic Documents.* Armonk, NY: Sharpe, 1990.

Jeffrey N. Wasserstrom and Elizabeth J. Perry, eds. *Popular Protest and Political Culture in Modern China.* 2nd ed. Boulder, CO: Westview, 1994.

Wu Renhua. 六四事件全程實錄 (The full record of the Tiananmen movement). Alhambra, CA: Zhenxiang chubanshe, 2014.

Dingxin Zhao. *The Power of Tiananmen: State–Society Relations and the 1989 Beijing Student Movement.* Chicago: University of Chicago Press, 2001.

Part Three: Massacre

Timothy Brook. *Quelling the People: The Military Suppression of the Beijing Democracy Movement*. New York: Oxford University Press, 1992.

Liao Yiwu. *Bullets and Opium: Real-Life Stories of China after the Tiananmen Square Massacre*. New York: Atria Books, 2019.

Andrew Scobell. *China's Use of Military Force: Beyond the Great Wall and the Long March*. New York: Cambridge University Press, 2003.

Wu Renhua. 六四事件中的戒嚴部隊 (The martial law troops in the June Fourth incident). Alhambra, CA: Zhenxiang chubanshe, 2009.

Part Four: Nationwide and Part Five: The Aftermath

Jean-Philippe Béja. *The Impact of China's 1989 Tiananmen Massacre*. New York: Routledge, 2011.

Rowena Xiaoqing He. *Tiananmen Exiles: Voices of the Struggle for Democracy in China*. New York: Palgrave Macmillan, 2014.

Louisa Lim. *The People's Republic of Amnesia: The Legacy of Tiananmen Square*. New York: Oxford University Press, 2014.

James Miles. *The Legacy of Tiananmen: China in Disarray*. Ann Arbor: University of Michigan Press.

James Tong. "The 1989 Democracy Movement in China: A Spatial Analysis of City Participation." *Asian Survey* 38, no. 3 (March 1998): 310–27.

Jonathan Unger. *The Pro-democracy Protests in China: Reports from the Provinces*. Armonk, NY: Sharpe, 1991.

Index

Books in the series

CPSIA information can be obtained
at www.ICGtesting.com
Printed in the USA
LVHW080537210122
708891LV00017B/549

9 781107 657809